THE CONTEMPORARY
WRITING CURRICULUM

Rehearsing, Composing, and Valuing

THE CONTEMPORARY WRITING CURRICULUM

Rehearsing, Composing, and Valuing

ROLAND HUFF
CHARLES R. KLINE, JR.

TEACHERS COLLEGE, COLUMBIA UNIVERSITY
New York • London

Published by Teachers College Press, 1234 Amsterdam Avenue,
New York, NY 10027

Library of Congress Cataloging-in-Publication Data

Huff, Roland.
   The contemporary writing curriculum.

   Bibliography: p. 187
   Includes index.
   1. English language—Rhetoric—Study and teaching.
I. Kline, Charles R.   II.   Title.
PE1404.H84   1987   808′.042.′0711   87-14315
ISBN 0-8077-2864-0
ISBN 0-8077-2863-2 (pbk.)

Manufactured in the United States of America

92 91 90 89 88 87   1 2 3 4 5 6

To
Jude and Marilynn

and to
David C. MacLean
(1959–1985)

This book is dedicated to the memory of David MacLean: musician, mimic, athlete, teacher, administrator, and dear friend. He was a gentle, caring person and an inspiring graduate student who constantly challenged us to rethink our basic assumptions. He was perhaps the finest natural teacher we have known; he could learn more from a mistake than any person we ever met.

Contents

Preface

During the more than twenty years the two of us have been teaching, we have seen very few publications purporting to advance simultaneously a curricular vision, a soundly researched pedagogy, and a rhetorically grounded theory of written composition. This book is our statement of what such a synthesis of vision, pedagogy, and theory might be. Crucial to our curricular model are the elements that frame the three sections of the book: rehearsing, composing, and valuing. A writing curriculum *must* provide daily and systematically focused rehearsal of writing skills; it *must* incorporate a thorough, well-grounded understanding of the composing process; and it *must* routinely assist students in developing skills to value and judge their own and others' writing.

R. H.
C. R. K., Jr.

Acknowledgments

We gratefully acknowledge the National Council of Teachers of English for permission to use Richard L. Larson's "Discovery Through Questioning: A Plan for Teaching Rhetorical Invention" (1968), portions of which appear in Chapter 3, and for permission to use Roland Huff's "Teaching Revision: A Model of the Drafting Process" (1983), portions of which appear in Chapter 4. We thank the School Council Publications of Great Britain and Macmillan Education Ltd. for permission to quote from *The Development of Writing Abilities* (1975, pp. 11–18), authored by James Britton, Tony Burgess, Nancy Martin, Alex McLeod, and Harold Rosen. We also acknowledge James Moffett for permission to quote material from *Teaching the Universe of Discourse* (1968). Special thanks go to Edye Johnson Holubec for reading Chapter 5 closely and providing invaluable feedback; to Amy Becker for the graphics that appear in this volume; and to Marilynn Kline for typing a basic draft of the manuscript, which allowed us to focus on the final version.

We also owe much to our professional colleagues. Professor Thomas Barton of Washington State University, Professor Donald Gray of Indiana University, Professor James Kinneavy of the University of Texas at Austin, and Dr. Judy Eekhoff, psychologist, played pivotal roles in the development of the vision that informs this book. A special debt is owed to Professor Michael Flanigan of the University of Oklahoma, with whom it all began. Major funding for our teaching and research came from the National Endowment for the Humanities (two grants) and from the University Research Institute of the University of Texas.

Above all, we are grateful to the students who through the years have tolerantly assisted us in conceptualizing the composing process and have given us permission to quote from their writing. Professor Huff, first author of this text, acknowledges an unpayable debt to the graduate research associates who staffed the Composition Research Laboratory at Washington State University (1979–1982) and subsequently at Eastern Washington University (1983–1985). It was in these research labs that the theories and concepts of this book were translated into practice, revised in sustained

dialogue, and field-tested under controlled conditions in some 200 sections of freshman composition. The Associate Directors of the lab during a six-year period were: Dana Elder, David Hadley, Jean Hegland, David Mac-Lean, Loyal Hanrahan, Kathy Ewing, and Devona Dawson.

Teachers College Press received various versions of this manuscript over several years. Always, Lois Patton was encouraging, and when she moved from her position as Acquisitions Editor, we were fortunate in her successor, Audrey Kingstrom. Thanks, Audrey, for working with us from final typescript through to publication. Your patience and simultaneous concern for deadlines were invaluable. We would also like to acknowledge the meticulous editorial work done by Nina George.

Finally, we wish to thank our consulting editor, Jude McMurry. She not only formatted the text to conform to Teachers College Press publication guidelines but also did the final stylistic editing, leaving us free to concentrate on what we were trying to say.

A Note on Language

Historically, when a third person singular pronoun was used to refer to an indefinite antecedent, the English language required the use of the masculine gender. Specifically, standard usage mandated in such cases the use of four masculine pronouns: *he* (subjective case), *his* (possessive case), *him* (objective case), and *himself* (reflexive). In 1975, the National Council of Teachers of English adopted a formal policy statement, "Guidelines for Nonsexist Use of Language in NCTE Publications" (NCTE, 1976). Since NCTE's prescription of nonsexist language in their sanctioned publications, a multitude of other professional organizations have followed suit.

The NCTE guidelines recommend four basic strategies to avoid the sexist use of gender:

1. Transform indefinite singular antecedents ("student") into the plural ("students") to avoid a masculine/feminine distinction ("they").
2. Substitute "one," "you," or "he or she" for generic masculine pronouns.
3. Alternate between using "he" and "she" when referring to indefinite singular antecedents.
4. Refer to indefinite pronouns ("everybody," "everyone," "anybody") with plural pronouns ("they ").

It is difficult to assess the implications for females and males of growing up reading and writing prose in which all indefinite singular antecedents automatically are referred to in terms of the masculine gender, but the argument of the NCTE guidelines is compelling and unanswerable:

> When we constantly personify "the judge," "the critic," "the executive," "the author," etc., as male by using the pronoun *he*, we are subtly conditioning ourselves against the idea of a female judge, critic, executive, or author. (pp. 23–24)

There is, however, another perspective on the issue. As writers, we have struggled with the difficulties of resolving the gender issue. We have turned our indefinite singular antecedents into plurals; we have tried alternating between "he" and "she"; we have used reluctantly the "he or she" construction; and we have even considered briefly the anathema of "s/he" (which does not resolve the "him/her" and "himself/herself" problem). Finally, we have been driven to agree with those writers who have argued that the gender issue is not *only* a sexist issue but also a stylistic issue of economy, convenience, and readability.

We propose an alternative solution to the gender issue that resolves both sexist and stylistic concerns. Four years ago, we started publishing a series of survey-of-research articles for regional NCTE journals. These articles were coauthored with graduate students, the majority of whom were women. Under the pressure of trying to edit the prose of as many as eight different coauthors, we decided to use the feminine gender whenever a pronoun referred to an indefinite singular antecedent. In all frankness, we were astounded at the overwhelmingly positive response by female readers; moreover, we received not a single complaint from male readers.

Upon reflection, we would like to propose an alternative solution to the NCTE guidelines as they refer to the sexist use of gender.

1. In the case of a single-authored text, the writer will consistently use his or her own gender when referring to indefinite singular antecedents.
2. In the case of a multiple-authored text, the writers will consistently use the gender that reflects that of the majority when referring to indefinite singular antecedents.
3. In the case of a multiple-authored text that has an even balance of male and female authors, a flip of the coin will determine the gender consistently used to refer to the indefinite singular antecedent.

There will always be exceptions. A woman writing for an all-male audience or a man writing for an all-female audience would likely use the gender of the audience as a courtesy. If the audience consists of an overwhelming percentage of one gender with only a few members of the other gender, courtesy might dictate a sparing use of the "one," "you," and "he or she" constructions. But in the main, the principle is clear: For lack of a generic or common-sex pronoun, authors will consistently use their own gender when referring to indefinite singular antecedents.

Quite apart from resolving the dichotomy of concerns about sexism in language and concerns for stylistic economy and simplicity, there are com-

pelling reasons for adopting this simple alternative solution to the sexist use of gender. First, it is important for young women and men to grow up reading and writing prose that automatically uses the feminine gender to refer to indefinite singular antecedents. This is a much stronger response to the stereotyping of male-female roles than the "he or she" construction. Second, it is easy to teach young writers to use their own gender when referring to the indefinite singular antecedent. Many a woman writer chooses to use "he" and "his" constructions in an attempt to reduce the stylistic complexities of indefinite plural antecedents and the "he or she" construction that can lead to the awkwardness of "himself or herself." Third, in many prose contexts it is valuable for the reader to know and be reminded of the author's gender. And finally, it is perhaps more significant than we recognize for authors, particularly very young writers, to "own" their text in terms of their gender.

The argument against this alternative solution to the sexist use of gender is that the solution focuses on the role of the writer instead of the needs and linguistic comfort of the audience. The counterargument is obvious: The fundamental problem of the sexist use of gender arises out of the English language's lack of a generic or common-sex pronoun. If consistent use of either the masculine or the feminine pronoun to refer to indefinite singular antecedents were *equally* acceptable, the problem would be resolved — essentially, we would have two generic pronouns.

To accustom readers to the use of the feminine pronoun as a generic pronoun, we have used it as such throughout this book.

THE CONTEMPORARY
WRITING CURRICULUM

Rehearsing, Composing, and Valuing

Part I

REHEARSING
IN THE WRITING
CURRICULUM

Musicians rehearse, athletes rehearse, dramatists rehearse, writers rehearse. Their rehearsals are focused, intensive, daily activities that build the skills, the confidence, and the accuracy that are manifested almost automatically during the pressures of a performance for an audience. Less skilled, less confident, and less accurate musicians, athletes, dramatists, and writers also need well-planned rehearsal periods. For both the beginner and the master, the rehearsal period is a time to work through the cognitive demands of the art or activity — first slowly, then more quickly as skill increases — while practicing the various aspects of the performance. For the beginning writer, regular focused and intensive rehearsal is essential. Thus, the importance of the journal.

During the sixties, journal writing was the vogue in high school and college composition classes. The Dartmouth Conference in 1966 (Dixon, 1967, and Muller, 1967) and the writing of Macrorie (1968) and Moffett (1968a, 1968b) encouraged many teachers to assign their students daily writings in a journal format. Typically, the student was given absolute freedom to write in any style about any topic. These entries were seldom read or, if read, were not graded by the teacher.

As a result of the backlash against the educational experimentation of the sixties (some would say "educational license"), many teachers reacted against the use of journals in the English classroom. In 1970, noted scholar and critic Professor Robert Heilman, then English Department Chairman at the University of Washington, commented in *College Composition and Communication*:

> I'm not against catharsis; the problem is only one of mistaking the study for the lavatory or the vomitorium. On the one

1

hand, we try to encourage growth by evaluation and control, on the other, we practice therapy by emetic, carminative, and laxative, and we supply, or even become appropriate receptacles. Hence perhaps the diary [journal], which seems to be having some vogue as a class surrogate for critical writing. (p. 236)

As a result of the educational tenor of our times, the use of the journal in the English classroom has diminished. Administrators and teachers often associate journal writing with undisciplined and unproductive student writing. Occasionally, they may associate it with "creative writing," making a clear distinction between practical, expository writing and impractical, although pleasurable, expressive writing. Journal writing, as many teachers understand it, is unproductive because it does little to improve students' basic writing skills.

It may be well to make a distinction between the terms "diary" and "journal," even though the two are often used interchangeably by both writers and teachers. Samuel Pepys and Anne Frank kept diaries; James Boswell and Katherine Mansfield kept journals. At its least, the diary may serve as a record of a teenager's social schedule. At its best, a journal such as Boswell's may describe the life of an entire society. Dictionaries offer the one as a synonym of the other and define each as a daily record of observations, transactions, events, or experiences. We tend, however, to make a connotative distinction between the two terms.

One normally thinks of the journal as a repository of commentaries on significant experiences and of elaborated descriptions of events along with the emotions that accompanied them. Journal entries can be made in any notebook. They may even be recorded on scraps of paper and allowed to accumulate in a drawer or box. The diary, on the other hand, has long been printed in the form of a small calendar book and favored as a suitable gift for adolescents. Such diaries are typically so small that they preclude any extended commentary; hence, the diary is commonly thought of as a place in which to make cryptic notations or short lists of important social events. A year later, even the writer may have difficulty decoding the significance of the entries.

Teachers who use journals in the classroom do not usually expect their students merely to cite events — to list what they did

on vacation or after the last basketball game. They expect students to record the specific details of a particularly vivid experience and to describe its impact. The word "journal" has been selected here to distinguish between the day-by-day notations, often of trivia, associated with the diary, and the more introspective descriptions of and commentaries on experience that are characteristic of many journals.

Keeping a journal is often erroneously regarded as the prerogative of the professional writer. To be sure, many writers do use journals, without concern for an audience, to record and explore the meaning of experiences later to be distilled and reshaped into work intended for publication. For example, between 1943 and 1963, Theodore Roethke filled 277 notebooks with his observations and reactions, and these journal entries served as the source of much of his later poetry. David Wagoner, the editor of Roethke's notebooks, comments on them as follows:

> As datings in his own hand prove, he returned to completed notebooks, often after an interval of several years, and hunted for what he could use, recombining old and new images, lines, or whole passages on related themes. These fragments in their turn would apparently suggest new rhythms, associations, and ideas, out of which a new poem would usually evolve. To put it mathematically: roughly a third of a typical poem written by Roethke in, say, 1955, would consist of fragments extracted from notebooks two or more years old, occasionally from fragments far older. (1974, p. 10)

Roethke's notebooks are an example of how the journal can serve to generate the peculiarities of form and authentic voice that constitute style.

But professional writers are not alone as journal keepers. Edward Weston, the photographer, kept a daily record of the visual discoveries that stimulated the photographic experiments for which he is now famous.

> *August 25.* Last eve green peppers in the market stopped me: they were amazing in every sense of the word, — the three purchased. But a *tragedy* took place. Brett [Weston's son] ate two of them!
> *August 27.* Well, I am joyful over my green pepper negative. If I can get some quality into the background it will

rank with my finest expression. I am not through with
peppers.

August 29. No—I am not through with peppers: now I
have another as fine or finer, — the same pepper from another
angle. It has amazing convolutions. (Millerton, 1973, p. 32)

Today, Weston's photographs of green peppers are among his
better known works, and his "daybooks" serve as a permanent
record of his visual discovery of and photographic experimentation with the phenomena of the everyday world.

It is important to emphasize that the journal or its equivalent
is an essential tool for many individuals whose professions have no
direct relationship to the fine arts. Researchers of all sorts keep
detailed, step-by-step records of their experiments and procedures;
doctors use the precisely scheduled entries of medical charts to
monitor physiological and emotional changes in their patients;
social workers keep case records on their clients. In addition to
those whose professions demand that they keep the equivalent of
journals, there are those who make sporadic use of journals
simply because their contents might one day be useful. Teachers
often take notes and describe classroom events when, for example,
they must deal with a particularly difficult disciplinary problem.
Many farmers record experiments with new seed varieties and
observations about growth rates or weather and soil conditions.
Historically, explorers and travellers have used journals to preserve
in all their freshness the details of new sights and experiences.
Individuals undergoing dramatic personal changes often keep
journals in which to document their feelings, sometimes at the
urging of therapists. Most teachers would agree that the skills
necessary to record observations and experiences accurately and
vividly, which are essentially the same in all these situations, are
"basic writing skills" (McCrimmon, 1970).

Why has journal writing been criticized? It is the therapeutic
model of journal writing that many teachers and administrators
condemn as inappropriate for classroom use. They have associated
the journal with undisciplined, cathartic outpourings of emotion.
Every teacher has known students who repeatedly and self-
indulgently confide their problems in written form: They confess
to hating their mothers or to being madly in love with an unap-
proachable person. Such outpourings may serve as useful releases
of emotion, but this sort of release in writing does not necessarily
constitute significant self-exploration. It certainly has little

relationship to the development of basic writing skills. (For a structured model of the therapeutic personal growth journal, see Ira Progoff, *At a Journal Workshop*, 1975.) In fact, we believe that mere cathartic writing has only a negative relationship to the production of competent prose.

But to dismiss the journal for previous misuse is to overlook an effective teaching method. Journals in the classroom need not be used only for catharsis. A skill-building model of journal writing is more appropriate for the writing classroom. In this theory of curriculum, the journal becomes the place where basic writing skills can be developed and where observations and experiences can be accurately recorded. The skill-building model (as opposed to the therapeutic model) depends on an intensive and ongoing interaction between the writer and the material in the journal. Professional writers often use the journal both for developing skills and for exploring the significance of their experiences, but in their case the self-exploration tends to be subordinated to the quality of the interaction between writer and recorded experience. One thinks of Thoreau and the "transcendental relationship" he maintained with his journals, or of the Latin grammar school student's "commonplace book" (Price, 1980).

Although it is not the primary function of the journal, self-exploration may occur in the writing curriculum as a by-product of the interaction between an individual student and her recorded experience. The primary function of the journal is to build writing skills. The journal is the vehicle for significant rehearsal of both the cognitive demands of the act of writing and the various aspects of the performance.

1

The Journal: A Vehicle
for Cognitive Development

Although the immediate purpose of the journal in the writing classroom is to develop basic writing skills, it has a larger purpose within the
context of cognitive development. When a child realizes that there are
people in this world who don't know who her father is, she has begun to
expand and elaborate the concept "father." The conceptual move from *my
father* to *father* to *progenitor* to *parenting* is an efficient metaphor for
cognitive development, the developing ability to apprehend the world as
an increasingly complex set of abstractions.

The journal can serve as an excellent vehicle for the type of "languaging" that promotes cognitive development. But before we can describe how
journal writing fosters cognitive growth, we must first establish a model of
cognitive development as it takes place in writing.

James Britton and four other British scholars (1975) spent five years
studying the development of writing abilities in children from age eleven
through eighteen. They concluded "that the [language] by which children
will govern their lives will require mental abilities that will best be developed by writing" (Britton, Burgess, Martin, McLeod, & Rosen, p. 201). To
determine what kind of writing would promote cognitive development,
they found it necessary to distinguish the *functions* of language from the
specific *modes* and *genres* in which it manifests itself.

The modes of language are typically defined as *descriptive*, *narrative*,
informative, *persuasive*, and *poetic/literary*. The first four are rarely
found in isolation. Rather, a mixture of two or more occur in a variety of
specific genres — for example, the letter, the technical report, or the newspaper article. Britton and his coworkers concluded that product-based
classifications of modes and genres helped little to define what kind of
languaging developed the cognitive abilities necessary to master particular
modes and genres.

After analyzing thousands of text samples written by students between
the ages of eleven and eighteen, Britton's research team concluded that the
functions of language were independent of mode and were derived from
the relationship between the writer and the audience. This relationship

results in three major functions of language: expressive, transactional, and poetic.

If the writer is writing primarily for herself or intimate acquaintances, the writing is defined as *expressive*.

> Expressive language is language close to the self. It has the functions of revealing the speaker, verbalizing his consciousness, and displaying his close relation with a listener or reader. . . . Much expressive language is not made explicit, because the speaker/writer relies upon his listener/reader to interpret what is said in the light of a common understanding (that is, a shared general context of the past), and to interpret their immediate situation (what is happening around them) in a way similar to his own. [And] . . . since expressive language submits itself to the free flow of ideas and feelings, it is relatively unstructured . . . (e.g., topical newspaper commentary in a conversational manner, some editorials, "interest" articles in specialist journals, gossip columns). (Britton et al., 1975, p. 90)

If the writer is writing for a more general and public audience, the writing is defined as *transactional*.

> [Transactional writing] is language to get things done: to inform people (telling them what they need or want to know or what we think they ought to know), to advise or persuade or instruct people. Thus the transactional is used for example to record facts, exchange opinions, explain and explore ideas, construct theories; to transact business, conduct campaigns, change public opinion. Where the transaction (whatever it is we want to do with language) demands accurate and specific reference to what is known about reality, this need constitutes a demand for the use of language in the transactional category. (p. 88)

If the writer adopts somewhat of a spectator role toward her own writing and is primarily concerned with its internal patterns (word-play, parallelism, thematic connections), the writing is defined as *poetic* or *literary*.

> Poetic writing uses language as an art medium. A piece of poetic writing is a verbal construct, an "object" made out of language. The words themselves, and all they refer to, are selected to make an arrangement, a formal pattern. . . .
>
> The phonetic, syntactic, lexical and semantic aspects of the utterance itself are the objects of attention, by the writer and the reader, in a way that does not hold of non-poetic writing. . . . Consonance and dis-

sonance between formal elements bind the writing into a complete whole, a single construct whether it be a sonnet or a novel, an epic or a curtain-raiser. . . . Poetic writing constitutes language that exists *for its own sake* and not as a means of achieving something else. (pp. 90–91)

The critical argument in the discussion of all these functions is that regular exercise of each serves as a vehicle for cognitive growth. Citing the work of James Moffett (1968a, 1968b) and Piaget and Inhelder (1969), Britton et al. conclude that cognitive development — the ability to process information at increasingly complex levels of abstraction — stems from on-going global interaction of the function categories. Given that development in any one of the functions of language tends to promote growth in the other functions, all the basic functions (expressive, transactional, and poetic) need to be encouraged and continually fostered in every writer — whether the second grader, remedial college student, or professional writer.

If Britton et al. had stopped here in their analysis of cognitive development, they would already have provided a strong justification for the role of the journal as a vehicle for the exercise of the expressive function. However, they go on to conclude that although cognitive development proceeds out of a global interaction of all three functions of language, the expressive function is primary in two respects. First, even though the very young child can use all of the functions of language in a rudimentary way, the expressive function serves as the primary vehicle for the acquisition of all of the functions. Second, and more importantly, Britton et al. (1975) conclude that the expressive function serves as the ongoing matrix for developing the cognitive skills needed for mature writing and thinking in all three functions.

[Expressive writing's] relationship to thinking . . . seems particularly direct and this suggests its importance as a mode of learning at any stage. It appears to be the means by which the new is tentatively explored, thoughts are half uttered, attitudes half expressed, the rest being left to be picked up by the . . . reader, who is willing to take the unexpressed on trust. Its use is not, of course, always exploratory, but exploratory situations seem to call for it. Thus, a study of the expressive elements in writing has been a continuing thread in our work. (p. 11)

Britton and his coworkers assert with considerable supporting evidence that expressive conversations with the self and intimate associates stimulate cognitive growth in all of the functions of language. Piaget and

Inhelder (1969) defined this elaboration of the expressive function into other functions as a decentering from an initial egocentricity. And Moffett (1968b) characterizes the move from the expressive to the transactional function in the following terms:

1. From the implicit, embodied idea to the explicitly formulated idea.
2. From addressing the small, known audience like oneself to addressing a distant, unknown, and different audience.
3. From talking about present objects and actions to talking about things past and potential. (p. 57)

Several points need to be emphasized in regard to these conclusions about the primary role of the expressive function. First, expressive writing, although written for the self and intimate associates, is not necessarily private in the sense that it deals with the merely personal events of the writer's life. Half-conceptualized questions of values, attitudes toward social issues, political opinions, and aesthetic responses often emerge for the first time in the implicit, associative structures of expressive writing. And second, the elaboration of the expressive function into the other functions is recycled again and again. As new ideas are explicitly formulated in transactional writing or balanced off against one another as formal elements in poetic writing, they serve to trigger new responses that need to be realized by an expressive function. The need to write expressively is lifelong.

This primary role of expressive writing in cognitive development has radical implications for the role of the journal within the composing curriculum. Expressive writing with its lack of concern for a public audience cannot be evaluated by the same standards by which we judge transactional writing. The implicit, free-wheeling associative structures of expressive writing are not what we want to see in a transactional essay written for a public audience. To apply the standards by which we judge the transactional function to the expressive function is to punish rather than reward the writer's emerging conversations with the self.

If we are to foster the development of the expressive function—and Britton et al. and Moffett tell us it is a primary stimulus for cognitive growth—we must provide regular opportunities for expressive writing in a format that encourages and rewards it (Emig, 1971). Whether you call it ten-minute daily writes or a daybook or a diary, what choice is there but the journal? Without ongoing practice in the expressive function, a composition course may actually retard cognitive development rather than pro-

mote it. Expressive writing is the matrix for the development and elaboration of all of the functions of language.

THE LOGIC OF EXPRESSIVE NONSTOP WRITING

The following discussion of expressive nonstop writing serves as a metaphor, a radical stalking-horse, designed to bring the developmental philosophy of the journal into a head-on collision with product-structured philosophies of teaching composition.

For the immature writer, expressive nonstop writing, or what Macrorie (1968) calls "free writing," is one of the most profitable journal exercises. The term "nonstop" is used literally. During nonstop writing, the students' pencils never stop moving. Students write nonstop on an associative basis, and if they get stuck for words, they simply write the last phrase or sentence over and over until the thoughts begin to flow again. By definition, nonstop writing is expressive writing.

This "free writing" has been criticized because its focus is not on grammar, punctuation, or spelling, but on getting the words down, going with the idea, finding an authentic voice. Nonstop writing, with its lack of focus on the conventions of standard usage, is precisely the kind of writing many educators are trying to eradicate. Yet, for a variety of reasons nonstop writing is an effective way to teach writing skills. First and foremost, nonstop writing provides students with the opportunity to write expressively on many subjects, time and again, with a minimum investment of time and energy. Second, nonstop writing allows students to make a wide variety of significant mistakes—false starts, wrong points of view, aborted arguments. Third, the associative structure of nonstop writing tends to lead students into a significant personal engagement with their own ideas and language. In nonstop writing, the students' predisposition to think of writing as a product is broken down, and they begin to see writing as a process of discovery and exploration. They learn that in the journal they are not expected to come up with a product; rather, they are expected to practice their writing skills in the context of the expressive function. They are writing for themselves.

Nonstop writing accomplishes a number of other objectives. It allows students to practice psychomotor skills that lead to increased scribal facility. As Scardamalia and Bereiter (1979) point out, there is a striking difference between how quickly people can write and how quickly they can dictate a paper on the same topic. Many students have had little or no practice in translating their thoughts rapidly into written form. Quite apart from being lazy in this respect, often their hands cramp up and

literally choke the flow of their ideas. In fact, numerous studies suggest that how much a student can write on a topic has some correlation with overall quality (Hillocks, 1986).

Nonstop writing—simply sitting down and writing an assignment for ten minutes without pausing—allows students to bypass the psychological entry barrier of confronting a blank sheet of paper. Moreover, students who get stuck for words begin to desensitize themselves in regard to writing blocks they may have simply by writing the last phrase or sentence over and over again. They learn that if they just keep writing, new thoughts and ideas will begin to flow again. Nonstop writing, like the artist's "quick sketch," is a vehicle to develop the fluency that is so important to control of subject.

Nonstop writing not only successfully bypasses students' writing blocks but also reduces their generalized anxiety toward the act of writing. Many students are afraid of writing because they associate writing, first and foremost, with being evaluated and judged. It is almost as though they have come to believe that a "C" on a writing assignment means that they are a "C" person. Nonstop journal writing helps to eliminate this anxiety because what the student writes is never judged as a product written for others. Nonstop writing is expressive writing; the audience is the self.

It is important to stress that in the nonstop exercise the student is not expected to be concerned with the mechanics of good writing or the conventions and rules of standard usage. The purpose of this exercise is to liberate the flow of thought and progression of ideas. When students continually break the spontaneous flow of content to consider questions of syntax and vocabulary, their writing often loses coherence and trails off into irrelevant and disconnected lists of information and opinions. This is not an argument against the importance of teaching standard usage, but an argument that the appropriate time to focus on coherence and correctness is *after* students have succeeded in getting their thoughts down on paper. Even mature writers are only occasionally capable of coherence *and* correctness in a first and often rapidly written draft. Do not expect this from young writers.

Students' lack of automatic certainty about the mechanics of standard usage can affect them negatively in another way. The spoken language that students use with one another often contains a richness and complexity of metaphor and argument not found in their written language. Their oral language often has the detail, imagery, and focus so desirable in written language. Yet when students write, their premature concern for correctness can lower the syntactic maturity and complexity of their natural voices. To avoid making mistakes, students often write in a voice that is less syntactically complex than their spoken language. This is an inversion of

the normal relationship between the written and spoken voice of the competent writer. Nonstop writing, with its lack of focus on questions of usage and its associative elaboration of ideas, leads students to use syntactic structures that more closely reflect the complexity of their thoughts and experiences. Nonstop writing is seminal in students' use and development of mature syntactic structures.

Students' premature concern for correct usage and the corresponding reduction of their written syntactic complexity also reveal themselves in the students' attempts to imitate the teacher's voice, leading students into awkward statements that represent an abortion of their own authentic voices. Half-mute and inarticulate as the students' voices may be in their tentative emergence in nonstop writing, they are nonetheless the students' own. Nonstop writing in the journal forces students to "speak for themselves." With continued practice, the students learn to listen to their natural voices and elaborate them into increasingly complex statements. In short, nonstop writing serves as an extraordinarily economic exercise of the expressive function of language—the function that Britton and Moffett consider to be a primary stimulus for cognitive development in transactional and poetic as well as expressive functions of language.

Those who have dismissed nonstop writing or free writing as an undisciplined enterprise may wish to examine Thomas Hilgers' (1980) empirical study that compared the effectiveness of free writing as an invention heuristic with the effectiveness of more rational heuristic procedures. Those students who engaged in focused free writing before drafting wrote significantly better essays than those who employed rational heuristics.

NONSTOP WRITING
AND THE SEARCH FOR A SUBJECT

Part of the theory behind nonstop writing is that as students' confidence increases, their facility with written language will become as automatic as speaking, and that with continued practice, students will learn to focus their thoughts into an organized statement. While it is true that there are students who learn quickly to focus their nonstop writing into comparatively organized statements, there are others who can go an entire term without finding a focus. One of the criticisms of nonstop writing is that students find it difficult to generate their own focus or subject within the writing. Critics look to these students' writing as proof that nonstop writing is undisciplined, unproductive, and noncumulative in terms of writing skills. At best it is merely a warm-up exercise allowing students to loosen up

their hands before getting into real writing. What the critics forget is that finding, engaging, and limiting a subject is a complex cognitive skill (see Chapter 3). Lack of focus is an endemic problem in student writing.

To dismiss nonstop writing as unprofitable because many students have difficulty in discovering their focus is to ignore the larger question of why it is so difficult for students to find significant subjects to write about—whether they are writing nonstop or spending half the term on a research paper. Our students are the best informed individuals who have ever lived. They have access to incredible amounts of information. Marshall McLuhan (1962) wrote of contemporary society as a Global Village, in which all kinds of information are transmitted almost instantaneously around the world. Students take for granted their knowledge of a variety of data. They have the latest information communicated to them via satellite; they understand and utilize complex economic systems when they use credit cards; most are aware of the local and national implications of an OPEC embargo; they are rapidly becoming computer literate and have access to electronic data banks. The Global Village is a reality.

Yet with all this information readily available, students still have difficulty finding something to write about. Why do they have so much trouble with a focus for their writing? The question is much larger than the issue of nonstop writing. McLuhan suggested that one of the reasons people in general have a difficult time in speaking with authority about their world is that they are overloaded with information. Students have encoded and stored an incredible amount of information, but they have not organized that information so that it is usable. They have not classified and subordinated that information into categories and subcategories that allow them to cross-reference information in such a way as to bring its significance to bear upon the events of their own lives. Indeed, students are bombarded with masses of information to which they cannot relate. Rather than information serving as a means of understanding their world, it becomes a source of confusion and as a result they often "tune out" the information coming in. They do not want to talk about it. They block. They do not even want to think about it. "Just let me be!"

Nonstop writing, with its concern for cumulative associative responses, begins to tap students' information banks. However, if students are overloaded with information that has not been meaningfully classified and subordinated into some coherent frame of reference related to their own lives, their associative responses may not enable them to perceive their own relationship to a subject. When nonstop writing serves only as a retrieval system for large amounts of unassimilated and extremely complex information, students tend to become bored with the exercise, anxious about it, or even hostile. This resistance can be overcome.

WRITING IN RESPONSE TO STIMULUS

To resolve the problems students have in discovering a focus for their writing, teachers traditionally have structured the writing in advance. The most successful approach we have found for nonstop writing is to provide the students with a stimulus designed to bring a variety of latent societal contradictions rudely into each student's consciousness. These "stimulus units" consist of stories and poems from anthologies, songs, cartoons, advertisements, and art work that portray differing beliefs or role models. These are organized into sets of two or more contradictory views on the same issue (approximately eight minutes of viewing, listening, and/or reading time). Each unit is relatively short, but it contains a large amount of information.

As an example, one of our favorite stimulus units is titled "Take This Job and Shove It." The unit consists of two songs and a short newspaper article. Students are provided with a stimulus packet including the lyrics of two songs so that they can read along as the songs are played on tape, and they are given the text of the newspaper article. The first song is Judy Collins' haunting rendition of a women's working song, "Bread and Roses." The lyrics, written from a feminist perspective, capture the basic human need for work that dignifies the spirit. The second song in the stimulus sequence is Johnny Paycheck's well-known, twangy, country version of "Take This Job and Shove It" — a parody of all low-paying, boring, menial jobs that reduce human consciousness. The final element of the stimulus sequence is a short news article that describes in terrifying detail the increasingly competitive nature of the job market and how difficult it is for the college graduate to find a satisfying job.

Once the students have read or looked at the materials and listened to the songs included in the unit, they write a ten-minute nonstop response. In reacting to the contradictions presented, students naturally draw upon their own experiences as well as the information from the unit, which is the *societal contradiction*. The result is focused writing, and it usually is characterized by a verve, a lively intensity that indicates personal involvement — the origin of Voice.

The stimulus units are constructed to foster students' expressive response to social concerns larger than the immediate events of their personal lives. Some stimulus categories are:

Education
Death/Suicide/Aging
Crime/Terrorism/War
Status of Minorities/Protest/Revolution

Politics/Economics
Work/Professions
Love/Marriage/Sex
Ecology/Population
Generation Gap/Cultural Values
Masculine/Feminine Stereotypes

During the progression of a course, a student may write in response to as many as 15 or 20 of these stimulus units. Not every stimulus unit strikes home, but most students find a considerable number to which they respond intensely.

If the stimulus unit successfully represents for the students a societal contradiction that they — as members of that society — have internalized and experienced, their nonstop, associative response to the stimulus unit tends to lead them to elaborate on their own experiences. It frequently culminates in an awareness of the discrepancies that exist between models for behavior. Once they begin to examine the effect of such contradictions and discrepancies on their personal thinking and behavior, students tend to seek resolution and closure in written responses that cannot be reduced to vague generalizations about truth, beauty, and justice for all. In their attempts to synthesize what is contrary to their experiences, beliefs, attitudes, and behavior, they are driven toward the attempted resolution and closure of organic form and argument. In short, expressive writing in response to carefully constructed stimuli fosters the elaboration of expressive writing into transactional writing.

The following example of a student's unrevised nonstop response to a stimulus unit on war demonstrates clearly how the student has organized a variety of associative responses into a focused statement. He is beginning to speak with authority about his world.

It's the easiest thing in the world to deplore the amorality of war without having seen or felt something of it. I have no first-hand knowledge, in the sense of having had to kill someone, but I have watched people die. All the A–6 pilots had flag decals stuck on their planes, but whether the flags got them into heaven or not is hard to say; in fact, it's hard to say whether it got them anywhere. Some people believe in the existence of a Soul, and this is the element of existence that makes it to the Afterlife, but it's hard to imagine even a Soul surviving the wreckage a human body undergoes after a jet crash. The pilot's body is often reduced to something like glue and is welded to whatever parts of the aircraft are left. Or if a plane misses the flight deck on a rough day, hits the ocean and immediately sinks, what the hell does the pilot think about this nifty little war as he sinks into the deep, green depths of the Pacific, trying to eject in a seat where some asshole neglected to check the cartridge? Is it the asshole's fault, or someone else's, something bigger? Or how about a guy from Fertile,

Minnesota, who tried to pull a pilot out of burning plane when suddenly it exploded and by God there wasn't enough of either one of them to bother about? Or what about the guy from Lawrence, Kansas, who failed to hear a warning shout on a stormy night and ended up lying on the flight deck, wondering what the hell happened to his lower legs? What do these guys think about that nifty little war, about America's need to save the world and preserve democracy? Not a squadron that goes out ever comes back fully-manned, and you want to know something? It's mostly the nice guys that get it. And that is not a cliché. *(Lee Atherton, Washington State University, Pullman, Washington, 1978)*

Writing in response to a significant stimulus is one answer to the criticism that expressive nonstop writing has a tendency to degenerate into a cathartic outpouring of personal opinion and experience. It also counters the assertion that nonstop writing is merely an associative stream of consciousness bearing little relationship to the considered judgments and nonlinear organization of competent prose. Because the stimulus units incorporate two or more dissonant and fairly intense views of the same subject — whether it be war or racial discrimination — the students' colliding responses to a stimulus unit force them to make a variety of logical distinctions and judgments. These logical distinctions and judgments represent a classification and subordination of their associative responses to the subject that begin to approximate the nonlinear organization of significant transactional writing.

JOURNAL FEEDBACK TERMS
FOR EXPRESSIVE NONSTOP WRITING

Critics of the journal and nonstop writing have raised another question. If the virtue of nonstop writing lies in its emphasis on process and in the fact that it is never evaluated as a product, how can students learn to assess their nonstop writing as a more or less satisfactory approximation of the nonlinear organization of competent prose? Certainly, nonstop writing gives students the freedom to make the false starts and mistakes that are necessary adjuncts of significant writing, but how is the student to assess her nonstop writing?

In *Zen and the Art of Motorcycle Maintenance*, Robert Pirsig (1974) suggests that students intuitively recognize quality in a finished piece of writing. But how does a student learn to produce quality, particularly in a nonstop writing situation where only rarely does a beginning writer "discover" a response to the subject that leads directly to a finished product? If students cannot learn to assess their nonstop writing, it will be difficult for

them to generalize to the nature of the composing process as it occurs in the considered production of competent prose. A few students may be able to generalize from their more successful nonstop approximations of good prose to a notion of how to write good prose consistently, but many other students will not. None of the students in a class is likely to gain much awareness of the nature of the composing process via unassessed nonstop writing. Yet to judge nonstop writing by the same standards that are applied to finished products is to destroy its function as a risk-free exploration of the student's expressive voice.

A response system is needed to encourage critical awareness and give students feedback about the basic writing skills involved in composing prose. It is possible to identify at least three basic writing skills above the syntactic level of the individual sentence necessary to writing competent prose: (a) limiting and defining a subject, (b) establishing a scene or thesis, and (c) supporting generalizations with specific details, examples, or evidence. Students' comparative mastery of these skills can be communicated concisely by using a number of journal feedback responses derived from film making. Students may not be penetrating analysts of the emotional and intellectual content of the cinematic composing process, but they have become sophisticated "viewers" as a result of thousands of hours spent watching television and films. Once given a description of film terms, most students grasp their meaning almost immediately and have little trouble applying them to the written composing process (Adams & Kline, 1975).

The primary purpose of the following feedback terms is not to evaluate any given journal entry or nonstop writing; rather, the terms are designed to point out the particular skills that need to be practiced the *next time* the student writes. The value of the feedback terms resides in what they can teach students about basic writing skills by defining those skills in the context of their own writing.

Words about Words—Show Us

"If You're in Love, Show Me" is the title of a song from *My Fair Lady*. Eliza Doolittle sings, "Oh words, words, words! . . . I get words all day through, first from him, then from you. Is that all you blighters can do?" The function of the camera's eye is to record a picture, usually in great detail. If the student is generalizing about an experience rather than describing its specific content, the comment, "Words about words" can be written in the margin. Other more precise hints can be offered: "Don't *tell* us you were a skinny teenager and hated it. *Show* us." The following paragraph is a student's response to such teacher feedback:

I think of myself as a teenager, really a pre-teenager, with no bustline to speak of—just plain skinny. I used to stuff nylons inside my bra to get a little more in the way of boobs. But it isn't the lack of a bustline I remember; it was being skinny. How many times I succumbed to a magazine ad: "Gain weight in this easy home program. Results guaranteed." And my Dad's irritation when a can of malt would arrive postage due. . . . *(Phyllis Jensen, NEH Writing Project, Richland, Washington, 1978)*

After students have internalized the concept "words about words — show us" as it relates to describing personal experiences, the concept can be elaborated to give students feedback on informative and persuasive writing. If the student is writing about abstractions rather than defining and demonstrating ideas and terms, it is appropriate to comment, "Words about words. Show us the process," or "Show us the causes/effects," or "Show us the comparisons/contrasts," or "Show us the evidence." The comment, "Words about words. Don't just *tell* us that Yellowstone National Park is being overrun with cars. *Show* us the evidence," led to the following paragraph by a student writer:

Within Yellowstone Park the network of roads was built for the motoring tourist. Beautifully smooth asphalt connects each major site, each complete with another parking lot so the tourist can conveniently leave his vehicle long enough to walk some few yards to see a waterfall. It is nearly as convenient as watching TV at home. Indeed, many visitors probably see most of the park world from their vehicle only, framed in glass as on TV. *(Derise Wigand, Washington State University, Pullman, 1979)*

Skimming the Surface: Roll the Camera In

When students write about their personal experience, they tend to bounce from one associative generalization to another without offering any significant development of that experience. Film terminology can again be used to give the student feedback: "Skimming the surface of your experience. Roll the camera in, focus on one scene or event."

After the student has grasped this concept and learned to focus when narrating a personal experience, the concept can also be applied to informative and persuasive writing. If the student is offering one abstraction after another, it is appropriate to comment: "Skimming the surface of your thoughts. Roll the camera in. Focus on one idea or concept," or "Focus on one comparison/contrast," or "Focus on one cause/effect," or "Focus on one argument."

Elaborate the Details: Give Us a Close-up

When the camera takes a close-up of a subject (a full-figure shot of one person, that person's face, a single flower), the particularity of the subject usually dominates the entire scene. Often students give a long shot of their subject (a person walking down the street) or a medium shot (a short girl walking down the street), when what they really need to give is a close-up.

In teaching this concept, it is helpful to explain the difference between a concrete detail and an elaborated detail. A concrete detail is any concrete noun modified by an adjective: "the short girl," for example. Students often think that the use of simple concrete details to describe a scene, a person, or an object is an adequate approximation of a perception or observation. They need to realize that it would be difficult to pick a particular "short girl" out of a line-up of ten other short girls. Students need to be persuaded to elaborate details so that the audience can apprehend the particularity of the subject: not merely "the short girl," but "the short, red-headed girl with the chocolate ice-cream stain down the front of her blue dress." If a student describes the details of a personal experience in general rather than particular terms, the comment, "Elaborate details. Give us a close-up," will usually be sufficient to define the problem.

Once the student has mastered this concept in descriptive and narrative writing, the same terms can be used to give feedback on informative and persuasive writing: "Give us a close-up. Elaborate the concept," or "Elaborate the example," or "Elaborate the cause and effect," or "Elaborate the comparison/contrast."

Establish Scene: Roll the Camera Back

In film terminology, an establishing shot is one that usually comes at the beginning of a film or scene and serves to set the time, place, and context of the action. Sometimes after students have begun to master the skills of using elaborated details and specific examples, they lose themselves in the specifics of the experience and neglect to set the scene before beginning to describe the characters. When this happens, students can be told, "Establish scene. Roll the camera back."

When the student understands the concept "Establish scene; roll the camera back" as it applies to descriptive and narrative writing, the terms can be used to give feedback about informative and persuasive writing. If students have defined specific causes and effects, carefully delineated a comparison or contrast, or presented concrete arguments but have failed to subordinate particular ideas to a thesis, a comment such as, "Establish thesis. Roll the camera back," will help them understand what is lacking.

Authentic Voice

The previously defined cinematic feedback terms serve primarily to show students what they are failing to do, but it is just as important to identify their successes. Students have difficulty in assessing their own writing, and whenever a student's voice comes through, it is helpful to reinforce the moment with the comment, "Authentic voice." This authentic voice may be only a few sentences interspersed throughout three or four pages of clichés and reductive generalizations, but it is important to begin shaping the students' responses by identifying those instances when they are speaking with authority.

Seed Idea

Nonstop writing is a skill-building rather than a content- or product-oriented exercise. Now and again, however, a student's voice will begin to emerge in a relatively focused and coherent discussion of her thoughts and ideas. When this happens, it is helpful to bracket the significantly developed section of the writing and comment, "Seed idea." This alerts the student to the fact that this portion of her writing is worthy of further development and could possibly serve as the basis for a considered essay.

Intra-Journal Response

One other comment that can often be made in response to students' nonstop writing is "Possible intra-journal response." Students make a variety of statements in their journals ranging from the absurd to the interesting, from the radical to the reactionary. If it would be profitable for the student to respond to her own statement, assign the student an intra-journal response to it. (This second assignment would not be nonstop writing.) Such an additional exercise may be valid for a variety of reasons. For example, the student may not be able to justify her statement and needs to discover that fact, or her statement may be a coded statement about herself that could be profitably deciphered, or the statement may embody a significant insight that could be elaborated into a possible seed idea. But more generally, it is helpful to assign intra-journal responses because the competent writer is characterized by the ability to interact with her own voice — linguistically, emotionally, intellectually. The intra-journal response raises the student's level and intensity of response to her own writing.

Most nonstops are "dead" writing in the sense that they will not be reworked, and the student has no responsibility to "finish" them. The

journal feedback terms draw attention to particular skills that need to be practiced and errors to be avoided the next time the student sits down to write. They are not intended to provide the basis for a grading policy. Because of years of conditioning by an educational system in which the overwhelming percentage of classroom feedback is graded evaluation, it takes time to convince students that they need not suffer the anxiety of judgment in return for an evaluative critique.

Consistent use of these feedback terms helps students to define in the context of their own writing those basic writing skills required to produce competent prose. Students learn how much more alive writing becomes if they recreate the components of their experiences and thoughts rather than merely generalize about abstractions ("Show us"), if they focus on a subject ("Roll the camera in"), if they use specific details, examples, or evidence ("Give us a close-up"), and if they establish a thesis ("Roll the camera back"). Although the feedback terms are designed to heighten students' awareness of writing skills they have not mastered, the same terms can be used to give immediate reinforcement when students successfully display a skill: "Excellent focus," "Good elaborated detail," and so forth.

Using these feedback terms to respond to journal and nonstop writing not only promotes fluency but provides a risk-free environment for the practice and mastery of essential writing skills. Although such writing is concerned more with recording the writer's thoughts than with communicating with a public audience, it serves as a rich seedbed for the discovery and development of authentic topics that can evolve into finished products. It turns out that students consistently produce papers of a higher quality when the sources of such papers are rooted in an earlier piece of writing.

What needs to be emphasized is that although the feedback terms are introduced early in the context of the journal and expressive nonstop writing, their use is not restricted to nonstop writing. Limiting and defining a subject, establishing a thesis, and supporting generalizations with specific details, examples, or evidence are *basic writing skills* that are required in all of the functions of language. The journal feedback terms are used to respond to all types of student writing throughout the progression of the curriculum.

The teacher, of course, is not limited to the journal feedback terms when responding to student writing. A stirring journal entry may prompt a personal response.

I was moved by your sharing of your grandfather's death. The detailed description of the intensive care ward with its intravenous tubes and computerized monitors was all too real. I think the piece is worthy of further development. I would

like more information about why your grandfather was important to you. Also needs an ending.

When responding to a finished piece of writing submitted to be read by a public audience, a capable prose stylist uses her entire range of critical awareness to define patterns of mistakes in usage, analyze logical problems, critique underdeveloped conceptualizations, and suggest alternative strategies of organization, tone, and style. However, if students have not begun to exercise a conscious mastery of those basic writing skills reflected in the journal feedback terms, it is unlikely that they will be able to make much use of such a sophisticated critical response. The journal feedback terms are a matrix for acquiring the basic skills required for the production of all competent prose.

Consistent use of these feedback terms in the writing classroom enables students, as they themselves report, to internalize "a director's voice." The director's voice should not be confused with the editorial voice that prompts many students to edit their writing for "correctness" while they are still engaged in the preliminary composing process. Editorial proofing becomes appropriate in the final stages of revision, when the student is getting ready to make the manuscript public. As the students write, listening to their own authentic voices and attempting to record the progression of their thoughts, they hear "a director's voice" urging them to "roll the camera back" or "set the scene." When this happens, students have become self-directed writers who will continue to evolve as the result of their self-directed interaction with their own authentic voices.

RESOLVING THE DICHOTOMY
BETWEEN EXPRESSIVE AND TRANSACTIONAL WRITING

By practicing nonstop exercises in response to meaningful stimuli and by attending to journal feedback, students acquire critical awareness of universal principles that are applicable to both expressive and transactional writing. Furthermore, with help, students can learn how their personal responses to the stimulus units can serve as the raw materials for a transactional statement.

Too often the relationship between expressive and transactional writing has been presented as a dichotomy. Too often teachers of "expository" or transactional writing have asserted that although nonstop writing may indeed serve as an excellent device for the development of students' expressive voices, it does little to promote the disciplined skills essential to compe-

tent transactional writing. On the other hand, too often the advocates of nonstop and expressive writing have been prejudiced against what they perceive to be the aridity of transactional writing. The split between those who inadvertently sacrifice discipline and method in their enthusiasm for promoting heartfelt expression and those who bypass the feelings and experiences of students in their zeal to implant rules and systems is apparent among teachers of every discipline. It is in the writing classroom that such biases are often most pronounced, and it is also there that they can be effectively eliminated.

The mind-set enabling us to perpetuate the artificial split between expressive and transactional writing is difficult to change because it is so deeply ingrained in our educational curricula. We tend to focus on expressive writing in our elementary schools to the neglect of transactional writing, and then suddenly shift, in our middle and secondary schools, to a focus on transactional writing to the neglect of expressive writing (Newkirk, 1977). The same dichotomy also manifests itself in the more limited context of college composition courses.

Ironically, the dichotomy tends to be most pronounced in precisely those composition classes modeled after the work of Moffett (1968a) and Britton et al. (1975). In such classes, students are encouraged to keep journals, and the major writing assignments follow a developmental sequence moving from an early concern with expressive writing to a middle and late concern with transactional writing. The stated purpose of such composition courses is to establish an organic bridge between expressive and transactional writing. In practice, however, there is a tendency among teachers to reinforce the notion that expressive writing is freeing, creative, and fun, and that transactional writing is stultifying and tedious. Such attitudes only constrict and negate the authenticity of voice that students feel they are beginning to establish in their expressive writing. Theoretically at least, expressive writing (story telling, descriptions of personal experiences) and transactional writing (logical exposition, definition, persuasion) are equally creative modes of writing. Few students would argue that Lincoln's Gettysburg Address was not a creative piece of transactional writing, yet their own educational conditioning and experiences have led them to the conviction that, for them, transactional writing is boring, artificial, tedious, and an utter waste of time.

Writing nonstop in response to well-chosen stimuli can serve to bridge the gap between expressive and transactional writing. If the stimulus represents a societal contradiction with considerable intensity, there is a natural tendency for students to begin to elaborate the expressive response into a transactional response. However, we have designed a specific exercise that requires students to elaborate their expressive response into transac-

tional writing. Consider the following example of a student's unrevised nonstop, produced in response to a stimulus unit on old age.

> Wow! My chest contracts! It really does! Pains! Really! And I fight for control. I'm on edge, anyway. To think of Grandma! I can't disintegrate here. Not in front of God and [the teacher] and everyone. But to think of Grandma!
>
> We ran around the yard like puppies, tumbling, rolling, chasing, ducking, spinning, boxing, hiding—Phil and I. The other cousins come, Doug and Bob and their baby brother. What's his name? They join us and we go over, shyly, to kiss their parent. And we four frolic. Like lambs, maybe. Far off, the baby cries. Everyone's laughing and talking and hugging some more, and it's all crazy and wild and fun. Grandma shuffles around and pats everyone. Grandpa grins and cries a little.
>
> Then Uncle Gene and Aunt Helen arrive with Donnie and the baby. And everyone laughs and hugs and kisses and talks. A baby cries. Grandpa wipes his eyes and Grandma pats everyone.
>
> It's time to get dinner on. Grandma has cooked for two days. Roast beef. ("It's stringy, I'm afraid.") One-egg cake. Other stuff. (That's all I remember: beef and cake.) As she's trying to get everything together and everyone started, it starts—another spell. She moans, "Oh! Oh! Oh!" Her eyes roll back. "Oh! Oh! Oh!" Two people support her to the bed and soothe her. "Oh! Oh! Oh!"
>
> I hate it! I run behind the barn. . . . *(Patricia L. Dick, Missouri Valley Writing Project, Columbia, Missouri, 1979)*

If everyone agreed with Moffett and Britton about the equal value of expressive and transactional writing, this type of expressive nonstop would be self-justifying. There is, however, a follow-up exercise designed to teach students how to transmute the more generally expressive or personal character of their initial response to a given stimulus unit into a transactional statement. After students have written a ten-minute nonstop in response to a particular stimulus, they are given a break to "shake out" their hands and count the number of words they have written. Counting the words written during a ten-minute nonstop is not a make-work task. After two to three weeks of writing nonstop on a regular basis, an average group of students will increase their individual production by 20 to 30 percent. This increase in scribal fluency is particularly important for the remedial or blocked writer. Counting the number of words serves as minimal reinforcement for the writer and also provides an ongoing benchmark by which to assess the writer's fluency.

After what amounts to a five-minute disengagement from their task, the students are asked to read back over their nonstops and identify one idea that they are willing to elaborate into a transactional statement. Subsequently, students spend another 15 minutes developing this idea. *This writing is not done nonstop*; rather, students are encouraged to write

in a more considered and deliberate fashion for a public audience. In this exercise, the expressive nonstop serves as a predrafting exercise for a transactional statement. The following transactional writing was done by the same student who wrote the expressive nonstop response to the stimulus unit on old age. The transactional response to her own writing was composed five minutes after the expressive response.

> How do people react to the tension they feel? Some suffer migraines: interrupted vision, grinding, pain, rolling stomach, out of it.
> Others get peptic ulcers or colitis or spastic colons. They worry about complications—cancer? They're bound up in diagnoses and treatments and prognoses.
> Some become accident prone. They drop things. They bung up their cars. They trip and stumble and sideswipe corners of their halls and misestimate the number of steps.
> Still others cry. Mama cried. Beth cries. Women cry. Do men ever cry, just from tension?
> Some pop pills. How "now!" How Americana now! Only Americana? Doctors do, I hear. Corporate executives do. Even young mothers do, I am told. Movie stars do.
> Some drink. School administrators drink. Joan Kennedy drank. *(Patricia L. Dick, Missouri Valley Writing Project, Columbia, Missouri, 1979)*

Having students write nonstop in response to a particular stimulus and then having them write transactionally in response to their own nonstop is an exercise that is best started at the very beginning of a composition course. If students are prevented from conceiving of a drastic split between writing for themselves and writing for others but are instead encouraged to experience the two functions as intimately related, they come to understand that they can speak powerfully in both expressive and transactional writing. Occasionally, we have students do a follow-up ten-minute nonstop in response to their transactional statement — just to demonstrate that, in a final sense, one function proceeds out of the other.

By repeating this exercise throughout the composition course, the teacher provides students with an opportunity to engage in regular, alternating practice in expressive and transactional writing. Meanwhile, the teacher is free to assign a developmental sequence of major writing assignments moving from expressive to transactional writing — without having the course break into the destructive dichotomy of "fun" writing and "serious" writing.

What should now be clear is that in our theory of curriculum, the journal serves three purposes. First, its immediate purpose is to promote the practice of basic writing skills as they are defined in the context of the student's own writing. Second, in the larger context of cognitive develop-

ment, the journal becomes the primary vehicle for fostering the expressive function. And third, it bridges the artificial, school-learned dichotomy between writing for the self and writing for others, encouraging the elaboration of expressive writing into equally authentic transactional statements.

The journal is to the composing curriculum as predrafting is to the polished essay: essential.

2

Integrating the Journal into the Composing Curriculum

The preceding chapter served as a justification for the value of the journal. It was an attempt, if you like, to retrieve in functional ways that radical belief in the self that illuminated the sixties and early seventies. This chapter describes how the journal can be integrated into a contemporary writing curriculum.

LIMITATIONS OF PRESENT PROCESS CURRICULA

We are fortunate that publishers are beginning to add process texts to their offerings of composition textbooks. Typically, the new process texts suggest a writing curriculum that consists of modeling an elaborated composing process for students and then having them write their way through that process repeatedly during the course. The goal of such a curriculum is clear; in theory, by the end of the course students will have internalized a comparatively sophisticated composing process that they will be able to use in their future writing.

Such a process curriculum with its concern for the elaborated composing of a limited number of essays, as opposed to the schoolboy writing of one required essay a week in an assigned organizational format, represents a light-years advance over the traditional composition textbook. Yet even the finest of these process texts, such as *Problem-Solving Strategies for Writing* (Flower, 1981), or *Four Worlds of Writing* (Lauer, Montague, Lunsford, & Emig, 1985), have some basic limitations. First, although some types of expressive writing may be suggested or encouraged in the predrafting and invention stage, the overwhelming preponderance of the major writing assignments are informative or persuasive. The politics of the English department and the exigencies of students' academic lives, particularly at the university level, require a heavy emphasis on informative and persuasive writing. But if this is the only type of writing allowed

for, the only type taught and rewarded in our composition classes, we are perpetuating that schizophrenic curriculum division discussed earlier — the split between "creative" writing and "school" writing, between private experience and public voice.

A second limitation of most process curricula is that although the predrafting, drafting, and revision model of the composing process presented in class may allow for or even require writing that ranges from the spontaneous to the carefully crafted and revised, the majority of this writing tends to be subordinated to composing a final informative or persuasive product that has been worked and reworked time and again in a highly conscious, if not self-conscious, manner. In the context of such a curriculum, it is easy to lose sight of the writer's need to write spontaneously, intuitively, and repeatedly in many styles, modes, and genres without concern for external evaluations of quality and correctness (Faigley, Miller, Meyer, & Witte, 1981).

A discussion of how to integrate the use of a skill-building journal into a contemporary process curriculum follows.

THE DEVELOPMENT OF THE WRITER'S VOICE

Chapter 1 described how the journal can serve as a matrix within the composition curriculum to establish both the interrelationship and the movement back and forth between the expressive and the transactional aspects of the writer's self. But the journal can do much more; it can serve as the primary vehicle for the development of the writer's voice.

New Romantic composition theorists and teachers of the sixties were fond of talking about the student's authentic voice. In fact, Donald Stewart wrote a very fine student textbook, well worth looking at, entitled *The Authentic Voice: A Pre-writing Approach to Student Writing* (1972). The authors of this book have roots in that tradition, and "authentic voice" is one of the feedback terms we use in responding to student journals. Yet without a functional definition, it is difficult to explain to students what an authentic voice is. We, as trained readers with a developed sense of taste, are left in the dubious pedagogical position of identifying examples of authentic voice in our students' writing — hoping that in time they, too, will be able to identify and strive for the elusive phenomenon of voice. What is needed is a functional definition of what we mean by the term "voice."

Vygotsky in *Thought and Language* (1934/1962) describes a move in the child's acquisition of language from exterior speech to inner speech and back to exterior speech. When a child is learning not merely individual

words but to converse, a high percentage of her language is vocalized in a comparatively unedited and egocentric form; exterior speech is the dominant vehicle of development at this point in the child's acquisition of language. The behavior is particularly clear when one observes a child of three or four playing alone; often she continues to vocalize in starts and stops as if she were carrying on a conversation with herself.

As children mature, an increasingly large percentage of their "languaging" becomes internalized as inner speech. Social convention undoubtedly has something to do with this internalization, but, more importantly, the child is beginning to construct interrelated chains of thought that would be difficult, time-consuming, and even impossible to vocalize — we can think faster than we talk. One of the primary results of this increasing internalization of speech is the more and more crafted nature of exterior speech.

Certainly, the child and to a lesser extent the adult continue to vocalize without prior thought, but exterior speech increasingly is derived from a monitored, censored, and edited complex of inner speech. To give an example, imagine driving home after a frustrating day at work when suddenly a flashing red light in your rearview mirror alerts you that you have been caught speeding. What half-articulated chains of thought run through your mind? *Damn! This is all I need. Should I play innocent?* "What's the problem, officer?" *Straightforward?* "It's been a hard day at the office." *This is gonna cost me. . . .*

This imaginary interior dialogue is overly developed; inner speech takes place in an almost cyphered format, half-consciously articulated fragments of a private language. The point, of course, is that the exterior "voice," which engages the officer in conversation, speaks out of the more or less elaborated context of inner speech.

We begin to arrive at a functional definition of voice. Certainly, every individual's voice is derived from an internalized complex of experience of all orders. But increasingly, the exterior voice of the mature individual is derived from an ongoing, focused interior conversation about the subject at hand. For the writer who is struggling to articulate a complex problem for an audience, the rehearsal of inner speech is essential (see Figure 2–A).

Figure 2–A illustrates in a simplified, schematic fashion the primary elements and interactions determining a mature writer's voice. The text produced by a competent writer is the tip of an iceberg, a visible product of numerous complex interior dialogues about the nature of the subject. The figure defines the writer's multiple conceptual perspectives on the content as an ongoing dialogue between two or more conceptual personas. When only one conceptual persona is explored or heard from, the writer

Figure 2–A: The Writer's Voice

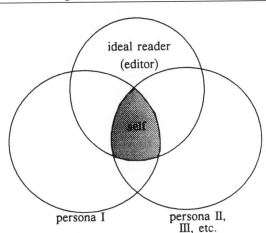

persona I

persona II, III, etc.

tends to speak in a series of broad, imprecise generalizations that reduce the significance of her experience rather than expand it.

The outcome and synthesis of writers' interior dialogues with themselves constitute the primary conceptual content of the text. But in the case of the competent writer, the conceptual content is not transcribed into the text in its raw form. Rather, the writer's internalized "ideal reader" critiques and gives advice about how to organize and represent the conceptualization in accordance with the needs and demands of an audience. Often, the ongoing critique of the "ideal reader" will generate further conceptual conversation; its concerns are not merely stylistic, but substantive — analysis of logic, concern for the quality of evidence, and demands for supporting details and examples.

Given this functional definition of the components of the writer's voice, Paul Simon and Art Garfunkel, in "The Sounds of Silence," crafted a memorable line: "The words of the prophets are written on the subway walls." Later, Simon elaborated the sentiment in a song entitled "Kodachrome Yellow": "My lack of education hasn't hurt me none; I can read the writing on the wall." Anglo-Saxon verbal gestures such as "Algebra sucks" or "Screw you, Teach" scrawled on bathroom walls may be authentic statements of authentic feelings, but the voices are inarticulate, almost mute.

Ideally, of course, we would guarantee that every child would grow up in a literate household, reading, writing, and talking with educated adults and peers. Lacking this, critical reading and writing across the curriculum

would be the first objective of the educational system. Lacking this, language arts programs, K through 12 and beyond, would be structured in accordance with James Moffett's (1968b) vision expounded in *Teaching the Universe of Discourse*, where all of the functions of language (expressive, poetic, informative, persuasive) were equally valued and taught in the context of increasingly complex modes, and genres (see Figure 2–B). Lacking this — the journal?

The concept of the journal as the primary vehicle inside the composing curriculum for the development of the student's voice is derived directly from the work of Moffett and of James Britton. Both Moffett and Britton maintain that the exercise of all functions of language in a rich proliferation of modes and genres is critical to developing the ability to derive increasingly sophisticated levels of abstraction. For Moffett, this exercise of the functions of language would take place most effectively inside a curriculum that moved students through a progression of listening, talking, reading, and writing in a developmental sequence of modes and genres.

One could argue with Moffett about his definition of the hierarchical order of modes and genres, although he argues cogently for the progression in *Teaching the Universe of Discourse* (1968b). But his assertion that the functions of language need to be exercised and developed in a rich divergence of modes and genres is indisputable. It is a large part of what we mean by education.

Language arts teachers do not have the control nor are they likely ever to have the control over the curriculum necessary to implement Moffett's developmental teaching of the entire spectrum of discourse. Nonetheless, within the limits of the individual classroom, it is possible to structure the journal in such a way as to allow for, encourage, and demand the expression of all of the functions of the student's voice in a variety of modes and genres.

STRUCTURING THE JOURNAL
AS AN EXPANSION OF VOICE

The secret is: There is no secret. We have designed a sequence of daily journal entries for the school week (Monday through Friday) in which the *form* but not the *content* is prescribed. With occasional modifications, this same daily sequence of journal assignments is repeated week after week throughout a course.

What is critical is not the particular exercises but rather the concept. The weekly journal with its daily entries in a prescribed form allows the teacher to design a sequence of assignments that demand the exercise of all

Figure 2–B: Moffett's Spectrum of Discourse

A highly schematic representation of the whole spectrum of discourse, which is also a hierarchy of levels of abstraction.

Interior Dialogue (egocentric speech)			P
Vocal Dialogue (socialized speech)	Recording, the drama of what is happening.	PLAYS	O
Correspondence Personal Journal Autobiography Memoir	Reporting, the narrative of what happened.	FICTION	E T
Biography Chronicle History	Generalizing, the exposition of what happens.	ESSAY	R
Science Metaphysics	Theorizing, the argumentation of what will, may happen.		Y

In Moffett's diagram of the spectrum of discourse (1968b; reprinted by permission), the move from the top of the left–hand column (interior dialogue) down to the bottom of the column (metaphysics) represents a ladder of increasingly complex abstraction. In *Student–Centered Language Arts and Reading, K–13 (Moffett & Wagner 1983),* Moffett suggests that this hierarchy of abstractions can be used to inform the language arts curriculum. Moffett believes that all of these forms of discourse can be read and written by very young children, at least in simplified forms. It is not a matter of teaching personal correspondence in the lower elementary grades and teaching metaphysics in college. Rather, the entire progression of discourse needs to be taught at every level and continuously recycled in increasingly complex terms throughout the progression of the student's development.

of the functions of the students' voice in modes and genres appropriate to the development of their writing abilities. The students are free to plug into these assignments whatever experiences from their private lives they choose, but the formal constraints of the assignments force them to voice their lives in a variety of functions, modes, and genres. And in theory, by

the end of the course students begin to assume command over the functions, modes, and genres that they have exercised so diligently week after week. As Yeats would ask, "How can we know the dancer from the dance?"—the students from their voices?

In terms of particular journal assignments, each teacher will probably want to design unique sequences to meet the needs of specific classes; however, theory and research mandate that certain *types* of journal exercises are needed. Students need:

- to write regularly, if not daily, in nongraded formats;
- to practice all of the functions of their voice in nongraded formats: expressive, poetic, transactional (informative and persuasive);
- to engage significant stimuli that demand expressive responses to events and ideas beyond their *immediate* personal experience;
- ongoing practice in moving from their expressive responses to public, transactional responses;
- practice writing in all of the basic modes of language, again, in a nongraded format: descriptive, narrative, informative, persuasive, and poetic/literary;
- particular practice in audience analysis and in the explicit definition and construction of rhetorical situations: the writer's stance, the needs of the audience, the definition and limitation of subject, and the purpose of the planned text;
- as much practice as time allows in a variety of genres: the essay, letters, poetry, and so forth.

JOURNAL ASSIGNMENTS

Before constructing specific journal assignments, teachers need to define for themselves the particular developmental needs of their own students. In general, however, the above list reflects needs common to all young writers, at least from middle school through the early college years. What changes from grade level to grade level, from one class to another, is the type of journal assignments that must be designed to meet these needs, assignments that take into account such variables as reading comprehension, syntactic maturity, and cognitive complexity.

The following weekly journal assignments were developed over a period of years to meet the needs of college freshmen who had been identified as remedial writers on the basis of their pre-college board scores. The first

term's weekly journal assignments* were for a remedial composition course; the second term's assignments were for a follow-up freshman composition course.

KEEPING A JOURNAL

Competent prose emerges staggering and stuttering out of a regular production of wastebasket prose. Writers need to write consistently, if not daily, in a format that allows them to express their feelings and ideas—without concern for external evaluations of quality and correctness. Keeping a journal and engaging regularly in nonstop writing allows for such consistent writing.

In this course, you are asked to make daily entries in a journal. Writing these journal entries will be nothing like keeping a "diary." Rather than the day-by-day *lists* of who did what to whom, when, and where, the writer's journal is an attempt to *record* experience and ideas vividly. If you go back and reread a diary three years later, it is often difficult even to remember what you felt at the time or whom you were with—mere names and dates tell us little. In these journals you will be asked to practice the skill of recording significantly your thoughts and ideas. Don't tell us you enjoy thunderstorms; show us.

> When I was a child growing up in west Texas, I fell in love with summer storms. You could see the promise of relief on those endless hot afternoons as the sparse clouds started to pile up, mushrooming slowly into towering thunderheads. The air would become unbearably humid and still—and then lightning walked like crooked giants across the flat land. . . . Finally, the torrential release of the rain.

To help you acquire those basic writing skills necessary for any significant writing, we have designed a sequence of daily journal entries.

DAILY JOURNAL ASSIGNMENTS

Monday's journal entry requires you to go to the Instructional Media Service in the basement of the Library, room 39. You go in, pick up the stimulus tape for that week and the typed transcript that accompanies the tape.

You then listen to the tape while reading the transcript. (A stimulus tape is approximately 5 to 10 minutes of music, poetry, spoken prose, graphics—enjoy.)

After listening to the tape, *immediately* write a 10-minute expressive nonstop in response. You are the primary audience for this entry, so explore and try to get down ideas and images that matter to you.

Tuesday's entry requires you to select an idea or image from Monday's journal entry and to spend 10 minutes developing your idea, refining it, or changing the perspective from which you originally viewed it.

---

*These journal exercises were developed with David Hadley, Washington State University, Pullman, Washington, 1982.

Your writing should consider the needs of an external audience. Try to explain things so completely that someone you've never met could understand exactly what you are talking about.

Wednesday's entry requires you to spend 5 to 10 minutes looking at or meditating upon an object, scene, person, or event. You are then asked to write a carefully crafted description of the subject of your meditation. Don't tell us *about* something; work to recreate it, to bring it alive through your writing by allowing your readers to see, hear, feel, taste, and touch what you experienced.

Don't just tell us about the hot, frustrated freshman standing in the refund line at the campus bookstore. Describe the odor of stale deodorant decaying in the late afternoon.

We suggest that you follow a general sequence of meditation/descriptions:

1. object
2. scene
3. person
4. event

After completing the sequence, repeat it, but draw your subjects from the past. Begin with a significant object from your past and on subsequent Wednesdays continue through the sequence, drawing your subjects from your memories of the past.

After the initial writing of your meditation/description, you are asked to set it aside for at least one day and then to return to it, revise it, type it, and hand it in the following Monday of each week.

Thursday's entry requires you to write a significant letter (not the brief note to your parents asking for money). What defines a "significant letter"? It is your need to communicate feelings, ideas, or information to someone in particular who is important—right now. It could be a letter to the registrar explaining why your tuition check bounced. It could be a "Dear John" or "Dear Susie" letter. It could be a letter inquiring about possible employment at a summer camp for academically deficient male cheerleaders, or it could be a letter to your father, whom you see at Christmas (sometimes), asking why he never writes. These letters do not have to be mailed, but they do have to be written to a real, important audience.

Before you actually write your letter, you are required to *justify* the importance of this rhetorical situation. *Define* in at least three or four sentences *each* of the following components of your rhetorical situation: (1) writer's stance, (2) subject (define and limit), (3) audience (needs, knowledge, attitude), (4) purpose/goals.

Friday's entry requires you to rethink, in writing, one of the week's journal entries. Try consciously to change perspectives. If you wrote a right-to-life entry, you might learn from trying to write from the point of view of someone who defines abortion as a civil liberty. If you wrote in favor of using higher sports fees to buy a better team, you might consider the viewpoint of someone who doesn't enjoy sports and already has difficulty making it on a limited income.

Consciously shifting perspectives is a valuable technique for learning; give it an honest effort.

Saturday's and *Sunday's* entries are optional but offer you the opportunity to write anything you choose. Suggestions include a poem, a song, or a description of the most important intellectual concept you've encountered during the week.

One of the ways we will be using journals this term is as a source for topics for papers, so you are encouraged to *write about subjects that really concern you.* Your instructor will label any entry that does not show a significant involvement with the process of writing as a "non-response" and will ask you to rewrite it. Your journal entries must be more than just words that fill a page.

Remember to identify each entry with the week of the term, the day of the week, and the date. For instance, if your previous entry was Week 1, Friday, September 23, your next entry would be Week 2, Monday, September 26.

REVISED JOURNAL ENTRIES

Each week you are to take Wednesday's meditation/description and revise it. Type your revision, paying particular attention to spelling, punctuation, and the conventions of grammar. Turn it in the following Monday.

The preceding journal assignments for a first-term composition course for remedial students teach students to write expressively; to derive transactional writing out of expressive writing; to write precise observations and descriptions; to write effective letters; and to learn how to rewrite and revise.

In the first term, heavy emphasis is placed on ensuring that students have something to write about. Thus, they are provided with stimulus units carefully designed to provoke them into a significant expressive response, and they are asked to write real letters that need to be written for real audiences.

Journal assignments* for a second-term regular freshman composition course were designed to teach many of the same skills. However, the assignments place an increasing emphasis on the students' responsibility to identify engaging subjects in the world outside their immediate experience and to respond significantly in both expressive and transactional writing. In addition, students are introduced to poetic writing in the form of the haiku, which is designed to sharpen their sense of word choice, economy, diction, and organic form. Collectively, the assigments demand a much more elaborated sense of audience than do the first-term assignments.

---

*These journal exercises were developed with Jean Hegland at Washington State University, Pullman, Washington (1983).

DAILY JOURNAL ENTRY SEQUENCE

Monday's journal entry is an observation/description. You are asked to spend 5 to 10 minutes observing or remembering an object, scene, person, or event. Then spend another 10 minutes writing a carefully crafted description of what you are observing. Try to write your description so that your readers can share the experience of your observation.

Tuesday's entry is a 10-minute expressive nonstop in response to a news article. You are to find a short article in a newspaper or news magazine discussing or reporting an event or incident that in some way concerns or interests you. Make a photocopy of the article and include it in your journal. Then write an expressive response to the article in the form of a 10-minute nonstop.

Wednesday's entry must be less than 17 words long. You are either to compose a slogan suitable for a T-shirt or a bumper sticker, or to write a haiku. In either case, the idea is word-play that makes a statement or captures a moment.

A bumper sticker slogan will probably be five to eight words long. A couple of only reasonably brilliant examples of bumper stickers are:

BLOW UP YOUR TV
A TREE FARM IS NOT A FOREST
LET AN EDITOR TOUCH YOUR TEXT

Most places that custom print T-shirts can fit only a limited number of letters on a shirt. For the purposes of this assignment, let's say that your slogan can consist of up to 33 spaces. On the T-shirt, that would be 3 lines of 11 spaces each. Remember that not only does each letter count as a space, but punctuation marks and the spaces between words also take up spaces on the shirt.

A haiku is a 17-syllable poem. (See attached explanation and examples.) *You are required to write a haiku at least every other week.*

Thursday's journal entry is a transactional response to Tuesday's nonstop. Reread the photocopy of your article and your expressive response to it. Identify the important, interesting, or unexplored ideas you find there. After defining in your journal who your audience is, write a 15 minute focused response in which you elaborate or explain those ideas so that the audience you've chosen will understand them.

Friday's entry is either a rethink or a free entry. At least every third week, you are asked to rethink something you've already written about in your journal. Try shifting perspectives in your rethink, so that you are getting at what you wrote about in your first entry from a different angle. A "free entry" means that you are free to write about whatever you wish in any way you like.

Saturday's and Sunday's entries are optional but offer you the opportunity to write anything you choose—for example, a poem, or a song, or a description of the most important intellectual concept you've encountered during the week.

One of the ways we will be using journals this term is as a source for topics for papers, so you are encouraged to *write about subjects that really concern you.* Your instructor will label any entry that does not show a significant involvement with the

process of writing as a "non-response" and will ask you to rewrite it. Your journal entries must be more than just words that fill a page.

Remember to identify each entry with the week of the term, the day of the week, and the date. For instance, if your previous entry was Week 1, Friday, February 11, your next entry would be Week 2, Monday, February 14.

REVISED JOURNAL ENTRIES

Each week you are to choose one entry from your journal and revise it until you are satisfied that it is a finished piece. Type your revision—paying particular attention to spelling, punctuation, and the conventions of grammar—and turn it in the following Monday. T-shirt slogans, bumper stickers, and haikus are not appropriate for this sort of revision.

INTRODUCTION TO THE HAIKU

The art of haiku began in Japan over 700 years ago. A haiku is an unrhymed poem that usually consists of 17 syllables: 5 syllables in the first line, 7 in the second line, and 5 in the last line. It is objective in that it is usually a short description of the natural world. Words like "love," "loneliness," and "happiness" are seldom used, but a good haiku is full of overtones and evokes feelings it doesn't actually mention. Basho, who was a Japanese master of haiku, said, "Haiku is simply what is happening in this place, at this moment." Of course, managing to capture in 17 syllables what is "happening in this place, at this moment" is no simple task. You will probably have to work very hard to come up with a good idea for a haiku, and then you will probably have to spend a lot of time fiddling with the words and syllables to get it right. Have fun and good luck.

A dragonfly darts
Across the mirroring pool,
Stops and starts of flight.

A branch scrapes the house,
relentless in the cold night:
Nobody lives here.

Leather seats and stars
A convertible on fire
In a summer night.

The weekly sequence of journal assignments is designed to provide exercise for all of the functions of the student's voice in a rich divergence of modes and genres. As a whole, the journal is structured to serve as a matrix for the development of an increasingly sophisticated "authentic voice,"

which fosters its own growth through increasingly complex dialogues with the self and the world that surrounds it.

THE JOURNAL FORMAT

The format of the journal page is important. To standardize the format, a teacher may decide to collect a small subsidy from students, cut stencils, and duplicate journal paper for the class. The sample journal page in Figure 2–C has been reduced, but the design should be clear: Turn a sheet of legal-size paper on its side and divide it into two major columns, each of which is accompanied by a small "sentence-level revision" margin. This format is designed to promote a mature composing process, even in the context of intuitive, spontaneous writing. The same format can be achieved by having the local bookstore order what are called "review note-

Figure 2–C: Sample Journal Page

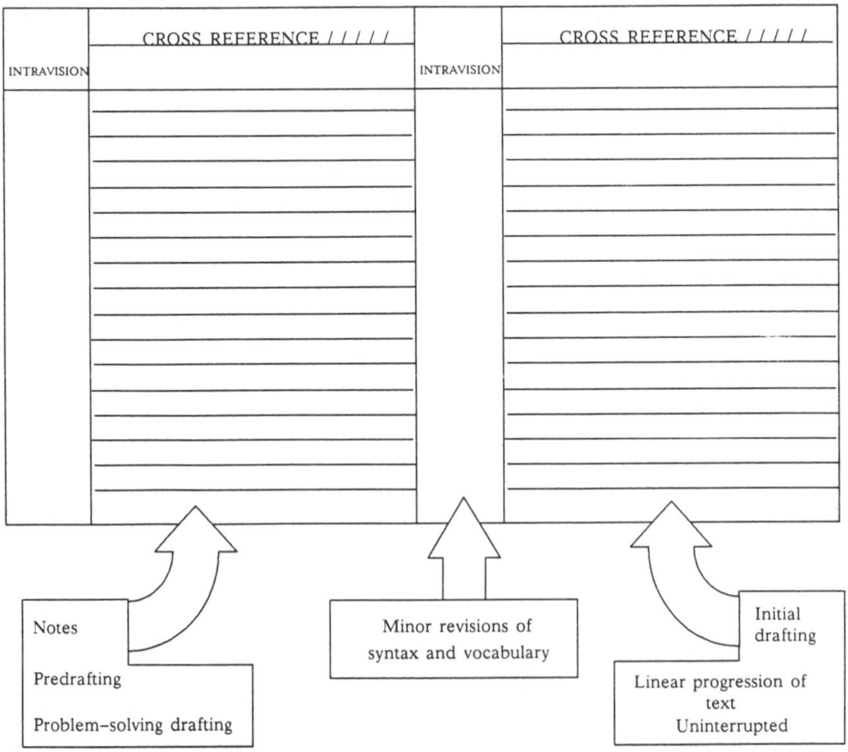

books," which have three-inch margins. The notebook is opened wide and the left-hand page and the right-hand page are used as if they composed a single sheet of journal paper. Some students prefer to draft on the typewriter. They can turn an $8 \ 1/2 \times 11$ sheet of paper sideways and divide it into two columns. The right-hand column is reserved for initial drafting, and the left-hand column is reserved for predrafting notes, problem-solving drafting, and no-fault leaps into complex syntactic structures.

Each journal entry starts in the right-hand column, and students are encouraged and exhorted to maintain the linear progression of their text in that column. The right-hand column is essentially a place for initial drafting, and students are reminded time and again that they should not be revising intensively during this initial realization of the text. The small margin accompanying this column is for minor revisions of syntax and vocabulary; most of these sentence-level revisions will take place after the initial drafting of the text.

The left-hand column of the journal page has quite a different set of functions. First, it is used to keep an ongoing record of the writer's plans for the evolving text. We know from the protocol research of Flower and Hayes (1980) that although mature writers seldom stop during the initial drafting of the text to rehearse what to say next at the sentence level, they do stop periodically and rehearse the development of the text as a whole piece of discourse: They consider audience, focus, and further definition and limitation of subject; they make notes about changes or additions to make later; they jot brief outlines of points that need to be covered in the subsequent development of the text. This ongoing rehearsal of the text as a holistic piece of discourse is absolutely crucial to the conceptualization of the evolving text as a precisely defined attempt to communicate with a specific audience. Essentially, the left-hand column serves in this respect as an organized record of the predrafting that takes place during the drafting process as the text folds back upon itself to investigate its own inherent possibilities.

Second, and perhaps most importantly, the left-hand column serves as the place where the writer engages in problem-solving drafting, devising major additions that will be inserted into or substituted for text in the right-hand column: Implicit ideas are developed; chains of reasoning are elaborated and supported with specific examples and evidence; and logical connectives and transitions are provided. During this problem-solving drafting, the initial draft in the right-hand column can undergo radical revision through addition, deletion, substitution, and reordering. In short, the left-hand column transforms the typically somewhat associative structure of the initial draft into a more logically organized statement.

Third, the left-hand column is the place to attempt to deal with

syntactic blocks. The vast majority of sentences constructed by the writer during initial drafting have their genesis in an act of syntactic faith, a launching forth into words that assumes that somehow the sentence will be brought home. For instance, the preceding sentence was not planned but was invented in the process of syntactic construction. But often during the initial drafting process, the writer finds herself blocked at the sentence level. She knows what it is she wants to say but simply can't make the sentence work — often it is a complex and/or compound sentence accompanied by a variety of modifying phrases. If the writer is trying to maintain the linear progression of the text at all costs, such syntactic blocks are extremely frustrating — typically indicated in the draft by numerous erasures and cross-outs. Eventually, the writer tends to get lost in her interior rehearsals of how to get it said and is reduced to silence.

If the writer moves over to the left-hand column and takes a no-fault leap into the sentence — without worrying about whether it will turn out all right — it is amazing how often the syntactic problem resolves itself in one or two attempts. Trying to get it said right in order to maintain progression in the text is a fundamental source of syntactic blocks — the writer can't afford to experiment. In the left-hand column, the writer can take risks in an attempt to find an adequate syntactic vehicle to express what it is she knows but is having difficulty saying.

The importance of the left-hand column as a no-fault springboard into complicated syntactic structures cannot be overemphasized. For some writers (including one of the authors), the simple act of switching to the left-hand column when they encounter a syntactic block can increase their production rate by 30 percent or more.

The format of the journal page serves to embody in microcosm the very model of the composing process that will be set forth in the next three chapters of this book (see Figure 2–D). The left-hand column records and promotes predrafting and problem-solving drafting, and the right-hand column is devoted to initial drafting and the linear progression of the text. The space limitations of the narrow sentence-level revision margins remind students that surface revision needs to be held to a minimum during the initial drafting of a text. Moreover, the format of the journal page serves to organize the writer's various drafting activities so that she does not enter the final drafting stage surrounded by a plethora of small notes scattered across the desk and flowing onto the floor.

In addition to the format of the journal pages, the sheer volume of writing that students do in the journal requires some form of overall organization. After the teacher has passed out journal paper to the students, for example, it is helpful to have them hole-punch the paper, buy notebook rings at the bookstore to bind the journal, and make covers out of poster-

Figure 2–D: Sample Journal Page with Entries

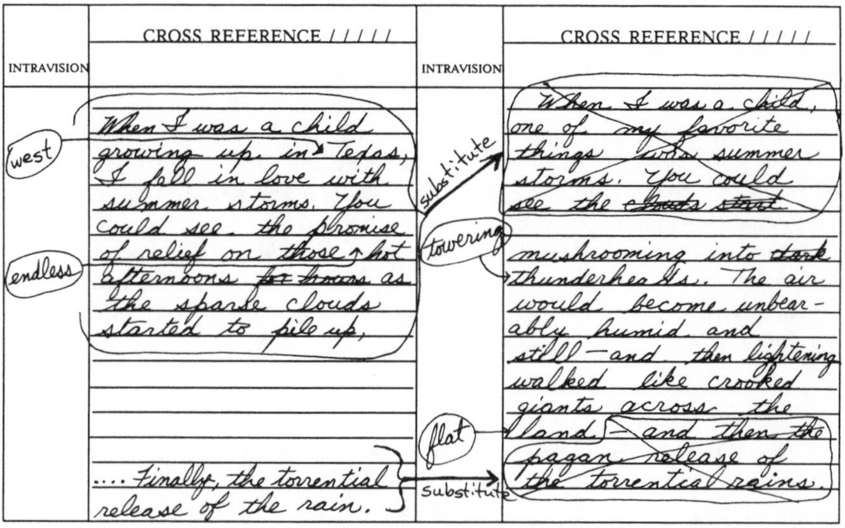
CROSS REFERENCE / / / / /
INTRAVISION
When I was a child growing up in Texas, I fell in love with summer storms. You could see the promise of relief on those hot afternoons as the sparse clouds started to pile up,
west
endless
.... Finally, the torrential release of the rain.
substitute
towering
flat
substitute
CROSS REFERENCE / / / / /
INTRAVISION
When I was a child, one of my favorite things was summer storms. You could see the clouds start
mushrooming into dark thunderheads. The air would become unbearably humid and still—and then lightening walked like crooked giants across the land—and then the pagan release of the torrential rains.

board. In addition, the students can make posterboard dividers to separate the journal into three sections. "section one" is for daily journal entries, "section two" is for special journal entries written in class or assigned as predrafting activities for major writing assignments, and "section three" is used for the actual drafting of major writing assignments.

In short, the overall organization of the journal encourages students to transfer the composing process that they have been practicing in sections one and two over into the actual drafting of major writing assignments in section three, and vice versa. The format of the individual journal page and the organization of the journal as a whole assist students to practice and engage the basics of the composing process on a daily basis.

STUDENTS' RIGHT TO PRIVACY

Given that daily journal entries are designed to foster the development of students' voices, on occasion students may find themselves writing about feelings, experiences, or opinions that they wish to keep private. To guarantee students' right to privacy, at the beginning of the class we hand out the following statement on journal privacy:

JOURNAL ENTRIES AND PRIVACY

1. On occasion you may write journal entries that you do not wish to share with other people. Your right to privacy will be respected.
2. If you write an entry that, for any reason, you do not wish to share with us, *remove* that entry from your journal and replace it with a blank sheet of paper marked *Private* and labeled with the date and number of the entry removed. Obviously, if too many of your entries are marked *Private*, you will be asked to start writing more entries that you are willing to share.
3. If you write in your journal about thoughts of suicide or describe your direct involvement in child abuse, hard drug usage, or violent crimes, the teacher has a *legal responsibility* to discuss the matter with you and refer you to professional help.

Establishing this journal privacy policy at the beginning of the class guarantees the rights of the students and the teacher. But just as importantly, the right to remove a journal entry avoids premature censorship of ideas and information that may be critical in the development of an authentic statement. Premature censorship based on a concern about who will read the evolving text can block the development of the fluency that the journal is designed to promote. Students are free to write anything they wish; they decide afterward who will be allowed to read it.

MANAGING THE JOURNAL

Today, structured journals designed to teach basic writing skills and develop the student's voice are an integral part of the authors' teaching. But initially, caught between the conviction that there was no substitute for students' regular production of large quantities of process writing and the realities of teaching multiple sections of over-enrolled composition courses, there seemed no bridge into practice. As we confronted a weekly flood of journal entries, the question of how to respond to so much student writing acquired a certain urgency. The situation was rather like that of Bill Cosby's outraged Noah, who complains bitterly to the Lord about living conditions on the ark. "Have you looked down in that hold lately? Who's going to clean that mess up?" To foreshorten a description of a somewhat frustrating period of experimentation, we split the question of "Who's going to clean that mess up?" into two parts: First, how was it possible to check that the students had completed the assigned journal

entries? And second, given the teacher's right to a private life, how could time be scheduled to respond to students' journals?

The first question, "How to check students' completion of assigned journal entries?" was a classroom management issue, the type of question teachers have been trained to answer, not so different from collecting lunch money. Our working assumption was that students as a group do not take writing assignments seriously unless they are checked regularly for completion, and we designed the following management strategies:

1. Completing all assigned journal entries is worth a significant percentage of the student's final grade. Although this writing is not graded as product, written "non-responses" do not count as completed assignments.
2. All journal entries are written in a notebook reserved solely for that purpose. Students can craft their own notebooks out of looseleaf paper, notebook rings, and posterboard. (Given supplies and instructional time, particularly at the elementary and middle school level, there are real advantages in having students turn their journal covers into collages that say something about themselves. A discussion of the process they went through to create their collages can serve as a metaphor for the written composing process.)
3. The journal notebook is subdivided into three sections. The majority of the notebook is reserved for the weekly sequences of daily journal assignments. A second section of the notebook is reserved for special journal entries that may be written in class or assigned as part of the predrafting of a major paper. The third and last section of the notebook is used for drafting major writing assignments.
4. At the front of the journal notebook is a checkoff sheet that identifies all assigned journal entries (see Figure 2–E). Students are responsible for checking off each assignment when it is completed. Every week at the beginning of the first class meeting, students exchange journals on a random basis and validate each other's lists of completed journal assignments. Each student turns in a half-sheet of paper that reports on the status of her classmate's journal. Missing assignments are itemized, and each report is signed.

Individual teachers must, of course, adapt and elaborate such basic management strategies and invent others to meet the needs of their particular students and classrooms. But once such strategies have been devised, teachers are past masters at implementing them.

Two key research findings made it both *necessary* and *possible* to answer the second question, "How could time be scheduled to respond to

Figure 2–E: Journal Checkoff Sheet

Writer's Name _____

Daily Journal Entries:

Week#	Monday	Tuesday	Wednesday	Thursday	Friday	Date Checked	Signature of Reader
1.							
2.							
3.							
4.							
5.							
6.							
7.							
8.							
9.							
10.							
11.							
12.							
13.							
14.							
15.							

Special Journal Entries

	Date Checked	Signature of Reader
#1		
#2		
#3		
#4		
#5		
#6		
#7		
#8		

Major Paper Drafts

	Date Checked	Signature of Reader
#1		
#2		
#3		
#4		
#5		
#6		
#7		
#8		

students' journals?" The first discovery has been validated by many researchers: Mere frequency of writing does not correlate with writing improvement unless that writing is *responded to* by a critical reader (Hillocks, 1982, l986). If frequent, nongraded journal assignments were to serve as a means of fostering the development of the writer, it was necessary to devise ways to respond to such writing. The problematic variable, of course, was teacher time.

Fortunately, a second research finding resolved the time variable by finding that teachers should give more emphasis to the guiding and careful development of fewer papers (Braddock, Lloyd-Jones, & Schoer, 1963; Stallard, 1974). In short, by reducing the number of major writing assignments that have to be *graded*, teachers salvage time with which to respond to journal entries and nonstop writing. Moreover, although journal writing needs to be responded to on a regular basis, not every individual piece needs such feedback, not every individual piece needs to be read, and the teacher is not the only person who can respond. There are a number of research studies that demonstrate the effectiveness of peer response (Beach, 1976; Lamberg, 1980).

With the time variable resolved, we found it surprisingly easy to schedule combinations of peer and teacher responses to journal writing. The following is simply one variation among many.

SCHEDULING RESPONSES TO JOURNAL ENTRIES

Week 1: Each student self-selects two journal entries to be read aloud to another member of the class. The listener responds orally to the first piece and responds briefly in writing to the second, using the journal feedback terms.

Week 2: Same as Week 1.

Week 3: Students turn in their journals, having identified four pieces of writing that they would like the teacher to read. The teacher spot checks each journal for completion of assignments, speed reads the four identified selections, and then responds in writing to two, using the journal feedback terms. The teacher's comments, of course, are not limited to the feedback terms.

Given that students are held accountable for the completion of all writing assignments, such a combination of peer and teacher responses, scheduled at regular intervals, is more than enough reinforcement to keep the class writing. In fact, as Glynda Hull's research (1981) demonstrates, such scheduled reinforcement actually helps students to internalize the self-management skills necessary to any consistent production of writing.

THE JOURNAL AS REHEARSAL

The role of the journal within the composing curriculum looms large.

- The journal is a place for the regular production of nongraded writing, a commitment that is essential to developing fluency.
- The journal feedback terms, when applied consistently to both expressive and transactional writing, promote the acquisition of basic writing skills.
- The journal serves as a vehicle for the development of the expressive function, a primary stimulus to cognitive growth in all of the functions of language.
- Writing transactionally in response to expressive journal entries provides a crucial bridge between the expressive and transactional functions.
- The daily journal assignments foster the elaboration and development of the students' voices in a variety of functions, modes, and genres.
- The format of the journal asks students to practice the basics of the composing process on a daily basis and to transfer that process into the drafting of major writing assignments.

Finally, all of these functions of the journal might be summed up in the term "significant rehearsal." Mature writers seldom, if ever, really start with a blank page. Their very perception of the world is structured as an ongoing rehearsal of what to say next. And typically, the mature writer brings to any subject, assigned or self-chosen, a prior canon of perceptions, thoughts, and previous writing relevant to the task at hand. Mature writers constantly integrate their past rehearsals, in terms of both form and content, into their present rehearsals of how to predraft, draft, and revise an evolving text.

For young writers, the rehearsal provided by the journal is essential. In terms of form and content, they have not yet mastered the skills required to produce finished prose to be read by others. And to assume that a series of graded writing assignments can serve as an efficient vehicle for learning as-yet-unmastered skills is a fatal pedagogical misjudgment. Any practitioner of a complex craft, whether she be a classical pianist, a pole-vaulter, or a computer programmer, would dismiss as absurd the notion that the basic skills of her discipline can be learned in the context of a judged performance. "Carnegie Hall is proud to present Leonard Bernstein *rehearsing* the New York Philharmonic Orchestra's performance of Beethoven's 'Fifth Symphony'. . . ."

In composition classes, the ongoing rehearsal of the journal is integrated into the larger context of the composing curriculum in immediately

practical terms. Students are required to derive at least half of the subjects for their major writing assignments from the journal. When students choose subjects from their journals, they are asked as the first step of their composing process to read back through their journals, cross-reference the entries, and identify related entries that constitute a focus of concern.

It should be noted that the assigned daily journal entries promote the writer's foregrounding of issues, ideas, and conflicts that represent true concerns. To encourage and assist students in this rereading of their journals, a cross-reference line is provided at the top of every journal page, as shown in Figure 2–C.

This cross-referencing of the students' own writing embodies a significant rehearsal of one of the most difficult cognitive steps of the composing process — finding/discovering an authentic subject. Moreover, given the fact that the students have likely written in their journals on their chosen subjects from multiple perspectives and in a variety of modes and genres, the journal serves as significant predrafting for the papers they will eventually write. In fact, we find that when our students derive their subjects from their journals, approximately 80 percent of them write adequate papers. When students derive their subjects from other sources, only about 50 percent of them write adequate papers.

In short, when students find/discover their subjects in the cross-referencing of their journals, they are beginning to act like mature writers, deriving their subjects from an intense interaction with an ongoing rehearsal of what to say next. As Robert Frost suggests:

> The conclusion is come to that like giants we are always hurling experience ahead of us to pave the future with against the day when we may want to strike a line of purpose across it for somewhere. (1964, *vii*)

There is no replacement for the journal within the composing curriculum. It serves as an ongoing rehearsal of skills and ideas that interact to ignite the composing process, turning it into an act of discovery — as opposed to the reduction of experience that characterizes the school-assigned essay. It is the half-lighted area just offstage, where the rehearsed and fluent actor prepares to step in front of a real audience.

Part II

COMPOSING
IN THE
WRITING CURRICULUM

Many of our students conceive of writing as an art for which they have no talent — a craft better left to those who have an innate and inexplicable ability to transform experience into words. Too often, students are shown examples of good writing and are asked to produce something "just as good," with little or no indication of how to get from the blank page to the finished product. While, certainly, an effective writing curriculum demands that students learn how to produce competent prose, it seems to us that competent writing can only be the result of a competent composing process. Almost without exception, contemporary composing theories and research on the teaching of writing agree that writing needs to be taught as process rather than product (Hairston, 1982).

While it is helpful for students to analyze models of good writing, models do not teach students *how* to write effectively. A superb essay represents the tip of an iceberg; what stands behind the essay is the time-consuming and often agonizing process of creating order out of a chaos of information, intuition, and half-formulated thoughts — a process in which draft after draft has folded back upon itself to generate a nonlinear crafted statement. When students try to imitate the finished products of professional writers, too often the results are ice cubes rather than the tips of icebergs. The ability to recognize good writing is insufficient for the unpracticed writer to produce good writing, as the ability to recognize good paintings does not equip the novice artist with the skill to paint well. Composition demands the mastery of a composing process, a process that students are capable of consciously controlling and directing.

Teachers need to present a model of the composing process that defines writing as a series of "tangible" steps while still

allowing students to discover and internalize their own unique variants. Those who would present the composing process as a set of lock-step procedures run the danger of forcing students into a straitjacket and denying them the right of discovering how to adopt these procedures to serve their individual styles and needs.

WRITING AS A CONVERSION EXPERIENCE

Drawing on what Dorothy Sayers called a "conversion of events from the world into experience in a person," Rohman and Wlecke (1964) characterized writing and the writer as follows:

> An "event" . . . is something that happens to one — but he does not necessarily experience it. You only experience a thing when you can express it to your own mind. . . . A writer is simply a man like ourselves with an exceptional power of revealing his experience by expressing it, first to himself and then to others so that we recognize this experience as our own too. When an "event" is so recognized, it is converted from something happening to us into something happening in us. And something to which we happen. (p. 15)

Rohman and Wlecke suggest that even though students have participated in numerous "events," they may not have converted those events into experience. They conclude that in order to be writers, students must first conceptualize the events of their lives — the raw data of their interactions with the world — before they can transform them into experience. The hasty conceptualization that characterizes so much student writing stems from the fact that students have not been shown how to form concepts of their own. Given a writing assignment, they merely clutch at the half-formed concepts they have inherited, almost osmotically, from their culture.

Without the formation of categories of events, without the recognition of the interrelationships between isolated events, experience remains a set of unrelated phenomena. When writing is taught as product, the conversion of event into experience tends to be aborted. Without a mature composing process, students have trouble in forming their own concepts. The results of this among poor writers, according to Rohman and Wlecke, is that "their hasty conceptualization of their subject obscure[s] rather

than illuminate[s] the nature of events for which concepts were supposed to provide insight" (1964, p. 6).

If we accept the suggestion that experience is converted into something "to which we happen," then *composing* the world also means controlling it to some degree. This sense of control over the elusive talent for writing is essential if students are to develop into competent writers. What is needed is a mature model of the composing process that allows for and demands that writing serve as a vehicle for the conversion of "events" into experience.

A FUNCTIONAL MODEL OF THE COMPOSING PROCESS

We divide composing into three major stages (see Figure II):

Predrafting: not merely thinking about the subject or assignment, but all of the activities that precede the act of drafting, including numerous activities that are written.

Drafting: not merely a one-shot, one-draft activity, but a process requiring a series of drafts that evolve toward a final draft.

Revision: not merely cosmetic touch-up of a draft, but *rewriting* to improve organization and transitions; *editing* to improve diction, sentence structure, and paragraph coherence; and *proofing* to correct errors in syntax, usage, and spelling.

Each of these three stages of the composing process is further subdivided into logically discrete steps that are interconnected and contiguous in the act of writing. The arrows that run in both directions between steps designate feedback loops showing students that at any step or stage of the composing process they may need to return to a previous one. For example, during the drafting stage a student may discover that she does not have enough factual information to develop a point she wishes to make; she may then need to go back and do additional predrafting before she can produce a draft. Moreover, steps can be added, reordered, or deleted to suit either the writer's or the teacher's needs. For a mature writer who has already internalized a complex composing process, the model may seem overly elaborated, but it is crucial for a young writer consciously to identify and analyze the components of a mature composing process. In fact, for young writers the ongoing analysis and elaboration of their

Figure II: A Functional Model of the Composing Process

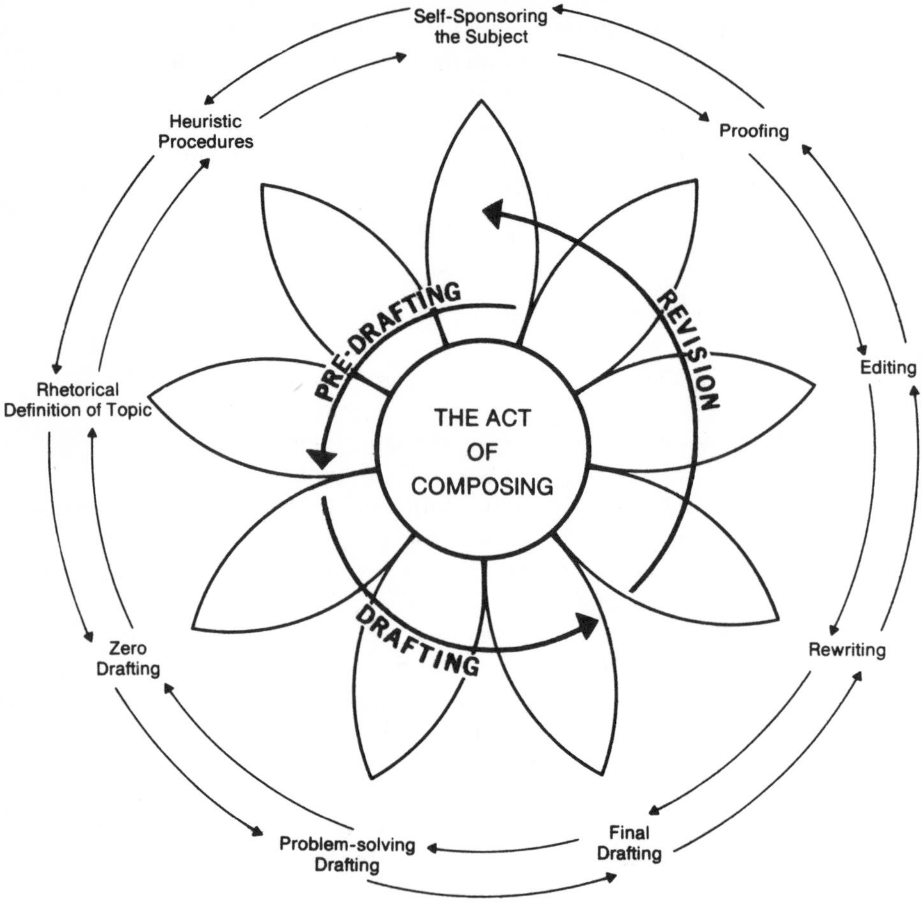

composing process may well serve as the primary "content" of a contemporary composition course.

INTEGRATING A MODEL OF THE COMPOSING PROCESS INTO THE WRITING CURRICULUM

The next three chapters consist of an in-depth discussion of the three major stages of the composing process: predrafting, drafting, and revision. But before engaging in that discussion, it

seems appropriate to suggest how such a model can be integrated into the day-to-day demands, concerns, and objectives of any writing curriculum. Certainly, we assume that by the end of a writing course, students need to have internalized a functional model of the composing process that provides them with direction during all stages of the writing process. However, it is important for teachers to realize that when they integrate a model of the composing process into the writing curriculum, it is not necessary to teach or assess predrafting, drafting, and revision in *each* assignment. We are concerned throughout this book with reducing the teacher's workload — not increasing it in the pursuit of some imaginary unicorn of excellence.

Early in a writing course, as might be expected, we spend a considerable amount of time teaching a sequence of predrafting strategies and providing in-class feedback on students' predrafting of a major out-of-class paper.

As the course progresses, we de-emphasize the teaching of predrafting strategies, *while continuing to hold students accountable for predrafting each major assignment*, and focus intensely on modeling and teaching drafting strategies in the context of the in-class essay. All of our in-class essays are written over a three-day period, and each day corresponds to a different step of the drafting process. Since these essays are written in class, they allow for continual monitoring, feedback, and instruction in the drafting process on an individual basis.

Teaching the revision stage of the composing process is perhaps the most difficult job of the composition instructor. Throughout the course we emphasize teaching revision, particularly in stylistic terms, by having students revise one short piece from their journal each week. Toward the end of the course, we place heavy emphasis on the substantive revision of one or more of the major out-of-class papers that they have written. It is impossible to receive a high grade in our composition courses without having written at least one major piece that is *worthy* of revision and *successfully* revising that piece.

Yes, it is possible to teach the entirety of the functional model of the composing process that follows in the next three chapters. But the model is taught in the context of the entire course, not in the context of individual assignments. What is important is that students have internalized a mature model of the composing process by the time they complete a composition course. When they exit, the model in their head is designed to replace us.

3

Predrafting: The Wellspring of Composing

That writing which is most exciting to read is that which seems to have been exciting for the author to write. Clumsy or well-drafted as the piece may be, we have the sense of an author compelled to write by her own enthusiasm for her subject.

Janet Emig (1971) makes a telling distinction between classroom assignments ("school-sponsored writing") and personal exigencies ("self-sponsored writing"). The distinction is critical. If a classroom assignment is merely "school-sponsored," the writer's engagement with the task too often reflects little or no concern for the effect of the writing on a real audience. To make writing more than a reductive plodding through "due-next-Friday" essays, students must somehow transmute school-sponsored writing into self-sponsored writing.

For teachers of writing, this poses an agonizing dilemma: How can we demand that our students become invested in their writing? If we were to wait for students to become engaged with writing on their own, often we would have to wait a long, long time. The only resolution to the problem that we know involves teaching students a variety of strategies for discovering, investigating, and analyzing the inherent possibilities in their chosen subjects. This approach to investing students in their writing involves teaching them how to engage in economic and creative predrafting.

Predrafting consists of all the activities that intervene between the initial decision to write and the beginning of a sustained first draft. It comes as a shock to most students to discover that for a professional writer much of what *precedes* writing a first draft consists of written activities. When we teach predrafting, we are teaching students how to convert the events of their lives into insight. When writing is based in predrafting, students tend to develop an intrinsic investment in exploring their ideas and emotions that seduces them into an attempt to account for themselves as human beings. Donald Murray (1978c) suggests that rather than rewarding those students who can "ejaculate correct little essays without

thought" (p. 375), we must give much more attention and consideration to what happens in that time "between receiving an assignment or finding a subject and beginning a completed first draft" (p. 380).

Chapters 1 and 2 discussed how the journal serves as an ongoing rehearsal of the self and can help students discover a variety of subjects that interest them. But after students have discovered a subject and perhaps even done some preliminary research, they must still explore, limit, and conceptualize the subject. Mere interest in or a passing acquaintance with a subject area does not necessarily equate with the right to hold an opinion. As many critics from other cultures have observed — most memorably, in the nineteenth century, De Toqueville and Dickens — one of the most irritating and apparently inbred attributes of Americans is their naive belief in their constitutional right to an *uninformed* opinion. Before a writer can express a real opinion or instruct or persuade others, she must first grapple with the diversity of information associated with the subject and discover or construct the logic that informs, limits, and defines it.

Too often students attempt to engage in drafting a text before they have adequately conceptualized their subjects. This observation is a pedagogical cliché but unfortunately a true one. The half-formed and often contradictory concepts adopted from parents or inherited from a popular culture often preclude making genuine statements. As Immanuel Kant, the high priest of reason, commented in the eighteenth century: "There is no art in being intelligible if one renounces all thoroughness of insight . . . it produces a disgusting medley of compiled observations and half-reasoned principles" (1785/1949, p. 27).

The bad news is that merely exhorting students to "think more" about their subjects is, in the main, ineffective. The hasty conceptualization that characterizes much student writing is not just a lack of time on task; more fundamentally, students have not been taught how to engage in systematic concept formation. The good news is that students can be taught heuristic procedures by which to explore, limit, and conceptualize their subjects systematically.

HEURISTIC PROCEDURES

A heuristic procedure is a set of operations designed to assist the writer in collecting information about a subject and inventing a logical structure to account for that information. (*Heuresis* is a Greek word meaning "discovery.") As Janice Lauer (1979) elaborates:

> A heuristic is highly generative if it engages the writer in a range of operations that have been identified as triggers of insight: visualizing,

analogizing, classifying, defining, rearranging, and dividing. [They] encourage the writer to generate increasingly richer symbolizations from which a new synthesis or insight can spring. (p. 269)

From one perspective, the entire functional model of the composing process set forward in the central section of this book is nothing more than an elaborated heuristic. But in a more limited sense, the conceptualization of subject is that point during predrafting where specific heuristic procedures are most helpful. In a fine article, "Classifying Heuristics," James Kinney (1979) defines three orders of heuristic procedures: intuitive, empirical, and rational.

Intuitive Heuristics

Kinney wrote, "Intuitive heuristics are based on that way of knowing articulated at least as far back as Plato and defined . . . as nonlinear immediate understanding" (p. 352). Intuitive heuristic procedures draw on the free association of seemingly unrelated knowledge and experience. The "free writing" strategies of Ken Macrorie (1968) and Peter Elbow (1973), referred to in this book as "nonstop writing," often yield the surprising or quirky connection between ideas that make the unique and engaging perspective for which a writer searches. A writer may simply "spill her mind," writing on whatever pops into her head, or she may choose to focus on a particular subject and write nonstop to discover what she intuitively knows about it.

As demonstrated in Chapter 1, nonstop writing is one of the most powerful and flexible instructional strategies in the composition teacher's repertoire. Research by Hilgers (1980) suggests that if students were to be taught only *one* predrafting heuristic, it might well be nonstop or free writing. Peter Elbow's (1973) "cooking process" is an extraordinarily effective procedure in which the student free writes a focused response to a subject, identifies a central idea in that free writing, and then free writes in response to that idea, continuing to recycle this process until the subject "pops into focus." Nonstop writing as a heuristic device self-engages the writer, bypasses the blank page, and promotes fluency. The associative nature of the response tends to prevent premature and reductive categorization, and the cooking process of free writing in response to free writing allows students to circle in on their subjects with increasing specificity.

Constructing extended analogies between apparently disparate ideas, events, or institutions is another intuitive heuristic. A perennial student favorite is "How is the American education system like a penal system?" Consider the sentencing of the repeat offender. . . .

One of our favorite in-class exercises when we introduce analogies is to

play Bette Midler's version of "The Rose": "Just remember, in the winter, far beneath the bitter snows lies . . . the rose." After listening to the song, students construct several analogies using the rose as a vehicle, complete with such attributes as flowering, thorns, fragrance, and withering. They are asked to use the metaphor of the rose to capture the essence of a specific, limited event in their own lives — with the *exception* of a love affair — and to envision the progression of their own lives from birth to projected death. As you might imagine, the writing of such predrafting exercises can become intense at the speed of light.

Another powerful intuitive heuristic is the negative analogy. After comparing the school to a penitentiary, students can be asked to define "How is the classroom *not* like a prison cell?" How is applying for welfare not like a merry-go-round? How is divorce not like death? How is unemployment not like impotency? Constructing negative analogies makes students aware of the way that clichés and metaphors can conceal a subject.

Brainstorming is an example of an intuitive heuristic that can aid the often difficult move from a general subject to a specific, manageable subject. Students brainstorm about a general subject, generate major categories, and then classify and subordinate the associatively retrieved information. Subsequently, students pick one of their categories and recycle the brainstorming and classifying and subordinating process. This sequence is repeated indefinitely until the students have limited and defined a manageable subject. For example, a student might begin brainstorming on the general subject of drunk driving and, in attempting to account for the wealth of her information, realize that she must focus on a more limited aspect of the subject. In the end, she might write an essay about why Mothers Against Drunk Driving should receive federal money to support their campaign.

If the teacher is interested in investigating in-depth a variety of intuitive heuristics, there are a number of "classic" textbooks for students that base entire writing courses on this approach. Perhaps the three best are Ken Macrorie's (1970) *Telling Writing*; Michael Paull and Jack Kligerman's (1973) *Invention: A Course in Pre-Writing and Composition*; and Donald Stewart's (1972) *The Authentic Voice: A Pre-Writing Approach to Student Writing*.

Empirical Heuristics

Whereas intuitive heuristics ask students to tap into their own knowledge, empirical heuristic procedures require students to interact with the world outside the classroom, collecting their information firsthand. When students explore a subject by interviewing individuals (a case study), by

polling others (an opinion survey), or by observing or participating in an activity (a field study), they are engaged in an empirical heuristic. As Kinney comments, empiricism is a "way of knowing through the senses, through direct physical experience" (1979, p. 352).

One effective way to introduce empirical heuristics at the beginning of a writing course is a version of the elementary school game of "Show and Tell." Students bring to class two easily portable objects that are highly textured and contoured, intriguingly visual, and richly connotative. Typically, students have arrived in our classes with items ranging from antique china dolls dressed in rich brocades to pieces of driftwood configured by waves and sun. All of the items are placed on a table, and students are asked to select any one item except their own. Students spend 10 minutes touching, smelling, experiencing, and meditating on their objects and then spend 15 minutes writing a description of the object that embodies the ways in which the object exists in time and space. Consider the following student's revised observation/description of a museum-quality Zuni basket. The student chose to "place" the object in time and space by adopting the stance of the Indian woman who wove the basket.

When the spring came it was time to call on the gods for rain and good weather. The old Indian squaw had worked on her offering basket throughout the long winter months. Between feeding the fire, trips to the river for water, and tanning the buffalo hides, she had sat in the shelter and steadily woven the sacred basket. Now after three months of hard work, the job was done.

The basket was approximately one foot across and five inches deep. Large enough for a generous offering of grain. She had made it from freshly picked reeds collected from the river banks after the first hard freeze of winter. The reeds were a rich amber color, but the design on the inside of the basket was what both gave it value and designated it as sacred. On the inside she had woven with painstaking care a diamond-back rattlesnake, the object of the upcoming ceremony. As she had woven throughout the winter, she had imagined again and again the snakes being brought in for the dance. She had tried to capture the intricate design of the coiled and striking snake. Now, the basket was finished.

This particular exercise also introduces students to the weekly journal exercise of writing an observation/description; the ability to describe sensory data precisely is a *basic* writing skill upon which more advanced skills of recording and reporting depend (Hillocks, 1975).

The previous empirical heuristic teaches students how to organize and structure descriptions of the physical environment. Each of the following heuristic procedures leads directly to writing a major transactional paper on a current social issue.

- Students in small groups are required to identify a social issue that concerns them. They then construct a questionnaire for a specific audience and poll a *representative* sample about their opinions on the issue.
- Individual students identify a social institution that intrigues them and spend time observing such environments as evangelical church services, hospices, pornographic bookstores — the list is endless.
- Students arrange an in-depth interview with an individual who is intimately involved with, connected to, or affected by a social issue.

Subsequently students write a major paper on some aspect of the social issue they have explored through these empirical heuristics.

We confess that the taped interview is our favorite empirical heuristic. The interview can serve as an extraordinarily powerful invention strategy, particularly if the person interviewed is truly interesting and if the questions posed have been carefully formulated, often with peer and teacher input. (See the description of the interview paper, including sample interview questions, in Appendix 3–B at the end of this chapter.)

Rational Heuristics

Intuitive and empirical heuristics assume that writers will generate organizing insights as they retrieve and collect information in the process of forming new concepts about themselves and their subjects. Rational heuristics do not deny the value of insight, but by contrast they emphasize exploring the *logical relationships* within a subject through *rule-structured* procedures. As Kinney (1979) suggests, "The essence of rationalism is a linear, step-by-step approach . . . that strives for a logical structure in which everything ties to everything else as one moves through the process of discovery" (p. 353).

Since Aristotle's *Rhetoric*, rational heuristics have been a major component of rhetorical systems. Aristotle's rational heuristics, which he called *enthymeme topoi*, consisted of 28 different perspectives on a subject that served to generate organizational and conceptual structure. Throughout rhetorical history to the present time, the topoi have continued to be taught under various guises as a means of exploring the logical relationships within subjects. Within introductory writing courses, however, unless the teacher is willing to spend considerable time defining the context of the Aristotelian topoi and explaining them operationally, the topoi are probably too complicated to be effective. However, as Edward Corbett (1971) demonstrates in his *Classical Rhetoric for the Modern Student*, the Aristotelian approach to invention can be profitably taught to the more advanced writer.

Richard Larson (1968) has clustered and restated the Aristotelian topics for a modern audience in a particularly effective manner. Each set of heuristic questions is *keyed* to specific types of subjects. The following is Larson's plan for teaching rhetorical invention.*

DISCOVERING THROUGH QUESTIONING

I. Subjects That Invite Comment

   A. *Writing about single items (in present existence).*
      What are its precise physical characteristics (shape, dimensions, composition, etc.)?
      How does it differ from things that resemble it?
      What is its "range of variation" (how much can we change it and still identify it as the thing we started with)?
      Does it call to mind other objects we have observed earlier in our lives? Why? In what respects?
      From what points of view can it be examined?
      What sort of structure does it have?
      How do the parts of it work together?
      How are the parts put together?
      How are the parts proportioned in relation to each other?
      To what structure (class or sequence of items) does it belong?
      Who or what produced it in this form? Why?
      Who needs it?
      Who uses it? For what?
      What purposes might it serve?
         How can it be evaluated, for these purposes?

   B. *Writing about single completed events, or parts of an ongoing process. [These questions can apply to scenes and pictures, as well as to works of fiction and drama.]*
      Exactly what happened? (Tell the precise sequence: Who? What? When? How? Why? Who did what to whom? Why? What did what to what? How?)
      What were the circumstances in which the event occurred? What did they contribute to its happening?
      How was the event like or unlike similar events?

*Adapted from "Discovery Through Questioning: A Plan for Teaching Rhetorical Invention," 1968, *College English*, *30*, 126–134. Used by permission of the National Council of Teachers of English and Richard L. Larson.

What were its causes?

What were its consequences?

What does its occurrence imply? What action (if any) is called for?

What was affected (indirectly) by it?

What, if anything, does it reveal or emphasize about some general condition?

To what group or class might it be assigned?

Is it (in general) good or bad? By what standard?

How do we arrive at the standard?

How do we know about it? What is the authority for our information? How reliable is the authority?

How do we know it to be reliable? (Or unreliable?)

How might the event have been changed or avoided?

To what other events was it connected? How?

To what kinds of structure (if any) can it be assigned? On what basis?

C. *Writing about abstract concepts (e.g., "religion," "socialism").*

To what specific items, groups of items, events, or groups of events does the word or words connect, in your experience or imagination?

What characteristics must an item or event have before the name of the concept can apply to it?

How do the referents of that concept differ from the things we name with similar concepts (e.g., "democracy" and "socialism")?

How has the term been used by writers whom you have read? How have they implicitly defined it?

Does the word have "persuasive" value? Does the use of it in connection with another concept seem to praise or condemn the other concept?

Are you favorably disposed to all things included in the concept? Why or why not?

D. *Writing about collections of items (in present existence). [These questions are in addition to the questions about single items, which can presumably be asked of each item in the group.]*

What, exactly, do the items have in common?

If they have features in common, how do they differ?

How are the items related to each other, if not by common characteristics? What is revealed about them by the possibility of grouping them in this way?

How may the group be divided? What bases for division can be found?

What correlations, if any, may be found among the various possible subgroups? Is anything disclosed by the study of these correlations? Into what class, if any, can the group as a whole be put?

E. *Writing about groups of completed events, including processes.* *[These questions are in addition to questions about single completed events; such questions are applicable to each event in the group and to literary works, principally fiction and drama.]*

What have the events in common?

If they have features in common, how do they differ?

How are the events related to each other (if they are not part of a chronological sequence)? What is revealed by the possibility of grouping them in this way (these ways)?

What is revealed by the events when taken as a group?

How can the group be divided? On what bases?

What possible correlations can be found among the several subgroups? Into what class, if any, can the events taken as a group fit?

Does the group belong to any other structures than simply a larger group of similar events? (Is it part of a more inclusive chronological sequence? one more piece of evidence that may point toward a conclusion about history? and so on.)

To what antecedents does the group of events look back? Where can they be found?

What implications, if any, does the group of events have? Does the group point to a need for some sort of action?

II. Subjects with "Comments" already Attached

A. *Writing about propositions (statements set forth to be proved or disproved).*

What must be established for the reader before he or she will believe it?

Into what subpropositions, if any, can it be broken down? (What smaller assertions does it contain?)

What are the meanings of key words in it?

To what line of reasoning is it apparently a conclusion?

How can we contrast it with other, similar propositions? (How can we change it, if at all, and still have roughly the same proposition?)

To what class (or classes) of propositions does it belong?

How inclusive (or how limited) is it?

What is at issue, if one tries to prove the proposition?

How can it be illustrated?

How can it be proven (by what kinds of evidence)?

What will or can be said in opposition to it?

Is it true or false? How do we know? (by direct observation, authority, deduction, statistics, other sources?)

Why might someone disbelieve it?

What does it assume? (What other propositions does it take for granted?)

What does it imply? (What follows from it?) Does it follow from the proposition that action of some sort must be taken?

What does it reveal (signify, if true)?

If it is a prediction, how probable is it? On what observations of past experience is it based?

If it is a call to action, what are the possibilities that action can be taken? (Is what is called for feasible?) What are the probabilities that the action, if taken, will do what it is supposed to do? (Will the action called for work?)

B. *Writing about questions (interrogative sentences).*
   Does the question refer to past, present, or future time?
   What does the question assume (take for granted)?
   In what data might answers be sought?
   Why does the question arise?
   What, fundamentally, is in doubt? How can it be tested? evaluated?
   What propositions might be advanced in answer to it?
       Is each proposition true?
       If it is true:
           What will happen in the future? What follows from it?
           Which of these predictions are possible? probable?
           What action should be taken (avoided) in consequence?
[Most of the other questions listed under "Propositions" also apply.]

Adaptations of Kenneth Burke's work (1969) offer a more immediately accessible rational heuristic approach for young writers. Burke translates and elaborates the journalistic questions of *where, when, who, what,* and *why* into the heuristic pentad of *scene, act, agent, agency,* and *purpose.* As Ross Winterowd (1975) demonstrates in his classroom text, *The Contemporary Writer: A Practical Rhetoric,* the pentad's five different perspec-

tives on reality can serve as powerful heuristic devices for exploring and constructing the logical relationships within any subject: *scene* (when or where was it done?), *act* (what was done?), *agent* (who did it?), *agency* (how did she do it?), and *purpose* (why did she do it?).

There are persuasive reasons for teaching beginning writers how to use the pentad as a rational heuristic. After students have begun to master the art of defining a subject from the perspectives of scene, act, agent, agency, and purpose, they can be introduced to the ratios, the way in which these perspectives interact to define the dynamic structure of a subject. But a word of caution. Kenneth Burke turned the art of constructing ratios within the pentad into an analytic device for constructing an entire, complex philosophical system. As Kristen Figg (1980) points out in her article, "Introducing Invention Techniques," the jargon and high level of abstraction typically characteristic of rational heuristics can confuse the young writer. If students are intimidated by the language of heuristic questions, their use is self-defeating.

Figg suggests that when rational heuristics are first introduced, they need to be translated into the students' language and heuristic questions need to be adapted and tailored to suit specific writing tasks. Taking her advice, we have devised an exercise (see Figure 3–A) to introduce the pentad's heuristic questions.

The exercise in Figure 3–A demonstrates how rational heuristics can be tailored to meet the needs of specific writing assignments. Such adaptation is of particular value early in the term. After students internalize the conceptual structure of rational heuristic questions as applied to specific assignments, they can learn to translate them and to apply them to self-chosen subjects.

Another effective rational heuristic asks students to examine their subjects from three *mutually exclusive* perspectives. This approach, adapted from the nine-cell, tagmemic heuristic of Young, Becker, and Pike (1970), is translated into effective classroom practice in *Four Worlds of Writing* (Lauer et al., 1985). In this student text, the "exploratory guide" accompanying each writing assignment provides students with a systematic way of exploring their subjects from three perspectives: static, dynamic, and relative. For example, if a student were to examine a classroom in light of these perspectives, she might look at its desks, chalkboard, and the color of the walls (static). She might think about how the room changes from hour to hour as classes of students enter and exit (dynamic). And she might consider the room in the larger context of the school building and the community (relative).

One of our favorite assignments when we introduce the rational

---

Figure 3–A: Using the Pentad to Analyze Grade Inflation

At the college level, we consistently encounter a considerable number of students with high school grades of C's or B's or even occasional A's in English who cannot pass the required freshmen composition courses. Meanwhile, many professors in other academic disciplines consider the exit standards for freshman composition to be far too low.

At many state universities as many as 25 to 35 percent of the entering freshman class must take noncredit remedial coursework in English and/or math. Yet the majority of these students graduate from high school with a C average or better. Grade inflation seems to be a reality.

But before you can take a position on an issue like grade inflation, you must first analyze the nature of the problem. The following questions are designed to help you explore and define the problem.

SCENE: Where does grade inflation take place––in all subjects? When does grade inflation occur––elementary grades, middle school, high school, college?

ACT: How does grade inflation take place? Are tests graded more leniently than they used to be? Are less complex tests given––multiple choice as opposed to essay tests? Are failing students passed regardless? Has the core curriculum been watered down?

AGENT: Who is involved in grade inflation––students, teachers, administrators, parents, college admissions offices?

AGENCY: How do those involved in grade inflation bring it about?

PURPOSE: Why do those involved in grade inflation do it?

---

heuristics of static, dynamic, and relative is to ask students to define "good writing" from these three mutually exclusive perspectives. From a *static* perspective, good writing is defined by the so-called "virtues" of writing— perspicuity, purity, propriety, precision, impressiveness. From a *dynamic* perspective, good writing is characterized by the mastery of a mature composing process that includes a broad range of predrafting, drafting, and revision strategies. From a *relative* perspective, good writing is defined by its functions in the larger contexts of education, work, and communication in general.

Using rational heuristic procedures to examine and construct the logical relationships within a subject will lead students into richer, more complex, and increasingly structured conceptualizations of their subjects. And when rational heuristic questions are presented in language that students can understand and with a level of specificity that makes them seem relevant to a particular writing assignment, students can learn to use them effectively.

Integrating the Use of Intuitive, Empirical, and Rational Heuristics

Valuable as these intuitive, empirical, and rational heuristics are in isolation, their real strength lies in the writer's combining them in the course of a single writing task. For example, a student might derive a generalized subject, "The Effects of Divorce," from an intuitive nonstop journal entry about her father's new wife. She might then brainstorm about this generalized subject and further limit the subject to "A Redefinition of the Nuclear Family." After considerable preliminary library research, she might apply the pentadic heuristic to discover the dynamic interaction of scene, act, agent, agency, and purpose.

Another student might use the empirical heuristic of the interview to investigate the implications of choosing a major in architecture. She might interview the Dean of the School of Architecture, a second-year architecture student, and a practicing architect. Subsequently, she might apply a simplified tagmemic heuristic to consider a career in architecture from mutually exclusive perspectives: *static* (what does a career in architecture require?), *dynamic* (what does an architect do?), and *relative* (how is architecture part of the life of the community at large?).

RHETORICAL DEFINITION OF TOPIC

The result of the rational, intuitive, and empirical heuristics is a self-sponsored subject that has been limited and defined and about which the writer has begun to realize a diverse set of ideas and potentially interacting connections. Most students think that they are now ready to begin drafting. NOT SO! An almost infinite number of essays can be written about any subject depending on the perspective the author adopts. Initially, this is a difficult concept for many students to comprehend. To make the point, we usually give an extended example. Consider the subject of "dating customs or mores among female undergraduates at university X." Depending upon the author's perspective, the writing assignment could be an objective sociological discussion of individual differences, subgroup patterns, and overall trends within a specified group. It could be a discussion of the implications of sexual relationships without long-term relational commitments. It could be a comparison and contrast of present dating mores to those of earlier generations. It could be a cause-and-effect analysis in the context of changing societal norms — ad infinitum. The point is that any subject consists of a diverse set of ideas and *potentially* interacting

connections. Mere subjects are inchoate, unruly, and so dynamic that young writers find it extremely difficult to derive an organizing focus.

Subjects are transmuted into write-about-able topics through the exploration and definition of the *rhetorical variables* that limit and inform all written communication situations. These variables consist of (a) the conceptualization of the subject, (b) the needs of the audience, (c) the organization of the text, and (d) the nature of the writer's stance. Until these variables are limited and controlled, the writer has no real *plan* for the context or content of the text, no map for the territory to be explored during drafting.

For lack of a sound rhetorical plan, the embodiment of a topic, young writers find themselves somewhat in the position of an amateur juggler who is attempting to keep too many different types of objects in the air at one time—three oranges, two wooden bowling pins, a dinner plate, and four kitchen knives. . . . Unfortunately, young writers have learned to resolve the problem of attempting to juggle too many undefined rhetorical variables rather efficiently by tending to:

- reduce the cognitive complexity of their conceptualization of subject to simplistic, declarative lists of non-interrelated generalizations that typically are only minimally illustrated with examples or demonstrated with evidence;
- sidestep the question of audience by writing for a completely undefined global audience (the result is what Britton et al. [1975] called "pseudo-informative" or "pseudo-argumentative" prose that denies any real relationship between the writer and the reader);
- abort the issue of the organic organization of the text by retreating to the quick-and-dirty, five-paragraph essay: introduction; points one, two, and three; and conclusion;
- avoid any investment or responsibility for their stance as writers by adopting what Britton et al. (1975) called the "student-to-the-examiner" persona; they produce a piece of writing composed to be read only by the teacher in her role as dispenser of grades.

If this analysis of what happens to student writing for lack of a sound rhetorical plan seems overly harsh, consider what happens when any human organism is cognitively overloaded with too many undefined, unlimited variables. We experience a loss of control that drives us to simplify the situation—almost at any cost. And remember that during drafting, students are not only involved in intuitively juggling the variables of the

rhetorical situation, but they are also simultaneously attempting to transmute thought into syntax (no easy task) as well as trying to remember
when to use "who" or "whom."

Rhetorically defining the topic is perhaps the activity in the composing process that provides the clearest insight into the difference between
good and poor writers. The necessity of elaborating and defining rhetorical variables has been noted by various studies, including Clifford (1981),
Cooper and Odell (1978), Maimon (1979), Marder (1982), and the National Assessment of Educational Progress (1977). Good writers examine and
reexamine, define and redefine the rhetorical variables of their topics
throughout the composing process. In this way, they continuously monitor
the sophistication, the breadth, and the depth of the writing problem they
"re-present" themselves (Emig, 1971). Poor writers do not do this (Stallard,
1974). That is to say, poor writers have not developed their ability to
define, to refine, and to redefine their topic.

Flower and Hayes' (1980) classic study, "The Cognition of Discovery:
Defining a Rhetorical Problem," defines the abyss of communication that
separates the good writer and the poor writer.

> Good writers respond to *all* aspects of the rhetorical problem. As they
> compose they build a unique representation not only of their audience
> and assignment, but also of their goals involving the audience, their own
> *persona*, and the text. By contrast, the problem presentations of the poor
> writers were primarily concerned with the features and conventions of a
> written text [spelling, punctuation, usage]. (p. 29)

In the same study, Flower and Hayes used protocol research to provide
striking evidence of the differences in perspective on the text adopted by
good writers and poor writers. They asked writers to tape record the types
of decisional thoughts that went through their minds during the actual
composing of text. (Both groups of writers had the same writing assignment.) They then analyzed the content of the protocols to determine the
nature of the writer's concerns about the emerging text. In the first 7 to 8
minutes of composing, the expert writer was concerned with the relationship between the audience and the assignment 18 times, while the poor
writers dealt with this issue less than half as many times. Moreover, in
regard to the goals of the text and the self, the poor writer evidenced no
concern whatsoever. The overall summary of the analysis demonstrated
that in the first 60 lines of protocol, the poor writers dealt with rhetorical
variables an average of only 17 times, while the expert writers dealt with
such variables an average of 42 times. Flower and Hayes concluded:

Good writers are simply solving a different problem than poor writers. Given the fluency we can expect from native speakers, this raises an important question. Would the performance of poor writers change if they too had a richer sense of what they were trying to do as they wrote, or if they had more of the goals for affecting the reader which were so stimulating to the good writers? People only solve the problems they represent to themselves. Our guess is that the poor writers we studied possess verbal and rhetorical skills which they fail to use because of their underdeveloped image of their rhetorical problem. Because they have narrowed a rhetorical act to a paper-writing problem, their representation of the problem doesn't call on abilities they may well have. (1980, p. 30)

Defining Rhetorical Variables

Clearly the answer is to teach students how to analyze, limit, and define the variables of the rhetorical situation *before* they engage in the drafting stage of the composing process. They must learn how to transmute an adequately conceptualized subject into a write-about-able topic. And by definition, a topic is the embodiment of a sound rhetorical plan. To recapitulate: Mature writers define and limit their topic by *rhetorically* defining their subject as a topic bounded by four variables: conceptualization of the subject, the needs of the audience, the organization of the text, and the writer's stance.

Conceptualization of the Subject.   Through the heuristic procedures presented previously, the writer begins to approach a self-sponsored, conceptualized subject. To transmute the subject into a topic, she must place it among the other three variables of the rhetorical situation, as illustrated in the communications triangle* in Figure 3–B. Between each pair of variables there is a tension, designated by a circled "T." The three tensions indicated in Figure 3–B are *Writer–Audience, Text–Writer,* and *Text–Audience.* As the writer continues to conceptualize her subject, the subject is seen as related to the interaction of the pairs of variables *as well as* to each of the other three variables per se.

In the phase of conceptualizing the subject as bounded by writer's stance, organization of the text, and the audience, the student poses questions to herself and makes *written note* of her answers: What can I as writer bring to this subject — what knowledge, point of view, specific examples do I bring? What does my audience expect me to relate? What does my projected organization of the text tell me about what its major points

---

*The communications triangle has been discussed widely, especially since Kinneavy (1971).

Figure 3–B: SUBJECT Composition Triangle

Writer ⓣ Audience

ⓣ SUBJECT ⓣ

Text

are, its key interrelationships? When she has answered these sets of questions, she has initially conceptualized the subject in the context of the three variables of the map; she has set the preliminary boundaries of the subject. Later she must return to the conceptualization of the subject and view it as a dynamic relationship among the other features of the topic (that is, she must review it within its "tensions"). But first, she must have worked through the other variables and set their boundaries.

The Audience. Texts exist for audiences, and an audience is not an abstraction. The audience is the set of anticipated readers or the known reader. The readers have expectations, desires for certain knowledge, and emotional, social, and intellectual backgrounds. They have likes and dislikes; they will tolerate certain forms and levels of language but not others. The writer cannot rhetorically define her topic without considering this audience in detail (see Figure 3–C). Undefined audiences lead to pseudo-informative or pseudo-argumentative prose that denies that any substantive relationship exists between the writer and the audience.

In this phase of rhetorically defining and elaborating the topic, the student poses and answers questions such as: What do I know about my audience; who are they, what do they wear, do they care about this topic, how can I reach them? What do they already know about the subject matter? How would they organize a text about this subject? If they were to have thought through this subject as I have, what topics would they be interested in exploring, what would they find relevant? Timely? Worthy of research? What level of language and what stylistic features would they expect? Having answered these and similar questions *in writing*, she will have set out the preliminary boundaries of the audience.

Figure 3–C: AUDIENCE Composition Triangle

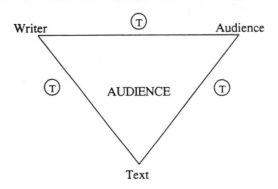

Organization of the Text.   Texts are not organized by lottery. All texts are not organized similarly (see Figure 3–D). When a teacher exhorts students to develop an "organic" arrangement of their text, she typically is met by blank-faced, dull-eyed stares. Unfortunately the term "organic" for many students refers to a type of gardening. What we needed to say is: Conceive the organization of your text as the result of studying the interrelationships among your stance, your audience's expectations, the conceptualized subject, and your text's organization.

As our writer continues to elaborate the topic by defining it, she asks: How many patterns for organizing my text can I think of — and which of these are appropriate for my topic as it is now emerging? Which of these do I feel most confident about (in terms both of my ability to use them and their appropriateness)? What does my audience expect? Does the subject

Figure 3–D: TEXT Composition Triangle

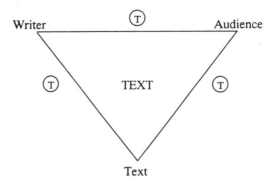

tell me how to organize major parts of the text (e.g., problem-solution, cause-effect, chronology)? And when I sum all these ideas, what should my finished text look like? How should it be organized? Again, it is important that the definition of the organization of the text that emerges from these inquires be written out. A well-thought-out definition of the projected organization of the text is the foundation of an "organically" arranged text.

The Nature of the Writer's Stance.   The writer herself is the fourth complex, multidimensional boundary of the territory of the text (see Figure 3–E). For a given text the writer may be an expert or a novice, an expositor or an explorer or a narrator (in one of several points of view — first person participant, third person, observer, and so forth), masculine or feminine in voice or bias, an introvert or an extrovert. The writer's stance is dynamic and is based on the other three variables.

In this phase of the rhetorical definition of topic, the writer asks and writes down answers for questions such as: What limits, what potentials does my subject allow me to explore? Does the subject demand that I be a radical? Apolitical? Logically exacting? More subjective in my evaluations? Neutral or biased? What does my audience expect of me? What "voice" are they expecting to hear in my text? Which of my many voices seems the most appropriate, authentic? Must I fulfill these expectations? How does my text dictate my stance (e.g., if problem–solution ordering is important, does that mean I should be neutral and analytic, and that my voice should be that of the expert who is delivering testimony to a congressional hearing)?

When the writer is seeking to elaborate her stance, she is visualizing

Figure 3–E: WRITER Composition Triangle

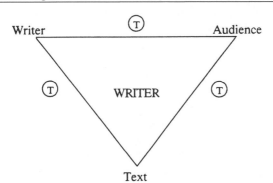

herself as the focal point of the interaction of the other three variables. Once the preliminary stance is established, the final boundary of the territory of the text has been staked out. What remains is the refining of that definition by reviewing each boundary as a dynamic feature; that is, the writer must refine the rhetorical definition of topic by studying the "tensions."

Addressing the Sets of Tensions.   While the writer was working through the steps above, she was elaborating her rhetorical understanding of the topic, but each point was approached singly. In fact, none exists only singly: Each interacts with each of the other three. We have labeled these interactions "tensions." There is a push-and-pull, give-and-take relationship between each pair of variables, and the three tensions that exist around any one of the four foci produce a dynamic set of boundaries. Reconsidering each set in turn allows the writer to redefine and thus elaborate and refine the rhetorical definition of topic.

The process is similar to that already presented. Writers must revisit each of the foci and confirm or alter their answers to the questions. For example, in the first step above — conceptualization of the subject — the questions now include: What writer-audience tensions must be taken into account as I conceptualize my subject? Perhaps I should consider myself more of a persuader than I had thought before I realized that the audience has sufficient knowledge but not the same perspective as the one I wish to use as a beginning point. If that is so, then I should reconceptualize my subject to include the presentation of background and arguments for my perspective. And next: What tensions between audience and the organization of the text assist me in refining my conceptualization of my subject? The text will be written at a lower reading level than I had originally thought, so. . . .

This process of revisiting the boundaries is cyclic; as each cycle is completed, the rhetorical definition of the topic is more precise, more focused. When the writer can clearly answer the following questions, she has rhetorically defined the topic with sufficient concreteness and substance to move ahead. The rhetorical questions are:

My stance is . . ..
My audience is . . . , and they expect . . ..
My conceptualized subject is . . . , and it comprises . . ..
My text is going to be organized into . . ..

We cannot overemphasize the importance of working through the rhetorical definition activity. Too many times we have watched students

begin to write with only a single word or phrase for a topic, an unexplored and unelaborated, low-level conceptualization unrelated to any orderly arrangement of ideas. And we have watched them abandon topic after topic after writing only a page, sometimes after only a paragraph. Writers with an unelaborated, undefined topic have at best one or two bones when what they need is the entire skeleton. How else will they know where the various parts go, which is which, how much each part weighs and how much weight it will hold, and what its role is?

INTEGRATING THE RHETORICAL DEFINITION OF TOPIC INTO THE CURRICULUM

The definition of rhetorical variables outlined in the previous section is precisely the process that writers must employ to limit, define, and establish control over their topics. Unfortunately, the ability to go through this process presupposes considerable experience in analyzing and writing for a variety of specific audiences — *experience that our students do not have*. Fortunately, as Flower and Hayes (1980) suggest, "The ability to explore a rhetorical problem is eminently teachable. Unlike a metaphoric 'discovery', [rhetorical] problem-finding is not a totally mysterious or magical act" (p. 31). In fact, entire courses have been based on teaching students how to analyze rhetorical situations and to identify rhetorical variables; they are often called "case book" approaches. Three recent textbooks reflecting this approach are *Cases for Composition* (Field & Weiss, 1984), *The Little Writing Book: Cases for Rhetorical Expression* (Veit, 1982), and *From Cases to Composition* (Woodson, 1982).

We question using nothing but the case approach as a global instructional strategy for younger writers or less capable older ones. They have so many things to learn: discovery and conceptualization of subject, fluency, defining and limiting the topic, drafting strategies, revision techniques, and matters of form and correctness. Yet without the ability to analyze the rhetorical situation — a key and essential step in the composing process — student writing is likely to remain, using Emig's (1971) terms, *school-sponsored* rather than *self-sponsored*.

We have, however, integrated the "case approach" into the curriculum in a shorthand fashion in order to provide students with the experience of analyzing and writing for a variety of specific audiences. We have devised a sequence of six rhetorical situations or "cases" that must be responded to in the format of a short letter to a highly specified audience. Each "case" is based on Festinger's (1957) concept of cognitive dissonance; it has a double bind in it that forces the accommodation of more than one rhetorical goal.

For instance, consider the following rhetorical situation* describing "The Copy Shop":

For over a year you have been working at the Copy Shop in the Student Union Building. The Copy Shop reproduces and collates materials for students and faculty. You work part-time, running the machines and helping out at the cash register.

Yesterday you learned that a similar position will be opening up at the Copy Shop. Your roommate, Terry, needs a job and has applied for this one. The manager of the Copy Shop has asked you for a written evaluation of Terry's qualifications for the job. You like your roommate, who has a special way with people. But Terry seldom hangs up clothes, is often late to classes, and spends a lot of time looking for misplaced books, lecture notes, telephone numbers, and the checkbook. You want your roommate to get the job because Terry is your friend and needs the income, but you do not want to jeopardize your own employment by misrepresenting Terry's qualifications to the manager.

Clearly, the writer does not wish to offend or "put down" her roommate, yet it is equally obvious that she must not ignore her roommate's shortcomings for the job. The double bind embodies cognitive dissonance, and as Festinger (1957) pointed out, the human organism has a built-in drive to reduce dissonance that tends to engage students in the task and drive them toward closure. In the progression of the course, the type of rhetorical situation that students are asked to respond to becomes increasingly complex, and the types of audience become increasingly distant from their immediate life-styles.

The specific progression of these rhetorical situation exercises has a number of steps. First, students read and analyze the rhetorical situation. Consider the following example of a rhetorical situation about dyslexia:

Dyslexia is a perceptual disorder that makes it difficult for a child to learn to read and write. Typically, during puberty (11–13 years of age), children suffering from dyslexia begin to "grow out" of the perceptual problem but are left with severe reading and writing problems.

Your 12-year-old son (or daughter) is beginning to outgrow his (her) dyslexic problems. He (she) has worked very hard over the past year and a half to improve his (her) reading and writing skills. For the last three weeks, his (her) seventh grade science teacher has been teaching a health unit on the skeletal structure of the human body. There is no textbook for this unit; students must take in-class notes, copying difficult terminology from the board. The lack of a classroom text has caused additional problems for your son (or daughter). His (her) poor writing skills make it

*The rhetorical situation exercises in this chapter were developed with David Abbot, William Ausmus, Dana Elder, David Hadley, Veronica Franklin, Linda Johnson, Paul Myers, Judy Sorem, and Linda Stairet; Washington State University, Pullman, Washington, 1980–1982.

difficult for him (her) to take in-class notes, and even when he (she) copies terminology directly from the board, he (she) often misspells essential terms; for example, "tebia" for "tibia." Normally, your son (or daughter) receives fairly good grades in science, but he (she) has just received a D minus on the test on the skeletal structure; 50 percent of the credit for each fill-in-the-blank question was deducted if the term was misspelled.

After students have analyzed the "case," they are requested to define *in writing* the rhetorical variables that structure the situation: (a) the conceptualization of the subject, (b) the needs of the audience, (c) the nature of the writer's stance, and (d) the organization of the text.

As you might imagine, the students' next assignment is to write a short letter responding to the highly specified audience, explaining to the science teacher about the child's problems with the health unit and suggesting that in the future the child should not be overly penalized for spelling problems.

The progression of the assignment to this point is valuable, but it provides the writer no feedback about how successfully she has accomplished her rhetorical goals. The next step of the exercise is elegant, economical, and extraordinarily powerful. Students are provided with eight fictitious letters written in response to the hypothetical case. (See the "Dyslexia Letters" in Appendix 3–A at the end of this chapter.) The letters represent a wide range of solutions to the double bind of the rhetorical problem. In their working groups of six (see Chapter 6, "Using Peer Group Instruction to Teach Writing"), students are asked to discuss the eight letters and reach a consensus ranking of the three best letters and the three worst letters. Invested in their own opinions, the students begin to interact intensely, and it is delightful to see them start to function as practicing rhetoricians. Their conversations are focused and include: Given the double bind, what constitutes the primary versus the secondary rhetorical goals of the letter? What are the audience's needs (both practically and psychologically)? There is considerable — and sometimes agitated — exploratory discussion about the likely nature of the audience's response to the tone, diction, and writer's stance of each letter. And, of course, the pressure is on because they must rank the letters high/low in terms of *effectiveness*. (The letters are not easily ranked, and there is no absolutely correct ordering.) The discussion, limited to 15 minutes, turns into a teacher's dream of a mini-workshop setting in which analysis of audience, definition of rhetorical goals, discussion of linguistic decorum, and style are discussed intensely.

After students have reached consensus on the rank-ordering of the letters, they are asked to redefine the rhetorical situation in terms of the conceptualization of the subject, the needs of the audience, the organiza-

tion of the text, and the nature of the writer's stance. What they are doing, of course, is redefining the rhetorical variables in terms of the *tensions* that interrelate them — the dynamics of the communication situation.

The final, inevitable step of the exercise is for the students to rewrite their own letters by drawing upon, integrating, and adapting the rhetoric they have seen employed by eight other writers.

The rhetorical situation letter is in many ways the most economical "exercise" in our classroom repertoire. First, it teaches students how to write effective letters — a highly potent accomplishment in a society that has almost forgotten the value of the epistolary act. We require that students learn to format the letter in terms of inside address, date, and return address. (The reader may remember that writing a "real" letter to a significant audience is one of the weekly journal assignments.) Second, the exercise engages students actively in the rhetorical enterprise of communicating with specified audiences (even if imagined). And third and most importantly, the exercise defines with exquisite functional precision the difference between the *initial definition* of the individual rhetorical variables that define the boundaries of the topic — the first letter — and the *redefinition* of the rhetorical variables, in terms of their dynamic, interrelated tensions — the second letter.

Students who have been writing pseudo-informative or pseudo-argumentative prose for unrealized, global audiences are surprised to discover that the structure of consciousness begins to unfold *organically* as an *arrangement* of the text once they have dynamically defined the interrelationship between the conceptualization of the subject, the needs of the audience, the organization of the text, and the nature of the writer's stance. Students are now ready to commit themselves to the journey of the drafting process.

PREDRAFTING: A FINAL WORD

Writing begins in self-sponsoring a subject, conceptualizing the subject, and defining the rhetorical situation. In a succinct article, "Prewriting Is the Essence of Writing," Boiarsky (1982) looks back over almost two decades of theorizing about and experimentation with predrafting. She suggests that, no matter what techniques are used, all predrafting is designed to lead a writer through four stages.

1. The writer participates in an event.
2. The writer gives meaning to the event.

3. The writer selects an angle for communicating the event's meaning.
4. The writer develops an organizational structure based on the angle to design an effective piece of written discourse. (p. 44)

Boiarsky suggests that if predrafting has been successful, unconscious thoughts and emotions have emerged into personal statements, and the expressive voice has become integrated into the student's public voice. She concludes that the reason predrafting is so effective is that it merely accelerates in an organized way the natural, creative process that we call learning. The question is no longer "Why predrafting?" The only question is "What type of predrafting strategies work with what types of writers for what types of assignments?"

During predrafting, students convert the events of their lives into insight. Without significant predrafting, student writing tends to reduce the implications of experience rather than to expand them into a vision of the self and its relationship to the world. When writing is based in predrafting, students tend to develop an intrinsic investment in exploring their ideas and emotions; this seduces them into an attempt to account for themselves as human beings.

APPENDIX 3–A
RHETORICAL SITUATION EXERCISE

Letters Written in Response to the Dyslexia "Case"

A. Dear Mr. Johnson,

I am writing with the hope that you will give our daughter, Emily Lou, some special consideration in the future. She suffers from dyslexia, which makes it hard for her to spell correctly and it was due to spelling errors that she did so poorly on her last test in your class. It doesn't seem quite fair that a child who studies so hard for a test should lose so many points simply because of spelling, especially when she has the kind of problem Emily Lou has. I helped her study, so I know she knew the material, but she just has trouble sometimes getting the right letters straight. It's not her fault.

Well, I just wanted you to know the situation, and I trust that in the future you will give her a break since she really is a hard working kid but just has trouble spelling. Maybe you would be so kind as to go back and change her last grade. That would make us all feel a lot better.

Sincerely,

B. Dear Mr. Johnson,

My son informed me that you penalized him 50 percent for each term misspelled on his science test, and as a result he received a D minus on the test. This does not seem fair in light of his hard work this past year and a half.

Have you forgotten that my son suffers from dyslexia? Surely, he shouldn't be responsible for spelling when you do not even provide a textbook from which he can study the necessary terms. After all, he cannot take in-class notes efficiently like the other students can.

If this unfairness persists, I will have no choice but to discuss the matter with your principal, Mrs. Spencer.

Sincerely,

C. Dear Mr. Johnson,

I am writing to you about my son Tom and the recent difficulty he had in your seventh grade science class. Tom loves science and has spoken so highly of you as both a teacher and a person that I felt the D minus he received on his skeleton test needed discussing. Tom suffers from dyslexia. As I am sure you know, this makes it hard for Tom to read and spell accurately unless he studies the material closely. Since the skeleton unit did not use a text, and Tom had to rely on his notes, he did very poorly on the

spelling aspect of the test. I understand the importance of spelling, but in this case, the penalty does not reflect Tom's ability, only his disability. Now neither Tom nor I want him to be given special treatment, and I would never ask you to change a grade. I would ask, though, for your understanding and confidence in this matter. I am sorry for not having told you sooner. Perhaps then you could have provided a study guide or tutorial help and so avoided this problem. If there is any way that I can help you to help Tom, please contact me.

Thank you for your time.

Sincerely,

D. Dear Mr. Johnson,

My son Tom is in your seventh grade science class. Tom is dyslexic. Because of his condition he did poorly on his test on the skeleton. He had difficulty spelling the terms. Perhaps you could reconsider his grade in light of this. Without the penalty for misspelling, he would have a B plus on the test. This reflects his efforts much better.

Sincerely,

E. Dear Mr. Johnson,

I don't see why my daughter Emily Lou should get poor grades in your class just for spelling. She has dyslexia, and this makes it hard for her to spell correctly all the time. Besides, your class is a science class, not a spelling class, and you should be able to tell if she knows the parts of the skeleton. When I was in school the main thing was whether or not you knew something, not if you could spell everything correctly. Well, she knew the answers to your test and still got a D minus just because of a few spelling errors. That just isn't fair as far as I'm concerned.

Since Emily Lou has this special problem, I think you should grade her on her answers and not on her spelling. She didn't deserve a D minus on that test because she studied for it. I guess you could give her a square deal on the rest of your tests.

Sincerely,

F. Dear Mr. Johnson,

I am writing with regard to my daughter, Emily Lou, who is in your seventh grade science class. While I consider Emily Lou a reasonably bright child, she has suffered from dyslexia, which has made it difficult for her to learn to read and write. Now our physician indicates that she is beginning to outgrow this perceptual disorder, and Emily Lou has evinced a strong love of learning by working exceptionally hard to improve her reading and writing skills. Along with our physician, Emily Lou's father

and I feel that it will be only a matter of time before she will be able to overcome her handicap. As I'm sure you appreciate, we are working hard to prevent her from becoming discouraged with her studies.

Generally, Emily Lou has done well in science, but recently she received a D minus on a test in your class on the human skeleton. It is my understanding that she lost a great number of points for her failure to spell many of the parts correctly. I can assure you that I agree with your desire to make the students become aware of the importance of spelling and I know that you are fair in your grading. Nevertheless, it is my hope that in the future you will be willing to take Emily Lou's special problem into consideration. Naturally, if she fails to learn her lessons then she should be penalized accordingly, but as I have indicated, her dyslexia creates problems, such as in the area of spelling, over which she has limited control. Again, this is a problem that we are working hard to correct, but in the meantime we worry that if she becomes too frustrated, Emily Lou might lose the will to persevere with the fight.

Thank you for your consideration. I would be most happy to discuss the matter further with you at your convenience.

Sincerely,

G.   Dear Mr. Johnson,

My son, Tim, has informed me that he received a D minus on his recent health test on the skeletal structure due to the unavailability of a textbook from which to study.

Tim has worked very hard over the past year and a half to fight his perceptual disorder, dyslexia, and to improve his reading and writing skills. Please do not put an obstacle in his path toward future improvement by penalizing him for spelling errors. He would have done better if he had had a textbook from which to study. Without it, he had to depend on in-class notetaking; given his perceptual disorder, he had difficulty copying words correctly off the blackboard.

Thank you,

H.   Dear Mr. Johnson,

Surely you are aware that my son, Tom, has a problem with dyslexia. For the last year Tom has worked with me, with his other instructors, and with several specialists on this problem, and he *is* making progress. Perhaps you don't realize that certain instructional situations are especially difficult for Tom. One in particular is the process of taking and copying notes written on blackboards. Tom is prone, in these cases, to miscopy words — not because he's lazy or careless, but because of his learning difficulty. Surely this is what caused him to misspell so many terms on the anatomy

exam he recently failed. In this instance what is done is done, and I don't ask that you change Tom's grade or allow him to retake the exam. What I do ask is that this occurrence serve as a point from which you, Tom, and I can start to help each other. All three of us want Tom to learn, and there is every reason why we should work together towards this goal.

Sincerely,

APPENDIX 3–B
THE INTERVIEW PAPER: PREDRAFTING

All of the events of our lives can be seen in a social context. For this paper, you will interview someone who is in a position to make a substantial statement about a specific social problem, issue, or concern. You may choose to talk with an important spokesperson for a particular group or belief, or you may interview someone whose life or life-style has been directly affected by social laws, expectations, or constraints. Both the welfare mother of three and the housewife will be able to respond to questions about the implications of "cheaper gas at the pumps," but the powerful and unusual perspective is apt to come from the geologist who has lost her job as a result of falling oil prices and now, after years of academic training, can only find work as a secretary. For this paper, you are asked to seek out and become engaged with powerful statements about difficult problems in our society.

If you choose to interview someone who is a victim of a social issue (hunger — a bag person; unemployment — a transient; drunken driving — a sole survivor), make sure that the interview is conducted in a safe environment for both you and the person you are interviewing. For example, if you choose to interview someone who lives or works in a rough neighborhood, don't go there alone.

Not only should the interview be conducted in a safe environment, but in many cases the interview will need to be conducted in a confidential manner. In your paper, you may need to change names and dates in order to protect the privacy of the person interviewed.

As you know, we suggest that you tape-record your interview so that you have a complete record of the conversation to refer to. Moreover, tape-recording the interview allows you to concentrate on listening to your subject rather than attempting to take notes at the same time.

You must have the person you interview sign the release of information form.

RELEASE OF INFORMATION FORM

I, _____, understand that I am being interviewed by _____ to provide background information for a paper to be

This assignment was developed with Jean Hegland at Eastern Washington University, Cheney, Washington (1983).

written for a freshman composition course. Eventually the paper could be published in a wider context.

This interview is subject to the following conditions:

	Circle one:
1. I give permission for the interview to be tape-recorded.	Yes No
2. I give permission for my name and any other identifying names, places, and dates to be used in written form.	Yes No
3. I wish my name and any other identifying names, places, and dates to be changed to conceal my identity.	Yes No
4. I understand that by signing this release of information form, I have given permission for _____ to use the content of our interview in published form, subject to the prior conditions.	Yes No

Name of person interviewed: _____

Signature: _____   Date: _____

Name of interviewer: _____

Signature: _____   Date: _____

POSSIBLE INTERVIEW SUBJECTS

Someone who has been unemployed for over 12 months
A director of a nursing home, and several patients
Observe a meal and worship service at a Salvation Army mission and interview someone who works there
A victim of sexual child abuse or battering
A *severely* handicapped person who is successful
A mother who has given up a child for adoption
Someone who was in a concentration camp during World War II
A welfare mother who does not work
A woman in a very nontraditional job (e.g., a mechanic)
A psychiatric aide at an institute for the mentally ill
Someone who has required hospitalization for a suicide attempt
A family member of someone who has committed suicide
A policeman who has had to kill someone in the line of duty
Observe a Pentecostal service and interview several members of the church
Observe an autopsy and interview the coroner
A Vietnam veteran who has served time in prison
An immediate family member of someone killed by a drunk driver
Someone who works in an "adult amusement" center
A prison inmate who has served at least five years

A quadriplegic
Someone in a halfway home
A rape victim
A battered wife
A political refugee
A tribal elder on a reservation
A judge on prison conditions
A bag person
A woman who has had a mastectomy
A terminally ill patient
Someone who works in a hospice
A private detective
A serious survivalist
A prostitute
An ex-heroin addict

HEURISTIC QUESTIONS FOR THE INTERVIEW

For each of the following categories of information, construct at least five specific questions that would be appropriate to ask the person you are going to interview.

1. Who is the person? What is his or her occupation, social and economic class, age, and other aspects of his or her personal history? (Don't forget to include a physical description of the person in your final paper.)
2. When did this person first become involved with the social problem or issue? How old was he or she? Under what circumstances? and so on.
3. Where does this person live, work, relax? What is his or her daily and weekly schedule?
4. What is the nature of the person's involvement with the social problem or issue: voluntary or involuntary? How does he or she feel about it? Does he or she want to change it? How has it affected his or her life? and so on.
5. Why is the person involved with the social problem or issue: What caused his or her involvement?

4

Drafting:
The Heart of
the Composing Process

In an important study of the drafting process, Sharon Pianko (1979) compared remedial and regular college freshman writers and established that better writers paused, rescanned, and reread more often and for longer periods of time. Moreover, Pianko discovered that the quality of reflection for the two groups of writers was quite different. Remedial writers tended to fill their pauses with a rehearsal of what to say next at the word and sentence level, while better writers tended to rehearse in the context of a holistic plan for the evolution of the entire piece of writing.

The protocol research of Linda Flower and John R. Hayes (1980) supported and elaborated Pianko's conclusions. Comparing and contrasting the taped reflective comments of novice and expert writers, actually recorded during the drafting process, they confirmed Pianko's findings that immature writers tend to rehearse at the word and sentence level. More importantly, they established that the expert writer's rehearsal of what to say next tends to be structured as a consideration of specific variables of the rhetorical problem: the writer's stance, the audience, the conceptualization of the topic, and the organization of the text. If drafting for the immature writer proceeds as the discovery of the linear flow of the text, expert writers are concerned with constructing the text as a realization of an increasingly specific and interconnected network of rhetorical goals (Sommers, 1979).

Teachers must allow student writers time for predrafting and must teach them predrafting procedures (heuristics) that assist them in the discovery and conceptualization of their topic. Yet even conscientious predrafting does not necessarily teach students to see decisions in the drafting

This chapter is adapted from "Teaching Revision: A Model of the Drafting Process," by Roland Huff, 1983, *College English, 45*, 800–819. Reprinted by permission of the National Council of Teachers of English.

processes as resolutions of rhetorical problems. In fact, as Flower and Hayes suggest, "The successful discovery of something to say is too often equated with successful writing, whether the [produced text] is appropriate to the rhetorical situation or not" (1980, p. 22). Clearly, immature writers need to be provided with a model of the drafting process that teaches them how to construct a text in response to the evolving definition of an increasingly rich and specifically designed rhetorical problem.

The model of the drafting process described in this chapter makes two major pedagogical assumptions. First, it assumes that the writer had discovered, limited, and defined her subject. Twenty-two of the twenty-three students whose final examination essays served as the source of writing samples for this chapter engaged in systematic predrafting. Typically, they brainstormed their subject and then generated major categories by which to classify and subordinate the retrieved information (a technique taught in class). If the defined subject seemed too large, they further limited the subject and repeated this procedure. Students' discovery, limitation, and definition of their subject (no matter what heuristic they use) are an important part of transforming a "school-sponsored" assignment into "self-sponsored" writing (Emig, 1971). Students need to own their subjects if they are to maintain any sustained engagement in the drafting process.

Second, this model of the drafting process assumes that students have defined and analyzed their "rhetorical problem" and, further, have formulated a preliminary rhetorical plan for the evolution of the written text. The students whose work is analyzed here had received intensive instruction in the definition and analysis of rhetorical problems: the demands of a specified audience as they relate to the author's own goals for (a) the writer's stance, (b) the audience, (c) the conceptualization of the topic, and (d) the organization of the text. Many of these students chose to construct a preliminary rhetorical plan for their final essays. Some of these plans were quite rudimentary, as shown in the following example. (None of the student writing samples has been edited for spelling, punctuation, or grammar.)

Writer's Stance: Writing to peer group (college undergrads)—trying to inform audience of how inflation affects the lower class.

Audience: (college undergrads)—middle class, age range 17 to 24. Those who work part-time or full-time and understand or have experienced the problems associated with work and inflation.

Conceptualization of the Topic: Inflation and how it affects the worker.

Organization of the Text: Show audience that though a recession may help big business in the end and also salvage a little of the nation's economy, it will most definitely hurt a great many Americans in a very big way.

Other rhetorical plans were more specific, particularly in terms of the writer's goals for the conceptualization of the topic and the organization of the text.

Conceptualization of the topic: showing effects of inflation on consumers, why, who, what, how—insight on recessions and examples.
Organization of the text: I. *Intro.* define inflation, consumers, and corporation, narrow in on consumer. II. *What's going on now?* A. recessions, B. three effects—money effects, political effects, snowball effects, C. Suggestions. III. *Concl.*

These preliminary plans, whether done formally or informally, are a critical component of the composing process. Without such a plan for the evolution of a whole text, the writer tends to focus during the drafting process on immediate and localized problems, often losing sight of both topic and audience.

In short, these plans are a product of the predrafting stage of the composing process. In practice, of course, the line of demarcation between predrafting and drafting is not so clearly defined. Even competent writers occasionally begin drafting with only a vaguely realized notion of what their topic is or even who will become their audience. Moreover, during the drafting of a major text, most writers have to return time and again to the predrafting stage of the composing process, rethink particular concepts, and do further research. In practice, predrafting and drafting are contiguous processes. Nonetheless, for the immature writer a somewhat artificial separation of the two steps is a helpful distinction.

The following model of the drafting process is necessarily theoretical in nature; the drafting strategies of mature writers are as multifarious as the divergent nature of their talents, tasks, and training. The purpose of the model is to teach students how to engage in the drafting of a text as a recursive process in which the linear order of the words constantly folds back upon itself to generate a nonlinear structure of ideas. If writing is to serve as an extension and elaboration of thought, students need to internalize a variety of drafting strategies that allow them to discover and reconceive the meaning and structure of a text as it evolves.

The model has three steps:

Zero drafting: The discovery and initial realization of the topic (Murray, 1968);
Problem-solving drafting: The identification and resolution of major conceptual and organizational problems;
Final drafting: The attempt to arrive at the best possible solution of a rhetorical problem.

Although these three steps are presented in sequential order, the intent is not to define drafting as a three-step process. Rather, the design of the model is to develop a critical awareness of the type of drafting strategy required at specific points in the drafting of a particular text.

INTEGRATING A MODEL OF THE DRAFTING PROCESS INTO THE WRITING CURRICULUM

To integrate this model of the drafting process into the curriculum of a single composition course, we focus on teaching drafting in the context of the in-class essay written over a period of three days (Sanders [Littlefield, 1975): day one = zero drafting, day two = problem-solving drafting, and day three = final drafting. To foreshorten the predrafting stage of the composing process, which is essential to engaged drafting, we provide students with a packet of approximately ten "source sheets" which focus on a variety of subjects ranging from inflation to high school illiteracy to sexual harassment on the job. Each source sheet cites 25 divergent facts or opinions (See Appendix 4–A at the end of this chapter for a sample source sheet.)

For each in-class essay, students are asked to read over the source sheets, which are designed to guarantee that the students have both context and content for their writing; to select a subject that engages them; to define a limited aspect of the general subject about which they have enough experience and knowledge to write; and to define their rhetorical situation.

All of the student examples in this chapter came from an in-class final examination in one section of a regular composition course. These students had received intense instruction in the drafting process throughout the term. For the final examination, students were provided with a source sheet that listed 25 divergent facts, opinions, and concepts about the general subject of inflation. Students then were given three 75-minute class sessions in which to produce a "concise, coherent, organized essay" on some limited aspect of inflation. They were encouraged to "spend time thinking, making notes, and brainstorming" before they wrote. To allow for substantive revision throughout the drafting process, students were provided with blue books and instructed to write the main body of the text on the right-hand pages and to use the left-hand pages for notes, questions, and major inserts. All writing was done in class, and work in progress was picked up at the end of each period.

ZERO DRAFTING

Young writers have been conditioned to believe that a proofread version of their first draft can serve as their final draft. Their freewheeling oral talk about their experiences often tends to be more complex and rich than their first-and-final-draft writing. If the first draft is conceived of as final, the writer cannot afford to take risks, explore, or make mistakes. Introducing students to the concept of zero drafting is a first step toward elaborating their drafting processes beyond an attempt to get it said "right" at the sentence level.

Zero drafting represents the writer's attempt to bridge the gap between an initial conceptualization of the topic and the organization of the written text. As Donald Murray (1968) indicates, this point of transition is a critical one.

> When [the writer] writes [his zero draft] he discovers the holes in his argument, the logical steps which are passed over, the sentences which grow tangled upon themselves, the paragraphs which collapse, the words which are inadequate. But still he must push on through the first draft. He cannot allow himself to be discouraged at this stage, or to be too critical. The happy accidents will be matched by the misfortunes, but still he must complete this piece of writing. He must achieve his destination.
>
> When he completes his first draft the professional writer has a feeling of relief, but this does not mean he feels he has completed his job. Now he can go to work on it, now he has begun, now he can become a craftsman. Before the completion of this first draft all was intangible; there were fragments of notes, bits and pieces of what he had to say, a sketch, a design, a plan, an idea, a hint. Now he has a piece of writing. And now that he has completed this piece of writing he can begin to write. (pp. 9–10)

The need for zero drafting occurs at a point when the writer realizes and accepts the fact that the time for predrafting is over and that what is needed is to produce a whole piece of writing. The task is to write an entire draft of her initial conceptualization as hard and fast as possible. The final product of the composing process will stand or fall upon the rhetorical plan more or less crudely realized in the zero draft.

Zero drafts vary in their completeness from writer to writer. And writers vary in their zero drafting from task to task. But given an extended writing assignment, students who have abandoned a first-and-final-draft

approach to writing typically use one or more of the following strategies to help them engage and complete their zero drafts.

Some students draft a rambling introduction, much of which is later discarded, as a warm-up exercise. Following is an example of a student's zero draft:

Inflation is an abnormal increase in the volume of money and credit resulting in a substancial and continuing rise in the general price level. Considering the past history of America as the wealthiest, most technologically advanced country in the world for most of history and looking ahead to the future America which the majority of American's perceive as continuing as in the past 100 years, upgrading, modernized technology, wealth and power, these periods of inflation should not come as any surprise. America as viewed by other countries is always associated with wealth and riches, and power that could not be easily held back. America has always been seen as a country of unlimited resources, technology, energy, wealth, and political power. Any dream could come true in America, this magnificent land of opportunity. With all of this potential which America was born with there seems to be no end, nothing out of her reach as a country. However in the last decade or so, various factors and influences have begun to prove this future ideal of America to be false. Has this land of opportunity and excess wealth transformed into a country of serious social, economic, and political problems?

This warm-up paragraph is an extreme example of impacted thought and syntax. Individual sentences run on and on with only minimal punctuation. The entire paragraph is almost a piece of associative nonstop writing. Nonetheless, the paragraph serves to plunge the writer directly into the topic. In the final draft, the writer deletes all of this warm-up paragraph, with the exception of the first sentence, and begins the essay with a terse definition of inflation and how the rate of inflation is calculated.

Inflation is an abnormal increase in the volume of money and credit resulting in a substancial and continuing rise in the general price level. The cost of buying a bundle of goods in the present year is compared to the cost of the same goods in the last base price year: 1968. The increase in price relative to the base price measures the inflation rate.

Figure 4–A shows three more zero-drafting strategies. Example 1 shows how, in contrast to a rambling, warm-up introduction, other students go directly to a statement of thesis and return later to frame the essay with a more general introduction.*

*Note: Revisions made by the student while generating a draft are indicated in the text in the following ways: (a) addition = [*Add.* plus textual addition], (b) deletion = [*Del.* plus textual deletion], (c) substitution = [*Sub.* plus textual substitution], and (d) reordering = [*Reorder.* plus textual reordering].

Figure 4–A: Zero-drafting Strategies

Example 1

Zero Draft of First Paragraph

There is definately a severe problem with a presidential [Add. economic] policy that will cut benefits from desperate people. In one case, a paralyzed man with a family of four was striped of [Add. all of] his [Add. social security] benefits, in another case a woman was forced to quit her [Add. union] job so that she would be eligable for welfare; her son needed a vital operation and his medicaid benefits had been dropped.

Later Draft

President Reagan has always promised that there would be a "safety-net" for [Del. the] low [Del. er]-income [Del. workers] [Sub. individuals]; this means that we [Add. in the lowest income bracket of industrial workers,] will never have to worry about sinking so low that we will starve to death. But could there be a chance of the net ripping out from underneath us? The threat of hitting the bottom is becoming more of a reality each day with [Del. the] high-inflation [Add. and] unemployment. High inflation is lowering the standard of living and unemployment is making total poverty a reality for many.

Example 2

Zero Draft

First off, ever since WWII prices have slowly been on the rise [Del. and] [Sub. but] it has only been in the last few years that it has really started to affect us. Most of us work just as hard for our money as we ever did but it is still worth less, so that in effect, something which cost one dollar several years ago, may now cost two, and that is definitely what you would call double digit inflation (*student's note to self in text*—USE FACTS #14 and #15 FROM SOURCE SHEET TO BACK UP).

Later Draft

"For the bulk of middle-class Americans, more and more family income now goes for the basics—energy, food, housing and health—which rose 13.8% last year." "Prices are still rising at an unparalleled rate." *SS no. 14, 15*

Example 3

Zero Draft

. . . Americans can't afford to save [Del. their] any substantial amount of their incomes because of the exhorbatant prices of food and other necessities. However, what money is left over from a check is usually spent on indulgences [Del. and] giving little thought to savings.

(*Student's note to self in text*— TRANSITION)

Our government leaders are not just sitting idly, [Del. bye,] waiting for something to happen to stop or decrease inflation. They feel its effects too, although not as harshly on their Bermuda-porsche salaries . . .

Later Draft

"The luxury items of yesterday have become today's standards and tomorrow's necessities."3 [Del. Perhaps the idea of cultural values is a main contributing factor to] Cultural values are a key contributing factor to the high cost of inflation.

The political system is a main focal point during times of high inflation because the power to change laws and taxes lies in the hands of the legislators.

During the zero-drafting process, some writers typically support their generalizations with specific evidence or examples. Other writers consciously focus on constructing the basic, logical progression of the text, returning later to support their generalizations, as shown in Example 2.

Example 3 shows how during zero drafting some writers cannot move forward until each paragraph has some form of transition to the next, while others occasionally jump over problems of transition, assuming that an intuited connection can be made explicit later.

In all of these zero-drafting strategies, the gestation of possibilities gives way — often painfully and crudely — to the generation of a text. It is extremely difficult for writers to develop their writing if their primary concern is "correctness" in terms of spelling, grammar, punctuation, word choice, and the linear progression of one sentence after another. Zero drafting's power derives from the fact that it is not error-avoidant.

Assuming that the writer has significantly limited and defined the variables of the rhetorical problem and has conceived a preliminary rhetorical plan, zero drafting represents the freedom and the responsibility to create meaning out of the innumerable possible permutations of thought and language. Perhaps the single most effective way to help immature writers improve their writing is to persuade them to stop trying to make a final draft of their first draft. At the beginning of the term, students can profit from being asked to compose their zero drafts orally for a live audience of at least one other class member. They can then transcribe a tape of this oral draft and elaborate it into a written zero draft. But no matter what techniques writers use to force themselves to complete their zero drafts, sooner or later they have to confront the question of whether they have anything to say.

As opposed to the reductive, one-shot drafts that tend to characterize student writing, in a true zero draft the writer discovers what she has to say about a topic. In Murray's words,

> The zero draft is the moment of revelation, of excitement and discouragement. . . . Happy accidents of language occur while he writes. He plays with a word and it leads to a phrase which in turn can lead to a revelation about the subject. . . . He has the feeling of giving birth, a sense of pride and a sense of embarrassment that the red and squirming thing is his. At the moment of composition all that he knows and doesn't know is there on the page. (1968, p. 9)

Teaching students to write zero drafts is effective because the zero draft cries out for rewriting — just as in Murray's implicit metaphor the

newborn child cries out for nourishment. The principle is the same: Writers are reluctant to abandon significant extensions, creations of the self.

Zero-drafting Strategies

To help students conceive and implement zero drafts, we provide them with the following summary list of possible strategies.

• Sometimes writers draft a rambling introduction, much of which is later discarded, as a warm-up exercise.
• Some writers go directly to a statement of thesis and return later to frame the essay with a more general introduction.
• During the zero-drafting process, some writers typically support their generalizations with specific evidence or examples. Other writers consciously focus on constructing the basic, logical progression of the text and return later to support their generalizations.
• During zero drafting some writers jump over problems of transition, assuming that an intuited connection can be realized later.
• Can you think of other strategies?

PROBLEM-SOLVING DRAFTING

When students have completed a zero draft, they can begin to understand Murray's assertion that writing is rewriting. Yet the mere fact that students want to rewrite their zero drafts is no guarantee that they have any notion of how to proceed (Flower, Hayes, Carey, Shriver, [Stratman, 1986). Most students want to jump directly to a final draft — often with disastrous results. The zero draft tends to be somewhat loosely, even crudely, organized both conceptually and rhetorically. Writers who attempt to convert their zero drafts into a final draft should be warned that major problems often occur later in the text and demand that the writer rewrite what was believed to be a "final" draft of earlier sections. Not only is such premature final drafting exhausting, frustrating, and time-consuming, but more importantly, writers' emotional investment in "finality" tends to short-circuit their ability to make substantial revisions. Deletions, additions, substitutions, and reorderings tend to be limited to revising an individual sentence or, at best, clusters of sentences.

Students have difficulty accepting the fact that certain sections of their zero draft may require a second and even a third or fourth rewriting before a final draft can be attempted. Part of their resistance originates in

Figure 4–B: Analyzing the Zero Draft

I. The Needs of the Audience
    A. How old are members of this audience?
    B. Where do they live?
    C. How well–educated are they?
    D. What do the members of this audience already know about the writer's subject?

II. The Nature of the Writer's Stance
    A. How well–informed is the writer about this subject?
    B. How well–educated is the writer in general?
    C. How is the writer dressed?
    D. How formal or informal is the word choice and syntax of the draft? Is the diction consistent?

III. The Dynamic Relationship between the Writer's Stance and the Audience.
    A. Is the identified audience likely to believe or accept what it is told by the identified writer?
    B. How might the writer change her stance to communicate better with the audience?

IV. Conceptualization of the Topic.
    A. Does the writer provide the audience with new information? If so, what new information is conveyed?
    B. Does the writer try to persuade the audience to do something? What would the writer like to have the audience do?
    C. Is this piece of writing designed to entertain the audience? How?
    D. How might a member of the audience be changed by reading this paper?

V. Organization of the Text
    A. Are there places in this piece of writing where what follows doesn't connect with what comes before––where the flow of the draft breaks? Identify these places with brackets.
    B. Are there places in the draft where the writer should elaborate or add examples? Identify these places with brackets.
    C. Does the introduction clearly establish the thesis or point of the draft? Does the introduction work to frame the piece of writing as a whole?
    D. Does the conclusion of this draft tell the readers what the writer expects them to do or think? Are the writer's expectations realistic?

These heuristic questions were developed with Dana Elder, Washington State University, Pullman, Washington, 1982.

their inability to define what a major problem is. To assist students toward the definition, identification, and potential resolution of the major problems in their zero drafts, they are asked to reread and critique their zero drafts in the context of various questions (see Figure 4–B). Students' rereading of an initial draft in the context of these heuristic questions constitutes an operational *redefinition* of their rhetorical situations: the needs of the audience, the nature of the writer's stance, the conceptualization of the topic, and the organization of the text.

After students have analyzed their zero drafts, they are asked to identify major problems by bracketing them off from the rest of the text. The definition of what constitutes a problem section is critical (Flower et al., 1986). Students are not asked to identify all of the conceptual problems (logic, evidence, theory) or rhetorical problems (sense of audience, organization, writer's stance). Rather, they are encouraged to identify those problem sections that are *critical* in determining what precedes and follows in the development of the text. During the beginning of the term, time is set aside in class for this analysis of the zero draft, and students are required to do a written critique that identifies and defines major problems. This in-class, written critique is followed up with an out-of-class conference during which the instructor does a formative evaluation of students' zero drafts and their critiques to point out major problems to be resolved.

After students have identified the problems that are crucial to a substantive rewriting of the text, they do a focused drafting of the problem sections. The examples of problem-solving drafting in Figure 4–C show how students respond to a somewhat typical range of problems and attempt to resolve them.

In the first example, the student elaborates a key paragraph by supporting a sequence of high-level generalizations with specific facts. The writer's problem-solving response to the zero draft paragraph is not entirely satisfactory. The revised paragraph still collapses a set of extraordinarily complicated relationships into a list of generalizations. However, the writer's problem-solving response is of a profitable order, and the resulting paragraph is much stronger than the original. Supporting generalizations through the addition of specific details, examples, and evidence is an important function of problem-solving drafting.

In the second example in Figure 4–C, the writer tries to resolve an obvious lack of connection between the first and second paragraphs of her zero draft. The first paragraph asserts that "uncontrolled spending" is the primary cause of inflation. Without transition, the second paragraph launches into a generalized description of the Great Depression.

Inserting the new paragraph and substituting text in the paragraph on the Great Depression do not completely resolve the problem of logical progression, but certainly these substantive revisions are moves in the right direction. In fact, having identified the difficulty, the writer will further attempt to resolve it during the final drafting process. This ability to add and delete major structural components allows the writer to reconceive the text. The possibility — sometimes the necessity — of radically reshaping the initial conceptualization of the topic is a critical aspect of problem-solving drafting.

In their zero drafts, students often establish logical chains of comparisons and contrasts or causes and effects, but frequently the individual links

of their argument are only minimally defined. The third example of problem-solving drafting in Figure 4–C shows a student's attempts to strengthen and develop the chain of effects that, the essay asserts, inflation has caused.

The problem-solving additions to the zero draft are organized by logi-

---

Figure 4–C: Problem-solving Drafting

Example 1

Zero Draft	Problem-Solving Draft
One of the main reasons why the problems of inflation multiply so rapidly is [Del. that] because the worker's wages do not keep up with inflation. ¶Industries pay their workers less so that they themselves can keep up with inflation, however this practice leaves the [Del. consumer] [Sub. worker] with less money to spend. As it is today, people are generally spending more of their earned paycheck at the time they receive it than before. There is less money being saved basically because there is less money to save. Large purchases are scarce and people are [Add. now] spending more money on necessities.	⌜Pay raises in the service industries (textiles, food processing, and retail trade) have been 70% to 80% below the average. From 1979-1980, wages and salaries in the private sector were 9% higher than in 1979—a big gain by past standards—but the gain was outstripped by an inflation rate of 12.4%. [In short, a dollar in 1979 was worth only ninety-six cents in 1980. The trend continues.] Source Sheet facts #10 and #25 ⌞ ⌜"For the bulk of middle-class Americans, more and more family income now goes for the basics—energy, food, housing and health—which rose 13.8% last year." Source Sheet fact #14 ⌞

Example 2

Zero Draft	Problem-Solving Draft
There is a quick-spreading disease infesting our [Del. nation] [Sub. country]—inflation. Americans have always been accustomed to a life of leisure. We've always been able to spend money and not think twice. This uncontrolled spending has lead to the high prices and low wages, the symptoms of inflation. 　The Great Depression of the thirties was the result of the easy-living, good times of the roaring twenties. During the twenties, money flowed like the illegal alcohol that supported it. ¶[*Text deleted during problem-solving:* At that time, Americans weren't thinking of the future, but in 1929, the fate of the stock market crushed their happy times.]	⌜Since the 1950's, the prices have been on a constant rise. Jobs always thought safe and dependable are now on the line. [Add. Before] Americans could get a loan from a bank with no problem, now with the high interest rate, we pay nearly double [Del. what] the original cost of the item. As the people cry out for help, the government sinks with us. All government support is being denied, its deficite is extensive. Public schools are getting little state support, and the result is massive staff reduction. There is not an area in society not hit by inflation. The entire country is chaotic. ⌞ ⌜Like America of today, they didn't think of the future. Their frivolous lives are like the lives we lead before inflation. All of a sudden the party's gone and all that remains is despair. ⌞

cal connectives. The added text contains six subordinate clauses beginning with "because" or "if," one sentence beginning with "Therefore," and the words "results" and "effects" are used once each. The writer's intent is clear: She has successfully attempted to strengthen the draft's analysis of causes and effects. One of the most valuable functions of problem-solving

---

Figure 4–C: (continued)

Example 3

Zero Draft	Problem-Solving Draft
In 1977, when mortgage interest rates were in the 8 to 9 percent range, 36% of homebuyers were purchasing a house for the first time. In 1979, a 12% mortgage interest encouraged only an 18% to purchase their first home. The present rate of 16% stimulates only the affluent, or those buying up from existing homes, to buy.	Because the interest rate has gone so high [Del. the] people do not want to take out extremely long term loans on houses because the interest will cost so much. [Del. So, they just don't buy.] Therefore they can't buy, so they don't.
Because of these extremely high interest rates, other producers in the economy are really hurting. Chrysler is a perfect example. It was forced to borrow from the federal government in order to keep from going completely bankrupt. Using given statistics, "Auto sales down 30% from 1980, home construction lowest since 1946 and 11,076 companies have declared bankruptcy . . . up 42% from 1980. Probably the biggest thing that this should mean to us is how many people those foreclosures and slow downs have effected. That is a lot of people out of jobs and into the unemployment lines *[Text deleted during problem-solving drafting:* which is very evident in the nation by looking at the standard rate of unemployment today. It grows every week of the year, all as a result of inflation.]	and a decline in the use of credit
	Because of such a high loss of production the company had to lay off thousands of workers. If the federal government had not stepped in [Del. however], many, many more people would be jobless now.
	Just one single company going out of business has [Del. a huge] an effect on others. That one [Add. single] company could owe a lot of money to others, and because of [Del. their] [Sub. its] [Del. its] foreclosure [Del. hurt the others] it results in the credit companies and others tightening up on credit and sales on credit in order to protect their well being. If a large company like Chrysler were to close down, more than just the factory workers would be out of jobs. Because so many people would be unemployed, sales to other companies would go down and they too would be forced to lay off workers. The statistics of [Del. the bank] [Del. the] [Sub. foreclosures] and bankruptcies, today, are very evident when looking at the unemployment rate that seems to go hand in hand.

(continued on next page)

Figure 4–C: (continued)

Example 4

Zero Draft

[The text is reordered during problem-solving drafting, and this entire paragraph becomes the essay's conclusion.] President Reagan's economic policy is clearly designed for the upper class income group—[Del. not for us] there is hardly any consideration for us at the bottom of the economic scale. In Reagan's [Del. pre] election speeches, he outlined his plan of action—we realized then that we were in serious trouble and fought for solidarity within the union to oppose his [Del. winning] [Sub. obtaining] the presidency. Unfortunately, even within our own rank, individuals doubted he would strike out at us. There can be no doubt now, after the [Del. pain] [Sub. knife] of his policy's cuts has been felt, that [Del. President] Reagan is an unacceptable president *[Text added during problem-solving drafting:* to be representing the blue collar worker for another four year term.]

President Reagan's policies are atacking the lower working class in two major ways. First, he [Del. is cutting] has already cut some social security and medicaid benefits. [Del. if he had his choice] [Sub. Given a free hand] Reagan would cut the social security program [Del. altogether] [Sub. completely] but he knows he would be committing political suicide by doing so.¶*[The rest of this paragraph was deleted during problem-solving drafting.]*

And second, Reagan's much-acclaimed tax cuts are just a nice-sounding knife in the back of the lower-income worker. The tax cuts are based on the marginal income scale used for computing income tax. The scale ranges from 14% up to 50%. When Reagan makes a 10% tax cut, it is the highest bracket that enjoys the increased income. [Del. This was not done accidentally, the Reagan administration wants the upper class to have more extra income.]

Problem-Solving Drafting

And second, Reagan's much-acclaimed tax cuts are just one more way to increase the differences between the white collar and the blue collar workers take-home salary. The take-home salary. The tax cuts are based on the marginal income scale used for computing [Add. income] tax. The scale ranges from 14% up to 50%. When President Reagan orders a 10% tax cut the lowest bracket enjoys only a 2.4% increase while the highest bracket take-home [Del. pay] [Sub. salary] increases by 5%—twice as much as the lowest bracket. The underlying issue, though is [Del. the] that as the lower income take-home pay increases, the individuals are pushed into a higher tax bracket. [Del. Explain why] Many people will try to work fewer hours, refuse to work overtime. [Del. turn down salary raises] [Sub. etc.,] in an attempt to avoid moving into a higher tax bracket. But in the highest income, [Del. bracket] 50% tax bracket, individuals can not be forced up into a higher bracket because there is no higher bracket. Therefore, it is these people who are backing President Reagan and his tax-cuts.

drafting often is the writer's identification and explicit development of an implicit or minimally developed structural pattern.

In the fourth example of problem solving, the writer makes minimal changes in the third paragraph of the zero draft and transports it virtually intact to the end of the essay, where it serves as the conclusion. To fill the hole created by this reordering, she deletes the last two-thirds of the fourth paragraph and substitutes an elaborated and extended chain of reasoning.

This freedom to cut and paste, to reorder the basic organizational structure of the text, and to insert new text to fill the gaps is a powerful aspect of problem-solving drafting.

The effectiveness of problem-solving drafting derives from the fact that it addresses the problems that the writers themselves have created in their zero drafts. The resolutions of specific problems tend to have global effects, forcing the writer to rework the overall structure of the evolving text in increasingly sophisticated terms. It is at this point in the drafting process that the writer can begin to take charge of the text — adding, deleting, substituting, and reordering major components in accordance with an increasingly realized and interconnected set of rhetorical goals.

If writers have immediate, even though rough, solutions to the problems in their zero drafts, their problem-solving drafting of these sections simply constitutes an elaboration of their zero drafts. However, the writer who sees no immediate solutions may have to return to the predrafting stage of the composing process and do further research. As these identified problem sections are truly integral to the development of the topic, the writer needs to draft solutions before writing a final draft of the text. Zero and problem-solving drafting are rather like rough-framing the interior and exterior of a house; the basic floor plan has to be adequately constructed before one can proceed to the wiring and plumbing and the installation of doors and windows.

Problem-solving Drafting Strategies

To assist students in conceptualizing and implementing problem-solving drafting, we provide them with the following summary list of possible strategies:

- Sometimes writers elaborate a key passage by supporting a sequence of high-level generalizations with specific facts.
- Some writers resolve a lack of connection between two ideas by adding a substantive insert.
- Sometimes writers attempt to strengthen logical chains of reasoning by further developing the individual links of their argument.

- Some writers reorder the basic organizational structure of the text and generate new text as required.
- Can you think of other strategies?

FINAL DRAFTING

Often students' problem-solving drafting engenders an initial engagement with the final drafting process. If while resolving particular problems in the zero draft, the writer has extended the implications of a chain of reasoning, supported a key assertion with specific evidence, or illustrated a series of generalizations with particular examples, there seems to be a natural impulse to revise other portions of the text until they approach the same level of elaboration. Even young writers have a reasonable sense of decorum when it comes to maintaining a reasonably consistent level of development.

Unfortunately, apart from this initial impulse toward elaboration, most students want to define final drafting as a minimal revision of the basic format of an earlier draft. As a result, final drafting at the intrasentence level tends to consist of correcting mechanics and usage, deleting redundancies or wordiness, and making additions or substitutions of word choice. At the sentence level and above, final drafting tends to be characterized by adding or deleting an occasional sequence of two or three sentences. Major substitutions or reorderings seldom occur.

Introducing students to the distinction between "a merely adequate final draft" and "the best possible solution to a rhetorical problem" helps redefine the final drafting process. In an adequate final draft the author has achieved her basic goals for the writer's stance, the audience, the topic, and the text. Major ideas are developed; information is logically classified and subordinated; the topic is introduced and concluded. In short, the writer has gotten it said — but it may not be said very effectively. One of the crucial differences between the immature writer and the mature writer is the degree of resolution for which they strive. Typically, the young writer is satisfied with mere conceptual closure and task completion, whereas the mature writer, given time and investment, is concerned with arriving at the best possible resolution of a self-defined rhetorical problem.

Brilliant writers are noted for the elegant, economical, and often unorthodox solutions they find for their rhetorical problems. Obviously, no group of students can be expected all to become brilliant writers, but students can be asked to resolve rhetorical problems satisfactorily within the context of their individual skills.

Reconceiving the Possibilities of the Text

Once students understand that final drafting is the mature writer's attempt to reach the best possible solution, the following list of heuristic questions — designed to help students reconceive the possibilities of the text and discover more effective means of communication — can be distributed.

1. Read your first paragraph aloud to someone else. If no real audience is available, read it aloud to an imaginary best friend. Does your audience want to hear more? Could you start your paper with your second paragraph? How could you rewrite your first paragraph in order to capture your audience's attention more effectively?
2. What is the thesis or point of your paper? Are all of your major ideas clearly subordinated to the point of your paper? Could one of your paper's subordinated ideas better serve as the central point? If your paper has three major ideas, could you get by with two or do you need a fourth?
3. Would the progression of your paper profit from a reordering of the sequence of your major ideas?
4. Are your major ideas related in ways that you have not shown — by means of comparisons and contrasts of size, number, duration; cause and effect, and so on? Would making such relationships explicit strengthen or enrich your paper?
5. As Ken Macrorie suggests in *Telling Writing* (1976):

   > Strong writers bring together oppositions of one kind or another . . . what they choose to present from life — whether it be object, act, or idea — is frequently the negative and the positive, one thing and its opposite, two ideas that antagonize each other. The result is tension. And the surprise that comes from new combinations. . . . Make it a habit to look for oppositions. You will find suddenly that you are wiser than you thought. Do it automatically. If you find yourself putting down *hot*, consider the possibility of *cold* in the same circumstances; if *simple*, then *complex*; if *loving*, then *hating*; etc. The habit will prevent you from oversimplifying people and processes and ideas. (pp. 79, 82)

   Identify the patterns of opposition in your paper. Could you profitably introduce others? Can you sharpen your patterns of opposition and increase the tension of your writing? Do you resolve your opposition in surprising or interesting ways?
6. Are all of your major ideas illustrated with concrete examples? Could you use more interesting or humorous examples?

7. Are all of your assertions or arguments supported with convincing evidence? Do you need to go to the library? (Don't kid yourself.)
8. Does your final paragraph serve to conclude the paper as a whole or simply to conclude the preceding point? Could you delete it? If your last paragraph is necessary, will your audience remember it? Could you rewrite it in a more interesting way?

After reconsidering their drafts from the perspective of these questions, students are asked to engage in the best possible final drafting of their essays.

It is extremely difficult to demonstrate the final drafting strategies of students by quoting short excerpts from the larger design of an essay. A single extended example of final drafting will serve to define the type of drafting strategies that students can learn to employ in their attempts to construct the best possible solution to a rhetorical problem.

At the conclusion of zero and problem-solving drafting, this particular student had produced a text that would have served — with judicious editing — as an adequate final draft. But in this case the writer chose to reconceive the structure of the essay in order to produce a much more effective piece of writing, part of which is shown in Figure 4–D. Both the earlier and the final draft consist of 12 paragraphs each; however, the paragraph sequence of the final draft was radically reordered from the previous draft. Paragraphs 1 and 12 remain in the same position in the final draft as in the earlier draft, but the sequence for all others was altered as follows: In the final draft, paragraphs 2 and 3 were derived from the earlier version's paragraph 11; final paragraph 4 came from the earlier paragraph 2; paragraph 5 was derived from paragraph 9, 6 from 10, 7 from 5, 8 from 4, 9 from 3 and 6, 10 from 7, and the final paragraph 11 came from the earlier paragraph 8.

The writer's global reordering of the essay's structure necessarily involved adding, deleting, and substituting text at the beginning and end of many of the new paragraphs of the earlier draft. Moreover, the writer divided one paragraph (11) into two (2 and 3), collapsed two paragraphs (3 and 6) into one (9), and substantively revised the content of others. A comparison of a sequence of four final-draft paragraphs with the five consecutive paragraphs from which the sequence was derived (Figure 4–D) demonstrates the effectiveness of the writer's final drafting strategies.

In this admittedly extraordinary case of final drafting, the writer radically re-envisions the topic. In addition to reworking the prose at the intrasentence level, the writer made substantive text revisions of every order — adding, deleting, and substituting individual sentences or clusters of sentences. And, of course, the writer's final drafting strategies are domi-

Figure 4–D: Example of a Final Draft

Paragraphs 3, 4, 5, 6, and 7
of the Zero and
Problem-Solving Draft

[Note: None of the revisions that were involved in the generation of the zero and problem-solving draft are indicated. What are identified are all those portions of this draft that were simply deleted in the final draft.]

(Paragraph #3)

Yet Congress cannot seem to agree on a course of action either. Because there are both Democrats and Republicans in Congress, there are a few different philosophies. [*Deleted during final drafting:* No one quite agrees on how to fight inflation. "Prices are still rising at an unparalleled rate (Source Sheet fact #*15.*"]

(Paragraph #4)

[*Deleted during final drafting:* The Republicans believe in spending only the money that the government has. In other words, they believe in balancing the budget. If people get in trouble by spending more money than they've got. So in the end they file for bankruptcy, why should the government think that they can get away with spending more than they've got. This is the philosophy of the *Democrats.*] They believe spending in deficit will cure the problems of inflation. This high rate of spending keeps the demand side of economics high, but this pushes prices higher and higher. The Democrats believe that, "High interest rates are needed to bring down inflation (Source Sheet fact #22)." This has not been shown to be true. [*Deleted during final drafting:* In fact, inflation kept climbing the whole time that the Democrats held the majority in congress and while there was a Democratic President. In the past few years while the Democrats were in office, the economy kept growing *worse.*]

(Paragraph #5)

"The pain of curing inflation is recession (Source Sheet fact #16)." This could be a painful truth. The Republicans believe that less spending, which causes recession, is the best plan of

Paragraphs 7, 8, 9, and 10
of the Final Draft

[Note: None of the revisions that were involved in the generating of new text during the writing of the final draft are indicated. What are identified are all those portions of the final draft that constitute additions to or substitutions for portions of the earlier draft.]

(PARAGRAPH #7 is a word for word transcription of paragraph #5 of the earlier draft.)

"The pain of curing inflation is recession (Source Sheet fact #16)." This could be a painful truth. The Republicans believe that less spending, which causes recession is the best plan of action to take. It may hurt people for a while, but this plan looks at the long-term goals. It is interested in the future, not concentrating totally on what is happening right this minute. "A recession offers one positive sign: 'It does tend to reduce inflation by putting a downward pressure both on wages and prices,' which seems to be the present state of affairs (Source Sheet fact #23)."

(PARAGRAPH #8 is derived from the central portion of paragraph #4 of the earlier draft.)

[Del. They] [Sub. The Democrats] believe spending in deficit will cure the problems of inflation. This high rate of spending keeps the demand side of economics high, and this pushes prices higher and higher. High demand may stimulate the economy but it causes interest rates to go higher. The Democrats believe that, "High interest rates are needed to bring down inflation (Source Sheet fact #22)." This has not been shown to be true.

(PARAGRAPH 9 is derived from abbreviating and combining paragraphs #3 and #6 in the earlier draft.)

Yet Congress cannot seem to agree on a course of action either. Because there are both Democrats and Republicans in Congress, there are [Del. a few] [Sub. basically the two] philosophies. There has been a battle in Congress and other places for political majority. Right now the Republicans

Figure 4–D: (continued)

action to take. It may hurt people for a while, but this plan looks at the long-term goals. It is interested in the future, not concentrating totally on what is happening right this minute. "A recession offers one positive sign: 'It does tend to reduce inflation by putting downward pressure both on wages and prices,' which seems to be the present state of affairs (Source Sheet fact #23)."

(Paragraph #6)

There has been a battle in Congress and other places for political majority. Right now the Republicans hold the Presidential seat and the majority in Congress. President Reagan has submitted a budget plan to Congress that even if passed in the way Reagan wants it, it could possibly be ruined. The Democrats hold enough seats in Congress and hold important positions in other places of government.

(Paragraph #7)

Congress is not too anxious to halt inflation anyways. They don't want the phenomenon of "bracket creep" to stop. What this means is that as inflation goes up, people's salaries go up to keep even with the rate of inflation. As this happens, people are put in higher tax brackets. Congress has no need to raise taxes [*Deleted during final drafting:* and neither do they wish to. It is very unpopular for them to raise taxes. It can also be devastating to their careers to do so during an election year.]

hold the Presidential seat and the majority in [Del. Congress] [Sub. Senate]. President Reagan has submitted [Del. a] [Sub. his] budget [Del. plan] [Sub. plans] to Congress [Del. that even if passed in the way] [Sub. , but they probably will not be passed in the form] Reagan wants it. It could possibly [Add. and probably] be ruined. The Democrats hold enough seats in Congress [Del. and hold important positions in other places of government] [Add. to at least partially put down Reaganomics].

(PARAGRAPH #10 is derived from paragraph #7 in the earlier draft.)

Congress is not too anxious to halt inflation anyways. They don't want the phenomenon of "bracket creep" to stop. What this means is that as inflation goes up, people's salaries go up to keep even with the rate of inflation. As this happens, people are put in higher tax brackets. Congress [Add. then] has no need to raise taxes [Add.; they get what they need from the 'bracket creep.'] [Sub. They have no desire to make raises in the unpopular taxes.]

nated by an extreme reordering of the organizational structure of the earlier draft.

Few student writers are capable of so completely re-envisioning their text. But given a real engagement with their topics during zero and problem-solving drafting, young writers can learn to make revisions of the same order — if not of the same extent — during the final drafting process. (Substantive text revisions were found in 22 of the 23 examination essays that

served as the source of writing samples for this chapter. Examples of substantive text revision from eight of the essays have been used.)

At the beginning of the term and periodically throughout the course, instructional time can be set aside for an "active appreciation" of the inherent possibilities of student texts. Students are expected to arrive in class with two copies of a final draft. For the first 15 or 20 minutes, they practice sentence-combining skills on the real vehicles of their own texts. The remainder of the class period is devoted to making an assigned number of substantive text revisions. For instance, early in the course, students might be asked to make three additions, three deletions, two substitutions, and two reorderings of at least one complete sentence each (by the end of the term, students may be asked to work with paragraph structures). Students are under no obligation to use any of these substantive text revisions in the version of the paper they eventually submit for a grade; they are required only to demonstrate an evolving ability to manipulate increasingly complex structures of their own texts. On the other hand, many a casual game of scrabble turns into demanding play; a single choice is capable of reordering the entire infrastructure.

Final drafting represents a crucial change in the epistemological status of the text. In zero drafting the writer's primary concern is to transform an initial conceptualization of the topic into a whole piece of writing; during zero drafting the writer's thoughts and ideas are often more engaging and real than the actual text reveals. In problem-solving drafting writers begin to wrestle with specific, unresolved problems that they themselves have created in their attempts to conceptualize a topic and communicate with an audience. During final drafting the raw data of the writer's experiences, thoughts, and ideas begin to be ordered into a text about which she has to think. As the writer struggles to achieve the best possible solution, the text itself becomes the primary reality, more interesting and complex than the original conception.

By definition, drafting as a recursive process involves an ongoing revision of the evolving text. Yet, to use Murray's term (1978b), this "internal revision" takes place in response to the demands of the topic and the writer's internalized ideal reader. After the writer has completed a best possible draft, it is time to submit the draft to the editorial judgment of a real audience and begin editing and polishing the manuscript for "publication." But that is the topic of the next chapter.

In using this model of zero, problem-solving, and final drafting, both teachers and students need to understand that the concern is not to define drafting as the writing of three discrete drafts—three drafts may not be enough. Rather, the concern is to teach drafting as the evolving resolution of an increasingly specified definition of the rhetorical problem, which is

likely to require different types of drafting. If, as Pianko says, "The ability to reflect on what is being written seems to be the essence of the differences between able and not-so-able writers" (1979, p. 277), the critical need becomes knowing what type of drafting is required at what specific points in the drafting of a particular text. The model presented in this chapter is an approach to ensuring that knowing.

APPENDIX 4–A:
SAMPLE SOURCE SHEET

Doubtful Diplomas: High School Illiteracy

1. Thirteen percent of all high school graduates are functional illiterates. They cannot read or write well enough to function in society. (Hechinger, 1979, p. 20)
2. Textbook publishers are revising high school texts to sixth grade reading level. (Hechinger, p. 20)
3. Surveys show that leaders of business and industry and the general public have lost faith in the high school diploma. They no longer feel that the diploma in any way shows that the graduate was competent in any of the basic academic skills. (Gilman, 1980, p. 19)
4. Citizens feel that the high schools' turning out large numbers of functionally illiterate will have serious negative effects on society in general and that it shows the students themselves to be individually incompetent. (Gilman, p. 19)
5. Students have lost the feeling that education is the best avenue toward success in the world. (Blackburn & Krajewski, 1978, p. 110)
6. Students today value immediate gratification over postponed gratification. Hence, going to school today in hopes of a better life tomorrow is ignored. (Nanebuth, 1978, p. 22)
7. Many students today are working. Time on the job is too often an excuse for not doing homework. (Kuehner, 1978, p. 135)
8. "Students are not buying into school. It isn't worth the investment." They can and do get good paying jobs without it. (Lytle, 1978, p. 77)
9. Columbia High School, Richland, Washington, instituted a five-point grading scale for honors classes to increase enrollment. Even honors students were refusing to invest time and energy in a course unless they could see some immediate advantage. So they received five grade points for an A, four for a B, etc. The honors curriculum was salvaged. (L. Stairet, personal communication, January 27, 1980)
10. Thirty percent of the students at Ohio State cannot write at acceptable college levels. (Zagano, 1978, p. 57)
11. Most high school students are not prepared to write college papers. (Kuehner, p. 135)
12. Nine percent of the 346,000 functionally illiterate high school graduates are attending college. (Cole, 1978, p. 11)
13. One out of five high school graduates functions with "difficulty" in

Compiled by Linda Stairet, Washington State University, Pullman, Washington, 1981.

today's society. This may involve difficulty reading a newspaper or job application, or writing a business letter. (Cole, p. 11)

14. Based on an Office of Education poll of 2,300 persons in adult education classes, 15 percent were high school graduates. Of all persons, 25 percent were below the fifth grade reading level; 65 percent were below the seventh grade. (Cole, p. 12)

15. The National Assessment of Educational Progress indicates that the essays of 13-year-olds and 17-year-olds have deteriorated from 1969 to 1974. (Zagano, p. 56)

16. Since 1964, the SAT scores for high school students have steadily declined. The SAT average over the past five years has gone down from 502 to 472. The largest drop was in 1975. This was the largest drop in 20 years. (Zagano, p. 56)

17. Forty percent of the parents responding to a CBS poll say that TV is a bad influence on kids, that it is a thief of time, and that watching TV is a deterrent to education, promotes passivity, and shortens children's attention span. (Blackburn & Krajewski, p. 112)

18. The electronic media have become so effective that some young people can no longer concentrate on a [teacher] who is just talking to them. (Blackburn & Krajewski, p. 111)

19. "There once was a sophisticated form of life on Mars, but alas, they had the misfortune of inventing TV 100 years ago." (Blackburn & Krajewski, p. 111)

20. Through TV and other instant forms of communication we are diminishing our potential to communicate, to interact with others, to imagine, and even to exist. (Blackburn & Krajewski, p. 111)

21. TV can never teach. There is only one way to learn — by reading. (Metcalf, 1978, p. 145)

22. Forty-one percent of parents surveyed in a 1,266-person telephone poll (3 ± accuracy) say that their children are not getting as good an education as they did. (Kuehner, p. 134)

23. Walter Cronkite said, "Our children deserve a better education than they are getting now." (CBS News Special, August 1978)

24. Teachers feel the child can be forced to go to school, but he/she cannot be forced to learn. (Frymier, 1978, p. 117)

25. Conclusions from the CBS News Special (August 1978), "Is Anyone Out There Learning?":
    A. Schools are not emphasizing reading, writing, and arithmetic enough.
    B. There is a lack of discipline.
    C. Grade promotion is too easy and is based primarily on attendance.

D. There is severe grade inflation. Students in honor societies cannot read or write.

E. Teachers are not as effective as they should be because they do not expect enough from the students and they are afraid of them. Teachers are not as dedicated as they used to be.

Sources Cited

Blackburn, J. E., & Krajewski, R. J. (1978). " . . . But who will listen?" *The High School Journal, 62.*

CBS News Special (August 1978). "Is anybody out there learning?" A report card on American Public Education" (W. Cronkite & C. Collingwood, Narr.).

Cole, G. (1978). "The chains of functional illiteracy." *Education Digest,* January issue.

Frymier, J. (1978). "Well yes, and no." *The High School Journal, 62.*

Gilman, D. A. (1980). "How can we improve high school education?" *Education Digest,* December issue.

Hechinger, F. H. (1979). "Schoolyard blues." *Saturday Review,* January 20 issue.

Kuehner, K. (1978). "Camera focused, focus blurred." *The High School Journal, 62.*

Lytle, J. H. (1978). "Are secondary schools meeting student needs?" *NASSP Bulletin,* November issue.

Metcalf, L. E. (1978). "The CBS Programs Reflectively Speaking." *The High School Journal, 62.*

Nanebuth, D. (1978). "Comments on 'Is anybody out there learning?'" *The High School Journal, 62.*

Zagano, P. (1978). "The great American writing crisis." *Education Digest,* January issue.

5

Revision:
The Realization
of Audience

When students are asked to revise their texts, they typically concentrate on cosmetic revisions at the sentence level and on proofreading for errors in mechanics—spelling, punctuation, and usage (Bridwell, 1980; Nold, 1982; Sommers, 1979). In contrast to students' limited operational definition of revision, Ellen Nold (1982) defines a threefold hierarchy of revision that describes the wide range of revision strategies employed by mature writers: the conventional, the mixed, and the intentional.

CONVENTIONAL
Motor — making letters
Graphical — using conventional graphemes, spelling, and punctuation
Usage — conventional written dialect, meaningful and complete sentences
MIXED
Lexical — word choice
Syntactic — producing and embedding grammatical strings
Formal — setting the form, the visual/typographical factors that call the reader's attention to main points and to relationships among main points
Generic — "determining the kind of writing that will best carry the message to the audience" [p. 16]
INTENTIONAL
Rhetorical — adjusting the audience–topic–writer–purpose balance to ensure that the audience's requirements as well as the writer's are met
Topical — researching the topic and evolving "a valid structure for that knowledge" [p. 16]
Purposive — "defining the purposes of communication" [p. 16]

THE DISTINCTION BETWEEN EXTERNAL
AND INTERNAL REVISION

It is important to understand that Nold's three orders of revision do not constitute a definition of the revision *stage* of the composing process. One of the major concerns of the preceding two chapters has been to demonstrate how the different orders of revision are contiguous and recursive, folding back upon one another to generate the structure of the emerging text. The model of the composing process presented in this book formally integrates revision into the predrafting and drafting stages through the use of heuristic procedures, the definition of rhetorical situation, and cumulative drafting. During predrafting and certainly in the early steps of drafting, the pre-text and text are in flux, always subject to alteration, improvement, and recasting. With every sentence and every paragraph the writer must strike a balance among audience, text, writer, and subject. This is as true for word choice as it is for organization of paragraphs and everything in between. But in these first two stages of composing, the hierarchy of revision activities that Nold describes are internally defined by the interaction between the emerging structure of the text and the writer's internalized "ideal reader." Real readers cannot respond to or critique that which has not been written. As Donald Murray (1978a) suggests:

> There are two forms of revision — one internal and one external. Internal revision occurs when writers are trying to find out what they have to say; external revision when they know what they have to say and are revising or editing their work so it can be understood by another audience. These two forms of revision, of course, overlap, but I believe they are distinct and significant. Writers must first understand what they are saying if others are to understand what was said. (p. 57)

The revision stage of the composing process is defined by "external revision." Obviously, there is no clear-cut line of demarcation between the internal revision of predrafting and drafting and the external revision of the revision stage of the composing process. One of the major concerns of the model of the composing process presented in the central section of this book is to demonstrate that the stages of the composing process represent interlocking feedback loops (see Figure II, p. 54); the writer may well discover during the external revision of a "completed" draft that there is a hole in her argument and find it necessary to re-engage the drafting stage or even the predrafting stage with their accompanying internal revision processes. However, for young writers it is helpful to distinguish formally between internal and external revision and to engage in a direct teaching

of discrete orders of external revision as they are embodied in the revision stage of the composing act.

During the revision stage of the composing process, the writer must re-access the entire hierarchy of revision activities — the conventional, the mixed, and the intentional — in the context of a completed text. The revision stage of the composing process assumes that a text exists that is adequately conceptualized and organized from the writer's point of view. Now the writer must shift her perspective and revise the text from the perspective of a real, specified audience. For the young writer, this shift to the stance of the critical reader is almost impossible without the informed responses of other readers.

WHY AUTHORS NEED EDITORS

After a writer has completed a best possible draft for a given audience, it is time to let the draft "cool" until the immediate indentification between the writer and her words has diminished. After this cooling off period, professional writers may be capable of shifting their focus on the draft to adopt the stance of their imagined real audience and proceed to "objective" revision of their texts. However, such objectivity requires not only extensive experience in writing for a variety of audiences but also a keen analytic eye and a rich repertoire of revision strategies. The ability to engage in this level of external revision is a late acquisition even in the development of the gifted, mature writer. Moreover, even professional writers characteristically seek critical responses from informed readers when they are highly invested in the readability and marketability of their texts. That is why publishing companies have editors.

It is common practice for magazines and journals to edit any author's manuscript in accordance with the editor's sense of style, the limitations of allowable length, and publication format. Many professional writers have long-term relationships with the editors of the companies that publish their work; the close relationship of Thomas Wolfe and Maxwell Perkins, the editor at Charles Scribner's & Sons, comes to mind. In addition to formal author-editor relationships, writers commonly seek out the responses of other writers to "work in progress." This informal critique may be as intensely detailed as Ezra Pound's editing of T. S. Eliot's "The Lovesong of J. Alfred Prufrock" or as casual as a quick reading by a friend who gives only a few comments about overall organization and style. The defining characteristics of the author–editor relationship are that the writing is considered to be "in process" and that the reader is attempting to help the writer fulfill the possibilities of the text. The reader tempers her judgments

about the present state of the text by suggesting ways in which the text may be improved.

Whether formal or informal, however, it is essential that revising be based on a sound, thorough strategy; research shows that unguided revision may *decrease* the overall quality of students' writings (Bracewell, Scardamalia, & Bereiter, 1978; Hansen, 1978).

The author–editor relationship is an important aspect of the composing processes of many mature writers, but it is an *essential* aspect for all young writers. Students' ability to make critical judgments about a final draft is limited for at least two reasons. First, they tend to have a more egocentric notion of their audience than does the mature writer, because of the chronological limitations of age and experience (Bracewell, Scardamalia, & Bereiter, 1978; Flower, 1979). Young writers are often amazed by what their audiences do not know and are even more astounded at some of the strange beliefs they hold—beliefs that often directly contradict the author's working assumptions (Kroll, 1978).

A second reason young writers have difficulty making critical judgments about their final drafts and revising accordingly is the limitation of their literacy (Beach, 1980, 1982; Flower et al., 1986; Rubin & Piché, 1979). Almost without exception, mature writers have read widely, at least in the area in which they write. Moreover, they have struggled through the composing process time and time again. As a result, they have internalized a set of expectations about what a finished text should look and read like. After the fervor of producing a final draft has cooled, not only can the mature writer identify significant problems but, more importantly, she has a considerable repertoire of reading and writing experiences from which to derive a solution. Even if young writers can identify significant problems in their final drafts, often they are clueless about how to resolve them (Bereiter & Scardamalia, 1982; Flower et al., 1986; Scardamalia & Baird, 1980; Scardamalia & Bereiter, 1983).

THE REVISION STAGE OF THE COMPOSING PROCESS

Just as mature writers profit from the critical responses of educated readers, young writers are in desperate need of such feedback. If our classrooms were structured in accordance with Mark Twain's definition of "a teacher at one end of the log and a student at the other," perhaps the teacher could serve as the educated reader who assists each writer in turn to realize the possibilities of her text. Given the constraints of numbers and time, a viable alternative is to utilize "peer responders" who have been

taught how to make informed judgments and to offer constructive feedback about how their classmates might revise their final drafts.

Since students have tended to think of external revision as a sentence-level operation, it is profitable to redefine the act of revision for them as readers as well as writers. Nold's hierarchy of revision (1982) can be simplified for students by translating her three orders of revision into revision tasks: (1) the intentional category (rhetorical and topical revision) becomes *rewriting*, (2) the mixed category (lexical, syntactic, and formal revision) becomes *editing and polishing*, and (3) the conventional category (motor, graphical, and usage revision) becomes *proofreading*.

Rewriting

Rewriting involves the writer's accepting that what she thought was at least an adequate final draft is in fact severely flawed conceptually and/or structurally. This can be a discouraging time for many writers since it involves a necessary recycling into earlier stages of the composing process. Sometimes the problems are local, confined to a particular but major segment of the text, and can be resolved through problem-solving drafting. At other times, the problems are pervasive and require redrafting the entire text. In extreme cases, the writer may need to return to the predrafting stage and redefine and limit the subject (Flower & Hayes, 1981), choose another audience, or even abandon the subject altogether and begin anew. The defining characteristic of rewriting is that the problems in the text cannot be resolved at the paragraph level or below by deleting, adding, substituting, or reordering.

Editing and Polishing

Editing and polishing a final draft is a much easier enterprise for students to accept at the psychological level; such revision assumes that the overall structure of the final draft achieves at least minimal conceptual closure. Yet although it is easier for students to accept the necessity of editing and polishing, the activity itself is more sophisticated. Rewriting involves the hard work of reconceptualizing the text, but editing and polishing brings into play the whole question of style. Some editing and polishing can take place at the local level: A more appropriate introduction or conclusion can be substituted, paragraphs can be elaborated or occasionally reordered or deleted, two paragraphs can be collapsed into one or one paragraph divided into two, better transitions can be provided between paragraphs and major ideas, elaborated details and examples can be added, awkward sentences can be disentangled, or a more precise word

can be substituted. These types of editing and polishing are high-level functions, and even if the young writer recognizes the need for such revision, she may not know how to do it.

Textual problems that require editing and polishing may be global instead of local: point of view, definition of audience, tone, diction, and syntactic structure, to name a few. (Shuman's 1982 analysis of H. G. Wells' revisions of *The Outline of History* offers an insight into this range of revisions.) Often such problems originate in the writer's lack of a mature writing style, yet they require a mastery of style to resolve them — Catch-22.

The defining characteristic of editing and polishing is that *particular* textual problems can be resolved at or below the paragraph level. But the *type* of problem may occur throughout — for example, an over-fondness for Latinate words or a habit of making paragraphs out of lists of simple declarative sentences. In our opinion, global editing and polishing is the most difficult writing skill to teach. Several texts are helpful, however, to introduce students to the concepts; Strunk and White's *The Elements of Style* (1972) is a perennial favorite, and William Zinsser's *On Writing Well* (1980) is a particularly effective introduction to stylistic concerns.

Proofreading for Mechanics

Proofreading is characterized by revisions at the sentence level and below that are made to standardize spelling, usage, and punctuation in accordance with rules that the writer already knows. This is the level of revision with which most writers seem to be most familiar (Bracewell, Scardamalia, & Bereiter, 1978; Bridwell, 1980).

For remedial or basic writers, proofreading is akin to some arcane form of medieval torture. After having agonized over correctness at the level of word choice and the individual sentence, they are now asked — no more sure of the rules than they were at the beginning of the writing task — to retrace that anxious path. Most basic writers do not proofread their texts, and, in all humanity, they should not be asked to engage in global proofreading at the beginning of a course. A more advantageous instructional approach is to teach a major rule of usage or punctuation, have students practice the rule in exercise format, give them a post-test to measure comprehension, and then have them proofread their own texts for *that particular error*. The instructional approach is cumulative; as the class progresses, students are held accountable for proofreading for an increasing number of rules.

For students functioning close to the norm or above, the first principle of proofreading is that the instructor refuses to accept copy that has not

been proofread. Real error is one thing; sloppiness is another. Every student needs to own a dictionary and a handbook of usage and punctuation. And yes, every teacher in every subject area should make the same demand. It is amazing how large a percentage of corrections will be made if a writing assignment is returned with the comment, "Unacceptable due to X type of errors. Correct and resubmit." A similar technique is Richard Haswell's (1983) "minimal marking." He finds that if he simply places checkmarks in the margin indicating lines of text where errors have occurred (one checkmark for each error), students are capable of self-correcting over 60 percent of their own errors.

More fundamental to the issue of proofreading for mechanics, however, is the need to clarify its purpose and disentangle it from the issue of teaching punctuation and usage. For the individual writer, instruction in punctuation and usage needs to take place before any attempt to proofread the text. The etymological roots of the word "proof" are instructive: Both the noun *proof* and the verb *to prove* are derived from the Old French *prouver* (to prove) and the Latin *probare* (to test, to find good). Literally, to proofread is to prove or test one's text by reading it to see whether it conforms to the rules of standard English. For the individual writer, proofreading is not an activity designed to teach spelling, usage, or punctuation; it is an activity designed to test the text against the rules that the writer already knows.

To confuse the writer's proofreading of her own text with instruction in usage and punctuation is disastrous. It is senseless to berate young writers for errors that they cannot identify. It is even more senseless to assume that the role of the teacher is to proofread student writing in the author's absence and identify errors with a swarm of red marks. Proofreading does not serve as significant instruction in usage and punctuation because it does not instruct or model.

The purpose of this brief taxonomy of external revision is to justify the importance of providing students with informed peer responses during the revision stage of the composing process. If rewriting, editing and polishing, and proofreading are demanding tasks for the mature writer, they are appallingly difficult for young writers (Beach, 1976; Windhover, 1982). Peer response groups can model, and thus teach, these very difficult tasks.

EDUCATING PEER RESPONSE GROUPS

Teachers who have committed themselves to using peer response groups to give formative feedback to the writer during the composing process are confronted first with the problem of how to establish and

maintain such groups. That issue is dealt with at length in Chapter 6, but to foreshadow: Establishing and maintaining small groups requires not just a decision but also the skills to make it work. The membership of a peer response group needs to be based on a variety of diagnostic data, collected either formally or informally, that include writing ability, usage skills, reading comprehension, cognitive complexity, imagination, personality traits, leadership potential, gender, and race. From these data, the teacher constructs heterogeneous groups of five to seven members—a number too large to be dominated easily by one or two students and yet small enough to discourage decision making by vote. Groups of six are particularly convenient because they can be subdivided into groups of two and three for certain types of tasks. The heterogeneity of the group is crucial if the students are to take upon themselves the role of providing critical feedback to each other: Weaker students must by necessity be tutored by stronger students, and a balance of gender and race provides a diverse experiential context. Except for shifts in membership due to personality clashes or group dysfunctions of other types, the integrity of the group needs to be maintained and fostered over sustained periods of time.

After peer response groups have been carefully established, the group members must be educated in how to give constructive critical feedback. The heterogeneity of the group provides diverse responses to a written text, but mere diversity is likely to be confusing unless it is organized in such a way that the author can cross-reference and evaluate it. Providing students with a response sheet consisting of a series of heuristic questions assists members of the peer response group to focus their comments (Denn, 1982; Hodges, 1982).

Specific response sheets can be generated for particular assignments, or they can be more general in design to produce and organize feedback for a variety of writing assignments. At the beginning of a writing course, groups may be given a fairly simple general response sheet (see Figure 5–A). After students have mastered the first response sheet in the progression of the course, it can be replaced with a second, more sophisticated version (see Figure 5–B).

No matter what type of response sheet the teacher generates, the peer response groups need to be taught how to use it (Kirby & Liner, 1980). Perhaps the easiest way to model the use of a response sheet is to make transparencies of papers written by students in other classes that exhibit particular types of common problems—for example, the topic is too large, the topic is never adequately defined, or the ideas are too general and need to be demonstrated with specific examples or evidence. If the sample papers are chosen carefully, the teacher can use the response sheet to model the distinctions between rewriting, editing and polishing, and proofread-

Figure 5–A: Response Sheet I

Author's Name   _____   Editor's Name   _____

Essay #   _____   Date   _____

1. Does the essay have a suitable introduction? Is it interesting? Does it make the reader want to read on?

2. Is the topic of the essay clearly established? Does the reader know, after reading the first paragraph, what the author is talking about?

3. Is the body of the essay arranged according to some plan? Is the plan easy for the reader to follow and understand?

4. Are the major ideas supported with specific details, examples, and evidence?

5. Does the conclusion follow from all that has gone on before? Is it free from new or irrelevant material?

6. Is the conclusion effective? Does it leave the reader satisfied?

7. Is the essay coherent? Has the author remembered that the audience may know little or nothing about the subject and that it is his or her responsibility to fill in the gaps?

8. Does the essay have an appropriate title? Is the title closely related to the essay's central idea?

<u>Reader's Overall Response</u>

I.   Positive Comments

II.   Recommendations for Rewriting

III.   Recommendations for Editing and Polishing

---

ing. Moreover, the teacher can identify particular types of problems in the text and make concrete suggestions about how they could be resolved. In this initial modeling of how to use the response sheet, it is crucial that the teacher note the *positive* aspects of each paper in addition to providing feedback about its weaknesses.

After the teacher has critiqued several papers, the class as a whole uses

Figure 5–B: Response Sheet II

Authors Name_____Editor's Name _____
     Paper# _____   Date _____

1. After the first paragraph does the reader want to hear more? How could the author rewrite the first paragraph in order to capture the reader's attention more effectively?

2. What is the thesis or point of the essay? Are all of the major ideas clearly subordinated to the point of the essay? Could one of the essay's subordinated ideas better serve as the central point? If the essay has three major ideas, could the author get by with two or does she need a fourth?

3. Would the progression of the essay profit from a reordering of the sequence of the major ideas?

4. Are the essay's major ideas related in ways that the author has not shown--by means of cause and effect relationships; comparisons and contrasts of size, number, and time; and so forth? Would making such relationships explicit strengthen or enrich the paper?

5. Are all of the major ideas demonstrated with concrete examples? Could the author use more interesting or humorous examples?

6. Are all of the essay's assertions or arguments supported with convincing evidence? Does the author need to go to the library?

7. Does the final paragraph serve to conclude the essay as a whole or simply conclude the preceding point? Could it simply be deleted? If the last paragraph is necessary, will the reader remember it? Could the author rewrite it in a more interesting way?

Reader's Overall Response

I.   Positive Comments

II. Recommendations for Rewriting

III. Recommendations for Editing and Polishing

the response sheet to critique other samples. The teacher leads the class in an oral discussion through the questions on the response sheet so that students can begin to internalize what defines an adequate critical response. After the class as a whole has critiqued several examples, all of the peer groups are provided with a sample paper. Each member completes the response sheet to critique the paper, and then the group discusses their responses.

Modeling how to use response sheets can become extremely sophisticated. Over a period of time, the teacher may collect a number of excerpts from papers to show in different ways a similar problem of introduction, transition, or conclusion. These excerpts can be contrasted and compared with successful introductions, transitions, or conclusions written by either students or professional writers. But whatever methods the teacher invents to demonstrate constructive critical feedback, the modeling needs to take place on an ongoing basis throughout the course. If peer response groups are to be effective, they must be educated. Group members learn to identify a variety of problems to avoid, and they internalize a variety of strategies to use in drafting a text.

Once peer response groups have been educated, the mechanics of peer criticism are fairly simple. The author numbers each line of her paper for easy reference, makes two copies of the typed original, and brings them to class. (At the high school and middle school level, where papers typically are not typed, teachers may wish to set aside class time for students to produce multiple clean copies using carbon paper. This copy time can serve as an occasion to emphasize the importance of legible handwriting.) Ideally, authors read their essays aloud while the members of the peer group follow along on the copies, two students sharing each copy. The importance of the author's oral reading of the text needs to be emphasized. Such an oral presentation forces authors to stand behind their work in a visible way. (No one wants to look like a fool.) After the oral reading, each student, including the author, uses the response sheet format to provide specific, written feedback, praising the strengths of the paper and making concrete suggestions about what type of rewriting or editing needs to be done.

At the beginning of the term, it is important that the entire peer group of six respond to each author's written text; it is likely to take six written responses for the author to spot significant correspondences in her audience's comments. If a minimum of fifteen minutes is allotted to each author, such feedback for a group of six will consume two entire fifty-minute class periods. One student in each group needs to be appointed timekeeper and help the group stay on task so that each author receives a fair share of the group's attention.

After the groups are familiar with the procedures of peer criticism and are increasingly capable of giving concrete, constructive feedback, the teacher may wish in the interests of time to subdivide the peer groups into triads. The procedures remain the same; the difference is that the authors receive feedback from only two of their peers. If classroom time is at a particular premium or if for some reason students have not made multiple

copies of their texts, the author's oral reading can be omitted and the papers can simply be exchanged, commented upon, and passed on to the next reader in the circle.

Once authors have received peer criticism of their texts, their obvious task is to evaluate that criticism and rewrite their texts accordingly. To put more direct pressure on the students to complete their revisions, they can be asked to bring their revised texts back to class for yet another group reading.

GROUPS PROVIDE INDIVIDUALIZED INSTRUCTION IN MECHANICS

Earlier in this chapter we asserted that neither the writer's proofreading of her own text nor the teacher's proofreading of texts in the author's absence could serve as significant instruction in spelling, usage, and punctuation. But on the other hand, five students proofreading the author's text can provide effective instruction in mechanics. The odds are right — five "instructors" to one author. But how do the students become instructors? They do so through *interaction*. The procedures are basically the same as those for the earlier peer criticism. Authors bring the original and two copies of their final texts to class, only this time someone other than the author reads the text aloud, sentence by sentence, while the other group members proofread along on the copies (two students to a copy) and suggest corrections and revisions. This leaves the author free to listen to what her text sounds like and to focus on what types of errors the group is correcting (Fulwiler, 1982). The author may disagree and is responsible for asking questions to clarify why a particular correction was necessary. The person reading the manuscript aloud makes agreed-upon corrections on the original, which the author turns in at the end of the class.

If the class is composed entirely of remedial writers or very young writers, the teacher may wish to hold the groups responsible for correcting only a particular type of error rather than holding them accountable for a global proofreading. But if groups in regular freshman composition classes have been constructed so that at least one or two members have the ability to write correct standard English, peer groups are capable of correcting the vast majority of errors of all kinds.

Our classes receive an all-but-memorized little lecture at the beginning of every course. The essence of it is as follows:

THE JANITORS OF LANGUAGE

Yes, you as students have the right to your own language. But if you have the right to your own language, you are also accountable for your spelling, grammar, and punctuation. You will be judged by the linguistic community at large in accordance with your ability to write and speak standard English.

This class is going to function very much like the real world. Excessive errors of spelling, grammar, and punctuation are not acceptable. Yes, we will review the major rules of grammar and punctuation in class. But it is your job to learn the rules, proofread your papers carefully, and correct your spelling, grammar, and punctuation. No paper that contains numerous, low-grade errors in mechanics will be read or evaluated for a grade. It will simply be returned to the author for correction.

English teachers are not janitors of language; it is not our job to spend our weekends proofreading and "cleaning up" your essays. Moreover, research suggests that red-marking your papers with a horde of corrections has little if any positive effect upon your writing.

In this class, you have a right to your own language, but you are also accountable for it.

After delivering this hard-line exhortation, we explain that although we will evaluate the work of each member of a peer group, we will award no grades until everyone's text in the group is acceptable at the level of mechanics. Unacceptable papers will be turned back to the group for further proofreading. For our freshman composition courses, we operationally define "acceptable" as no more than one spelling error per typed page, no more than two usage errors per typed page, and no more than two punctuation errors per typed page.

This, so to speak, places the fox among the chickens. We admit to a certain amount of perverse satisfaction when the shock on the students' faces indicates that they realize that we mean it. And it is a delight when students arrive at that first group proofreading—armed with dictionaries, handbooks of usage, and punctuation guides—to watch them begin to function as "grammarians." They now have a high investment in getting it written "right." Not only are they immediately concerned with correcting their own papers, but they are directly concerned with correcting their peers' papers, since no one's paper will be graded until all of the group's papers are acceptable at the level of mechanics.

Group proofreading is one of the single most effective ways to move from a passive memorization of the "rule" to an active production of correct sentences. Not only is the author confronted with five proofreaders who are determined to serve as her instructors, but if the author continues in future papers to make the same type of error, the peer pressure that the group exerts is enormous. "Look, Jane, how many times do we have to go

through it? If you have more than two items in a series, you *have* to use commas." In addition to the author's learning about what types of her own errors need correcting, each member of the group, in the role of instructor, corrects a wide range of errors in the papers of others.

A Disclaimer

This approach to group proofreading, we must admit, is not as doctrinaire as it may sound. We tend to overstate the case a bit for the benefit of students. If students encounter questions of usage during group proofreading that are too complex for them to handle, the teacher needs to be available as a consultant. Also, there are likely to be a number of bidialectal or ESL students in every class whose usage problems cannot be dealt with by their peers. While the members of the peer groups are correcting each other's papers, the teacher can work individually or in small groups with those students who have extreme problems at the level of mechanics.

If group proofreading were instituted in the upper elementary grades and maintained in every English classroom throughout the college curriculum, not only would students write and speak more correctly — but people would no longer move away from us at cocktail parties when we answer the question, "What do you teach?" The classic response to our confession that we teach English is, of course, "Oh, I'd better watch what I say. I was never very good at grammar." More importantly, once released from the janitorial function of proofreading student papers, teachers can get on with teaching literacy — the ability to communicate significantly with others through listening, speaking, reading, and writing — as the defining characteristic of an educated human being.

MANAGING THE COMPOSING ACT

This chapter has dealt with presenting students with a hierarchy of revision and teaching them how to reaccess the entire range of revision tasks from the perspective of the critical reader. Specifically, this involves teaching students to discriminate among rewriting, editing and polishing, and proofreading. Perhaps more importantly, the chapter demonstrates how to integrate final revision into the composing process through a systematic use of informed peer criticism. This peer criticism is sequenced and focuses on discrete aspects of revision in separate group sessions. (Peer criticism simply will not work if students are concerned primarily with errors in mechanics in their first response to a writer's draft.)

This model of recursive peer criticism is logical and teachable. And as John Clifford (1981) reported in his empirical study of peer criticism, "Composing in Stages: The Effect of a Collaborative Pedagogy," those students who received *informed* peer criticism wrote substantively better texts than those students who revised their texts by themselves.

Yet, as the authors of this book adopt the perspective of the critical reader and go back over this chapter and the two preceding chapters, a fundamental issue remains unanswered. How is it possible to integrate this recursive, three-stage model of the composing process with its various sub-steps and exercises into the day-to-day curriculum of a real classroom? How do you avoid overloading the students with a plethora of concepts? How do you avoid overloading the teacher with extensive record keeping for a complex sequence of predrafting, drafting, and revision tasks? How do you avoid cognitive burnout?

The answer of how to avoid meltdown on the part of the curriculum, the students, and the teacher emerges if we split the problem into two parts. First, "How do you avoid overloading the students conceptually?" As suggested at some length in the introduction to this section, the instructor does not teach nor do the students attempt to learn the entire model of the composing process in the first week of the term. Rather, it is important to focus on teaching a variety of specific predrafting strategies early in the term. Thereafter, the teacher simply holds students responsible for doing significant predrafting for every major written assignment. The direct teaching of zero drafting, problem-solving drafting, and final drafting is implemented in the writing of the three-day, in-class essay, and the in-class format allows the teacher to monitor the actual drafting processes of the students and to provide ongoing individualized feedback. The direct teaching of revision takes place in the context of the modeling and in the sequencing of critical tasks for the peer response groups. In short, the teaching of the model of the composing process is spread over the progression of the term; on any given assignment, students implement only those aspects of the composing process that they have been taught. The curriculum, of course, is cumulative. By the second half of the term, students are responsible for predrafting, drafting, and revising each major writing assignment.

The second question, "How do you avoid overloading the teacher with complex record keeping?" is easier to answer. As with the journal, it is not necessary for the teacher to read and critique each stage of the students' composing process. It is only necessary for her to hold each student responsible for having gone through the various stages.

There are two simple ways to hold students responsible for going

through the composing process. First, each stage of a major writing assignment is to be completed by a specified deadline. On the day that the predrafting, drafting, or revision of an assignment is due, the teacher plays gatekeeper at the door and visually checks that each student arrives with the appropriate completed work. (We validate this check by rubber stamping the student's work with a fire-breathing dragon, *rampant*.) At the college level, we have been known to deny students entry to class for lack of a problem-solving draft. Students catch on quickly: Each stage of the composing process must be completed on time. Otherwise, some students will try to cram predrafting, drafting, and revision into one desperate all-nighter — thus aborting the unconscious processing, perspective taking, and incubation that characterize a mature composing process.

The second check of the students' engagement of the various stages of the composing process takes place when they have completed the final version of their texts. When students hand in their rewritten, edited and polished, and proofread copy, we require that they also attach all predrafting tasks, multiple drafts, and revisions that interacted to generate the final text. (This policy, for all practical purposes, eliminates even the possibility of plagiarism.) Each packet of materials is turned in with an assignment checklist (see Figure 5–C). This checklist concisely validates that the packet contains the required predrafting, drafting, and revision stages of the written assignment. Each author checks off the completed stages of the composing process that are included in her packet.

Before students pass their packets of materials and final texts to the teacher, they exchange packets on a random basis and examine each other's checklists, thumbing through the packet to make sure that the author has in fact included all of the written materials indicated on her checklist. The checker then signs her name and the date.

The assignment checklist allows the teacher to manage the complexities of keeping records on predrafting tasks, multiple drafts, and revisions with comparative ease. The teacher need not read through the entire record of the student's composing act, yet students consistently are held responsible for engaging in a fully elaborated composing process. Moreover, if the teacher encounters complex writing problems while evaluating a student's final text, having the complete record of the student's composing act is invaluable in diagnosing the origins of the problems and explaining them to the student.

If a functional model of the composing process is fully integrated into the writing curriculum, students are taught how mature writers engage in the act of writing — a first step toward curing the neurosis of the one-shot-draft confrontation with the blank page. And if students write through all

Figure 5–C: Managing the Composing Act: Assignment Checklist

Writing assignment #_____   Writer's name _____

PREDRAFTING
_____a. Nonstop writing
_____b. Brainstorming
_____c. Outline of subject
_____d. Other

DRAFTING
_____a. Zero draft
_____b. Problem–solving draft
_____c. Final draft

REVISION
_____a. Rewritten on basis of peer criticism
_____b. Rewritten on basis of teacher's suggestions
_____c. Proofread by writer for mechanics and spelling
_____d. Proofread by peers

Checked by _____, date _____

of the stages of the composing process *repeatedly*, they begin to internalize and master a model of composing that reflects, channels, and organizes the nature of consciousness itself.

The payoffs for integrating a mature model of the composing act into the writing curriculum will be reflected immediately in the quality of student writing. But more importantly, as students continue to practice, to elaborate, and to master the composing process in the subsequent writing tasks of other classrooms and in the work environment, they will continue to develop and evolve as writers and as human beings. The internalization of a mature composing process constitutes the primary content of a contemporary composition course. When students exit our courses, the model in their head is designed to replace us.

Part III

VALUING
IN THE
WRITING CURRICULUM

The writing teacher and the students exist in an all-too-artificial world: Class periods come and go, terms begin and end. Yet the fact remains that classrooms are filled with people. Sometimes we forget that interactions between the teacher and the students and among the students themselves are personal. And certainly the individual writer's encounter with her journal, her subject, and her composing process is in every sense of the word "personal."

The curriculum presented in this book structures and demands the personal, intense involvement of students and teacher alike in exchange for rewards of growth and learning. In addition to rehearsing and composing, the curriculum requires *valuing* — of product, of process, of self, and of others. "Valuing" is a more inclusive and humane term than "evaluating," "ranking," "testing," and "grading" — all of which most teachers must do at some time. For students to learn to value, as they have learned to rehearse and to compose, they need a framework to support optimum personal interaction. Crafting such a framework involves at least four components: (1) implementing group-based cooperative learning, (2) blending formative and summative evaluation, (3) teaching students to critique and to judge, and (4) establishing for the teacher a fair, defensible method of evaluating the students' work in the class.

Group-based cooperative learning is important because valuing begins with individuals' getting to know, to accept, and to listen to each other. Quite apart from the personal gains that occur in cooperative learning, research indicates that cooperative learning accelerates and focuses formal instruction. Virtually all aspects of the curricular model presented in Parts I and II require or may require group work. Cooperative learning and group work do not just happen automatically when the teacher moves the

students out of straight rows and into small groups, but that is a starting point. Chapter 6 provides an in-depth discussion of peer group instruction.

Blending formative (*ongoing*, periodic, instructive) evaluation and summative (*final*, total, reflective) evaluation is critical because the individual's growth as a writer involves more than the dimension of one class period or one term. A student's grade at the end of a course may be summative evaluation from the teacher's perspective, but for the writer it is also formative evaluation, an "in-progress check" on how well she is developing as a writer. In a sense, summative and formative evaluation are but different sides of the same coin. Further, a rigid distinction between the two becomes an artifice that insulates the teacher from the students by segregating the students from the evaluative system.

Teaching students to critique and to judge their own work and that of others is a critical requirement in the writing curriculum. Because students' development as writers is in process, they need ongoing, consistent formative evaluation from the teacher and the audience of their peers. Because the act of judging clarifies the writing being judged, they need ongoing, consistent summative evaluation from the teacher and the audience of their peers. Taste is not immediately available to all, and neither are standards and criteria for judging. Evaluative criteria are learned; they must be taught.

Establishing a fair method of evaluation that is consonant with the goals and the procedures of the writing curriculum outlined in Parts I and II is not easy. However, the curricular model contains within its framework its own evaluative methods. But to go on now would be to leap to the conclusion before the final elements are in place. Invested writing and a mature composing process cry out for a self-integrating evaluative model — and the key to that is peer group instruction in the writing curriculum.

6

Using Peer Group Instruction to Teach Writing

Think back to learning the skills to ride a bicycle. . . . What was needed first was not a lecture on how to ride a bicycle. Nor was it a manual on how to ride a bicycle. The first thing needed was — a bicycle. What one needed next was someone who would walk alongside giving constant feedback: "Johnnie, don't lean forward so far" or "Slow your pedalling down and then you'll have more control." *When students are learning new skills, they need immediate feedback and individualized attention.* One learns to ride a bicycle by riding a bicycle and by getting feedback. One learns to write by writing and by receiving feedback. Perhaps the most elegant case for this point has been made by Peter Elbow (1973). Unfortunately, few students of writing receive the individualized and immediate feedback necessary to master fundamental composing skills. They write their assigned essays in isolation, turn them in to the teacher, and are awarded a final grade. And there is little evidence that students understand the teacher's written commentary on their finished products, never mind internalize those comments as principles to be integrated into the next act of composing (Knoblauch & Brannon, 1981).

Because teachers have twenty to thirty students and may teach two, three, or even more composition classes a day, it is impossible for them to provide the quantity and quality of feedback their students need. Yet it is by writing, receiving immediate feedback, and responding that students master composing skills.

The single most under-used resource in most classrooms is the students — especially students working in peer groups. Using peer groups to evaluate student writing not only decreases the teacher's grading load but also increases the amount of students' writing (Peckham, 1978).

In the majority of high school and college classrooms, a teacher transmits information that students receive, reflect upon or memorize, and return to the teacher in oral or written form. Occasionally, the teacher stops to ask questions to which students are expected to respond; the teacher may comment upon the students' answers before proceeding to make another extended statement. In this interaction there is little cross-fertiliza-

tion of ideas in terms of students talking to one another or reacting significantly to a peer's response to the teacher. The teacher knows the answers to
the questions; the main function of student participation is to verify how
well the teacher's answers have been learned. No matter how skillfully the
teacher creates the illusion of exchange or discussion, the primary instructional method in such a classroom is the lecture.

An interesting exercise for both novice and veteran teachers is to tape-
record a class period, then later that day replay the tape and fill in a
classroom interaction chart (Figure 6–A), noting for each minute during
the period whether the teacher, a student, or no one was speaking. Whether or not the sentence dealt with the class topic can also be marked on the
chart.

Such a chart often reveals uncluttered visual proof that in many/most
classrooms the primary role of the teacher is to transmit information by
talking. Teachers also talk to discipline students, direct activities, remind
the class of important assignments that are soon due, and so forth—note
that in the third minute on the chart in Figure 6–A, the teacher had to
work to get back onto the topic for the day.

None of this is to say that it is unprofitable for the teacher to function

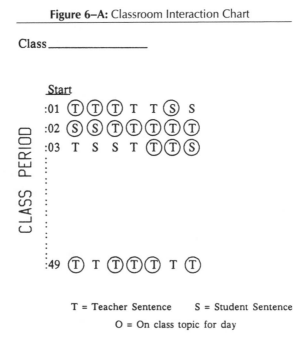

Figure 6–A: Classroom Interaction Chart

Class_____

T = Teacher Sentence   S = Student Sentence

O = On class topic for day

as an information dispenser and the student to function as an information receiver. Often the most efficient way to present new concepts, elaborate familiar concepts, point out interconnections among concepts, or identify and explain the significant ideas in assigned readings is through lecture. Yet a classroom in which the teacher is primarily a lecturer and the student primarily a passive listener is not an efficient environment in which to learn skills. Writing is, above all else, a learned skill.

RESEARCH ON PEER GROUP INTERACTION IN THE CLASSROOM

Why is it so important to emphasize peer group instruction in the writing classroom? What benefits might a teacher who uses extensive group work expect? Researchers find that properly structured peer group interaction is one of the most effective avenues for academic and social learning in any classroom. In an essay in *The Social Psychology of School Learning* (1980), David Johnson comments:

> Teaching and learning do not typically take place within a dyadic relationship between an adult and a child. Students' learning takes place within a network of relationships with peers, and it is these relationships that form the context within which all learning takes place. Student–student relationships are an important and vital aspect of classroom learning and students' development and socialization. There is considerable evidence that peer relationships within the classroom contribute to . . . internalization of values, acquisition of perspective-taking abilities, and achievement. (pp. 156–157)

These three elements — internalizing values, acquiring perspective-taking abilities, and achieving — are the cornerstones of successful group work. Achieving "cooperative learning" requires that a group develop social skills and that it have positive interdependence ("we sink or swim together"), individual accountability ("everyone does her share"), and processing time ("did we succeed at what we just tried?") (Johnson, Johnson, Holubec, & Roy, 1984).

One goal for all teachers is to help the student become a better and eventually a complete critic of her work. We have all heard tales of "miracle cures" that teach the craft of writing, but only infrequently have we heard of miraculous methods for improving students' perceptions of their own work. This is, however, one of the major impacts of cooperative group work. As students interact with one another, they begin to develop the

ability to adopt a variety of perspectives and roles. The young writer becomes an editor who assists her colleagues in revising their work, a proofreader who checks the writing of others for errors in mechanics, and a critical reader who evaluates the finished essays of her peers. As the student becomes increasingly able to adopt the perspective of a critical reader of others' writing, she begins to comprehend the "ideal reader" of her own work more and more precisely, and through this becomes more aware of the standards of the reader/evaluator. Inevitably, this internalization of the critical reader role interacts with her role as writer to produce better writing (Hawkins, 1980).

Studies of how students function in a problem-solving situation reveal that when students work within a cooperative learning framework, they will set out to discover more information than students who have the same assignment but are working in a competitive framework (Crawford & Haaland, 1972). Students working in the cooperative framework will make better use of the information they get from other students (Laughlin & McGlynn, 1967). Writing is a problem-solving exercise. Peer groups can function at various levels in the broad solution of the problem—brainstorming and inventing, coaching and supporting, first-draft reading, proofreading, and evaluating. Cooperatively, these groups can mount a formidable attack on "the writing problem."

When students work in groups, the students who are less motivated to complete the assignment are bolstered by the others. A considerable body of research has demonstrated that students working together on assignments have more success in completing them, remain motivated longer, build a sense of group purpose that provides additional motivation, tend to continue into other, higher tasks in the same subject area, and view the instructor more and more favorably as learning and success rates improve (Blake & Mouton, 1961; Garibaldi, 1979; Gunderson & Johnson, 1980; Johnson & Ahlgren, 1976; Johnson, Johnson, Johnson, & Anderson, 1976; Kline, 1975; and Wheeler & Ryan, 1973).

Growth through Controversy

Another dramatic outcome of the cooperative learning enterprise is growth through "controversy." As a group works toward its goal, differing points of view and different ways to solve the problem are brought up by individuals within the group. The resulting controversy prompts learning. We have known for years that cognitive reasoning cannot be taught directly (see, among others, Inhelder & Sinclair, 1969; Turiel, 1973), but achieving higher levels of cognitive reasoning remains one of the most important

goals of education. The cooperative learning framework with its inevitable controversies establishes situations that encourage cognitive development.

The group setting allows the give and take necessary to prompt discussion about how to resolve the problem and dissolve the controversy. At the same time, it breeds curiosity to decide which of the competing ideas is most valuable for the group. This reaction, labeled "epistemic curiosity" by Berlyne (1966), prompts the student to consider alternatives, and this reflection upon possibilities is apparently what stimulates cognitive growth. Controversy in the context of group interaction also stimulates the development of moral reasoning (Blatt & Kohlberg, 1973; Rest, Turiel, & Kohlberg, 1969). This epistemic curiosity causes students to take new perspectives — one of the cornerstones of cooperative learning. Not only achievement but also cognitive and moral reasoning are enhanced through cooperative learning.

Social Growth

A further benefit of peer groups is that students who work in cooperative settings are more likely to get along with students from other ethnic groups. In a meta-analysis, Johnson, Johnson, and Maruyama (1983) conclude:

1. Cooperation, with intergroup competition, promotes more positive attitudes between majority and minority students than does interpersonal competition. (p. 17)
2. The social judgments which majority and minority students make about each other will increase or decrease the constructiveness of their relationships. . . . When majority and minority students are placed in the same classroom, they carry with them the prejudices and stereotypes prevalent in our society. (pp. 37)
3. When heterogeneous students interact within a context characterized by positive goal interdependence, a process of acceptance is prompted, resulting in promotive interaction, . . . accurate understanding of others' perspectives, . . . feelings of success, [and] self-esteem. (pp. 37–38)

Group Work vs. Other Learning Frameworks

The definitive research on achievement and cooperative learning is a meta-analysis by Johnson, Maruyama, Johnson, Nelson, & Skon (1981) based on 122 studies with research conducted at various levels of schooling and in various subject areas. Their comprehensive results leave little doubt

that we as professionals have scant choice but to employ cooperative learn-ing principles in the classroom. Those results may be summarized as fol-lows:

1. Cooperation without intergroup competition versus cooperation with intergroup competition — no real difference in achievement.
2. Cooperation versus competition — cooperation promotes higher achievement than does competition.
3. Cooperation versus individualistic effort — cooperation promotes higher achievement than do individualistic efforts.
4. Competition versus individualistic effort — no significant differ-ence.

Interestingly, Johnson et al. (1981) found that these results do not vary according to the subject field — they are as valid for English as for mathe-matics. The researchers offered these statements in their conclusion:

> Currently, interpersonal competition and individualistic work are com-monly found in education in the United States. . . . Given the general dissatisfaction with the level of competence achieved by students in the public school system, educators may wish to . . . increase the use of cooperative learning procedures to promote higher student achievement. (p. 58)

STAGES OF GROUP DEVELOPMENT

Groups must move through predictable stages if they are to function properly, and the teacher needs to arrange a series of tasks that will take these developmental stages into account. It is important for the teacher to realize that time spent initially in establishing groups and in task sequenc-ing will pay off later in terms of the quality of peer instruction within the groups. (See especially Johnson & Johnson, *Joining Together: Group Theo-ry and Group Skills*, 1975.)

Involvement Stage

The initial stage in group development is that of *involvement*. Here the group comes together for the first time. Under the supervision of the teacher, the group comes to know itself and its members. (Knowing names is only the beginning of the process of understanding roles.) The rules of the group are established at this time. It is important, however, to under-

stand that there are always two sets of rules operating simultaneously: those formally laid down by the teacher and the group, and the unspoken tacit agreements that evolve as a result of the interaction among individual members. This is a particularly busy time for the teacher in that some mediation is necessary to ensure that the individual rights of the members are not subsumed by the group as a whole or by one or two strong individuals who tend to monopolize and thereby inhibit group processes.

During this first stage, members of each group test the limits of their willingness to become involved with each other. At first they may show little empathy or active concern for each other (though we have found that students are usually eager to escape the patterns of anonymity and isolation found in large classes). They may be unwilling to participate actively in group tasks and are reluctant to exchange views. Yet, talking together produces empathy, and empathy reduces inhibition. Ideally, empathy is a two-way flow of awareness between individuals. It requires a response that says, verbally or nonverbally, "I'm with you." To interact empathically with each other, group members must come to trust that the empathy and support they extend will be returned.

As empathy and support grow, members come to respect each other as individuals — respect but not necessarily agreement develops. At first, the group may establish norms that require the unanimous agreement of all members; as the group develops, group norms tend to be replaced by individual norms. Eventually members are respected more for their individual differences than for their willingness to conform. Groups develop through a process of constructive disintegration and positive reintegration; in this way they are much like individuals as they adapt to change and chart new values (Dabrowski, 1964; Frondizi, 1963).

During the stage of initial involvement, members may find it difficult to be "genuine" within the group. Process-oriented activities that encourage students to interact without fear of ridicule or rejection help the members through this necessary stage. A climate of trust is established in which members feel safe to be what they are and say what they feel and think. Once students can drop their defenses, they are generally willing to take risks within the group (Corey, Corey, Callanan, & Russell, 1982).

Transition Stage

Increased risk taking marks the movement of the group from the tentative involvement stage to the *transition* stage. In the transition stage, the group internalizes the rules it has established. Members begin relating to one another in more genuine ways. Often, a signal that the group is in the transition stage is the willingness of members to confront each other

and to challenge the teacher's role and opinions (Corey et al., 1982). Members feel increasingly confident in expressing their own opinions. Group norms of superficial consensus are gradually replaced by a consensus that values individual differences. As students learn that they receive more feedback as a result of these differences, they come to value and respect the unique contributions each individual offers the group. As a result, individual members suffer less anxiety about sharing ideals with the group as a whole and about participating in group activities. They also gain a sharper awareness of their responsibilities.

Working Stage

When the group realizes that the individuality of its members is the source of its strength, it begins to take responsibility for itself. Different leaders appear from within the group, depending on the present task or need (Egan, 1973), and groups that are functioning well require little teacher intervention. Group autonomy is indicative of the final stage in group development: the *working* stage. In the working stage, individual differences are utilized to accomplish group goals. Group goals, in the form of tasks assigned by the teacher, are now both process- and product-oriented. Groups are able to accept a task and direct their cooperative efforts toward the completion of that task.

If groups within the writing classroom are to be used successfully for peer instruction, they must move through these three stages of involvement, transition, and working. It is *essential*, therefore, that the teacher maintain the same group membership over extended periods of time. Very little work can be accomplished if groups are not given the time to move through the initial involvement stage, then through the transition stage, and into the working stage. Altering the composition of the groups daily or even weekly aborts the developmental process and negates the purposes for which the groups were established.

GUIDELINES FOR ESTABLISHING
AND MAINTAINING CLASSROOM GROUPS

Classroom experience and research (notably Johnson, 1980) suggest that there are four guidelines for establishing groups, which can be summarized as follows:

1. Groups need to be large enough to ensure a diversity of opinion and talent, yet small enough to control and to keep on task toward the goal.

2. The groups must be involved at various points in the learning process, not just at the beginning or only at the end.
3. The teacher needs to structure group tasks in such a way that (a) only one major point is involved in each, (b) each occurs when the students have sufficient background to deal with it, and (c) each has a definite format in which the solution/product is to be presented.
4. The other work in the classroom and the criteria for evaluating students' achievement must not conflict with the role and the criteria for the groups.

These guidelines provide a framework for the following discussion of how to establish successful peer groups.

Group Membership

If groups are to function productively, it is important that each contains a heterogeneous mix of students. Groups that are composed of one personality type or one intellectual level or one gender will not have as much productive interchange; they tend to have a limited perspective. Heterogeneous groups offer new and different insights to their members.

On the first day of class, students should write. The assignment might be: (a) Describe your most successful writing experience, (b) Describe your least successful writing experience, or (c) Tell how you feel about writing about either of these two questions. The teacher can use these writing samples to gain some sense of individual skill development and personality variables. Students are then grouped on the basis of individual differences. In the writing classroom, the teacher should attempt to have in each group at least one student who demonstrates a mastery of the conventions of standard English usage, one student who shows cognitive complexity in coherent and organized writing, and one student who has some verve, passion, and insight. (These three types of writer may have overlapping skills, but they are not necessarily the same person.) Obviously, students who give evidence of having problems with writing are best matched with individuals who are strong or imaginative writers.

Size of Groups

Research on small-group interaction suggests that the best group size for the types of tasks exercised in a writing classroom is from five to seven (Hawkins, 1976). Such groups satisfy the dual necessity of providing a

large enough pool of information for meaningful feedback and a small enough number for efficient teacher monitoring. Very small groups often do not generate sufficient affective and cognitive interaction to propel the group into substantive problem solving. In three-member groups, two members often join against the third. Four-member groups often split two against two. A five-member group is a safeguard against the two-against-two or the two-against-one configuration; in a six-member group one rarely finds a three-against-three subgrouping, since under the pressure to function as a group such a coalition tends to break down rapidly. Any group larger than seven tends to discourage the type of individual investment by each member necessary for highly cooperative interaction in the process of completing a task. It is too easy for the shy or noncommitted student to hide within a group that is too large. Furthermore, in large groups one or two students tend to take over in the name of efficiency and impose an agenda that may not reflect the concerns of the group as a whole. We prefer to establish six-member groups when possible because of the ease with which they can be further subdivided into dyads and triads for certain exercises.

Using Groups to Structure Classroom Space

The straight, military rows of the classrooms we grew up in have done more to stifle interaction between the teacher and students and interaction among students than any other single factor. Students have only peripheral eye contact with the students to their left and right — if they are "sitting up straight and paying attention." They have only occasional direct eye contact with the teacher, who is trying to communicate with 20 to 30 students and who may be as far as 20 feet away. Characteristically, in American society individuals do not feel comfortable discussing issues with those who are more than four or five feet away.

The single most effective change that a teacher can make in a classroom to upgrade the quality of learning is to restructure classroom space on the basis of group interaction. Feedback will go up a thousand percent or more, and if that interaction is channeled precisely into peer instruction, the quality and quantity of learning will rise dramatically.

As Figure 6–B demonstrates, students sit, live, and learn in their groups. The students form closed circles for group work and open up into horseshoe-shaped groups facing the teacher and the board for full class instruction. Students have access to immediate eye contact and interactive awareness of the other five members of their group at all times. Clustering the students in groups also creates large, open spaces in the classroom. The teacher is then freed to play a "thrust stage" out into the classroom even to

Figure 6–B: Restructuring Classroom Space

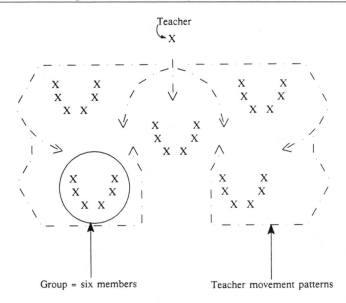

Group = six members   Teacher movement patterns

deliver formal lectures, emphasizing points by advancing and retreating. It is necessary to return to the board only to demonstrate a point visually in writing or with graphics. With practice, a teacher modifies the thrust stage into a theater in the round and can give instruction from any point in the classroom; there need be no "back row." Moreover, the teacher can automatically move toward and intensify interaction with groups that are confused or need restraint.

Let's discuss discipline. Certainly students who sit, live, and learn in groups talk more. When the students are actually engaging in group work, the room is full of talk, laughter, shifting chairs . . . (close the door). But when the teacher is lecturing or when students are working individually, there is no more reason for irrelevant conversation in a group-structured classroom than in a traditional classroom. In fact, the notion that it is more difficult to maintain discipline and control in a group-structured classroom is sheer nonsense. It is much easier to monitor the behavior of five or six groups than it is to monitor the behavior of thirty students the teacher can't even get close to. Moreover, the teacher can "isolate" problem students from the class as a whole, almost from a Machiavellian perspective, by placing them in highly academic-oriented groups where their disruptive behavior will not be reinforced but will be actively discouraged by strong

personalities. The entire classroom no longer serves as a stage for the class clown or inveterate whisperer.

What about the physical logistics (moving desks and chairs) of establishing a group-centered classroom? We all know that the janitor rules the school, and the instructor of the next class is likely to expect/demand straight rows. The solution is simple. On the day that the teacher spatially establishes groups (the second day of class?), she arrives early and places an X on a small piece of masking tape on the floor at the front of each row and writes on the tape the number of chairs in each row. Then she restructures the classroom space by placing the chairs in five or six carefully arranged horseshoe-shaped groups. When students arrive, they are assigned and placed into their groups, and the logic and purpose of sitting in groups is explained. The teacher makes it clear that the students' first responsibility upon entering the classroom each day is to move chairs and physically form their assigned groups. And most importantly, their last responsibility is to reorder the classroom into neat, straight rows using the masking tape X's as a guide. No one leaves the classroom until it is impeccably neat! If the teacher will monitor and reinforce consistently the deconstruction and reconstruction of the straight rows, reordering classroom space is no problem (Wiener, 1986) — as one of our graduate students used to say, "a piece of cake."

Group Rules

Carefully established groups that are prepared to adhere to clearly articulated group rules are usually more productive than randomly chosen groups that attempt to operate on the basis of implied or poorly defined rules (Egan, 1973). Once the "parent" groups have been established, it is important that the teacher discuss the rules by which the groups are to abide; these may be formulated in advance or they may be devised cooperatively by the students and teacher. Once decided on, these rules need to be written down and duplicated, and a copy should be given to each student; the teacher then needs to discuss them with each group and/or the class as a whole.

The following examples illustrate how a few basic rules can be worded so as to make clear to students that they are expected to participate in all group tasks, to be willing to share feelings and ideas, to be supportive of others, and to be willing to negotiate compromises.

1. Everyone should agree on a definition of the assigned task so that the purpose of each group session is clear.

2. Everyone is expected to contribute. Consistent nonparticipation (silence) on the part of a group member is *not acceptable.*
3. Everyone should try to stick to the point. All comments are expected to be relevant to the topic.
4. Everyone has valuable contributions to make. All members are expected to listen carefully to each other and to try to understand each other.
5. Everyone is expected to respond to the comments made by an individual in the group.

If rules are clearly defined and discussed prior to assigning group tasks, it is easier for the teacher to correct the uncooperative behavior of a member who is aggressive or hostile, competitive, or given to withdrawing or straying from the point or to monopolizing discussions. Moreover, clearly articulated and agreed-upon rules reduce the initial frustration and even hostility that can result from confusion about how to behave in the group (Egan, 1973). It is often helpful to print these rules in the form of a contract and have students sign it.

Initial Group Exercises

After the teacher has assigned students to their groups, the students need to group themselves spatially. Group assignments can be announced by the teacher orally, but we have found it more effective to post lists of group membership on the board and ask students to find the other members of their group without talking. Since students often do not know each other, the task of finding other group members without talking requires some nonverbal interchange between class members. Usually, students succeed in finding their group by displaying their names. This exercise not only functions as an ice-breaker but also immediately places responsibility on the group to take care of their own business. The first principle of group work is that any task the group can accomplish on its own is left to the group.

At the outset, when students are still getting to know each other, it is important that the teacher provide tasks that are not product-oriented (Healy, 1982). A premature engagement of the group with a product-oriented task tends to inhibit its members. During their initial contact with each other, students try to determine what behavior is appropriate within the group (they wonder: "How far can I go? Whom can I trust? What is my role here?"). A task that requires too much personal investment is seen as a risk; if the risk of failure is great, little investment will be made. Instead, the teacher needs to provide initial tasks that are process-oriented,

tasks that will inform students about the meaning of purposeful communication rather than require them to focus on producing a well-made product. (See David Johnson's *Reaching Out*, 1986, for a variety of communication exercises appropriate for initiating and modeling group interaction. The teacher needs to select one that suits her style.)

Changes in Group Membership

Establishing group membership is at best a chancy procedure. The teacher may find that some groups are not working efficiently. At such times she needs to be straightforward. The teacher who acknowledges that a group is not functioning and then takes firm action to aid better interaction demonstrates that each group is expected to be productive. A student may be moved from one group to another, or several students may need to be rotated. There need be no apologies for this; the teacher need not feel uncomfortable about being tactfully honest about such issues. If there are two overwhelmingly strong students in one group, for example, it is better to confront the situation: "It's not working. You two are always involved in an argument. I'm glad you come prepared, and I'm glad you speak out. I do not think, though, that you should stay in the same group. This other group needs someone who will speak out, so I'm going to move Kevin to that group." After group membership has been established, it should be altered only in extraordinary circumstances.

Monitoring the Groups

The teacher needs to monitor and guide the progress of the groups as they move toward responsible autonomy. Independence can be encouraged by the care with which the teacher becomes involved with each group. While it is appropriate for the teacher to answer questions of definition or procedure, a group should not be assisted to complete its tasks. It is particularly important that the teacher redirect task-related questions back to the group, and then (by physically moving away from that group) signal the expectation that the group will function competently on its own.

Proximity Monitoring.   The simple act of moving around illustrates the concept of proximity monitoring. Merely by walking from group to group, pausing now and then to observe the interaction between members or to answer a procedural question, the teacher encourages the groups to remain on task. Proximity monitoring allows the students a measure of

independence without engendering the feeling that the teacher has abandoned them.

Observer Monitoring.   Another means of monitoring small groups is to encourage them to develop means by which to monitor themselves. Here the small group is asked to form a circle. One member sits off to one side of the circle and observes the group in action, paying close attention to each individual. The observer keeps a record of how well the group follows group rules — for example, recording how many times each person speaks. Such information immediately and objectively reveals who is monopolizing the discussion and who is not contributing at all. Other records can be kept of how well the group adheres to the point and how efficiently it monitors its time, how many positive and how many negative comments group members make, and how willing they are to negotiate compromises. One particularly valuable observation exercise is to monitor and record whether individuals are listening to each other. Do members respond to each other's statements or does the conversation consist of members "taking turns," making unrelated remarks showing no comprehension or appreciation of the previous speaker's statement? After the observer has finished recording the nature of the group's interaction, it is her responsibility to reflect her observations back to the group.

It is important to rotate the responsibility of observing among group members. Once they have had an opportunity to step out of the group and watch the group process, they return to the group as more fully participating members, more aware of the rules and group process and of how they, as individuals, function within the group.

Tape Recording.   Another simple way to monitor is to place a tape recorder in the middle of the group so that the teacher can be entirely out of the picture. This allows the group to feel independent, yet it permits the teacher to listen later to what has happened within the group. This is particularly effective with groups that are having problems. The teacher does not intervene directly to solve a problem but instead has a record of the interchange from which segments can be played back to illustrate why the group may be failing to function well (George, 1984).

Teacher Participation.   Once the groups are functioning independently and have moved to the working stage, another effective way to monitor their activities and model appropriate interaction is for the teacher to participate, as a group member, within each group in turn — to share writing samples and accept critical feedback from the group on how to revise a given sample. This not only gives validity to the task and to the

value of group feedback but also provides the teacher with an opportunity to demonstrate how to give and receive constructive criticism.

USING SMALL GROUPS
TO "PARENT" OTHER GROUP STRUCTURES

Although in most cases groups of five to seven students are the most efficient size to stimulate peer instruction within a writing classroom, other types of structured groups can also serve a useful purpose (Hawkins, 1976). In such cases, the original groups of five to seven students play a "parental" role by guiding the participation of their members in situations in which it is advantageous to divide the small groups into even smaller units or to merge them into larger group structures.

The following outline of instruction, designed to teach the use of journal feedback terms (see Chapter 2), shows a few of the ways in which small groups exercise a "parental" influence over several larger and smaller group structures:

1. *The framework.* The teacher lectures to the whole class on the rationale and use of the journal feedback terms.
2. *Teacher demonstration.* The teacher demonstrates the use of the journal feedback terms with an overhead projector, applying the terms to an actual sample of student journal writing and commenting on their meaning.
3. *The group critique.* The teacher asks the small groups to critique, cooperatively, an anonymous sample of student writing by using the journal feedback terms.
4. *Defining terms.* The teacher then assigns members of the small groups the task of discussing and clarifying among themselves the significance and use of the journal feedback terms. A recorder is appointed by each group to keep a general record of the discussion and a particular record of any unclarified issues or unresolved questions.
5. *The inside-outside group* (used primarily to focus group discussion and to demonstrate group processes). The teacher uses the recorders to form a seated "inside" group circle of which the teacher is a member. The rest of the class is formed into a standing "outside" group circle around the "inside" group. The teacher engages the inside group in a discussion of the journal feedback terms and responds to the particular questions of the recorders. Only those in the inner circle can talk, which serves to intensify and focus the discussion. Members "outside" the group listen

to the discussion but may become active participants at any time by tapping into the inner circle. The person tapped relinquishes her chair and joins the outside circle.

6. *Feedback in smaller groups.* The teacher has the class members return to their original small groups and subdivide themselves into groups of two or three. If there is a leftover member when a "parent" group subdivides into smaller units, it is usually better to add that student to one of the parent group subdivisions rather than pair students from different groups. The members of these small units then give each other feedback on a self-selected sample of their own journal writing. After 15 to 20 minutes, the teacher recycles this process by having the sub-groups exchange members. The members of these new units then give each other journal feedback on a second self-selected journal entry. The process, for a six-member "parent" group, can be repeated almost indefinitely.

7. *The debriefing.* The teacher reconvenes the class and forms it into two equal groups. Half of the class is seated in a circle; the remaining students stand outside the circle. First, the members of the inner group discuss their experiences in giving and receiving feedback while the outer group monitors. Then the outer group discusses its experiences and relates them to those of the inner group. This allows for an extended discussion of the students' collective and individual experiences in giving and receiving journal feedback.

While this model of a particular sequence of instruction can be modified in an infinite number of ways, it serves to illustrate how the small groups can exert a parenting influence in the class as a whole. (See Appendix 6–A, "A Taxonomy of Group Structures," at the end of this chapter for a schematic discussion of the variety of group structures that can be implemented in the classroom.) If the teacher bypasses the parenting function of the small groups and attempts to hold full-class exploratory discussions before the parent groups have been convened and their members have become invested in them, the situation will almost inevitably revert to the instructional mode in which the teacher is relegated to the role of an information dispenser. Similarly, if the teacher attempts to divide the class directly into groups of only two or three for such purposes as exploratory discussion or peer tutoring, a large percentage of these group interactions tend to disintegrate into irrelevant conversation. If the groups of two or three emerge from a parent group, the latter then assumes responsibility for monitoring its own subgroups, holding them responsible for the completion of their assigned tasks. The parenting function of the small groups

enhances the quality of participation among the members of both larger and smaller group units (Johnson & Johnson, 1975; Johnson & Johnson, 1980).

FOSTERING PEER RESPONSES
TO STUDENT WRITING

Peer instruction is an effective way to provide students with opportunities to do more writing and receive more feedback on that writing than a single teacher can provide. But too often the first task assigned to small groups in the writing classroom is to edit a major paper: "Each member will read her paper aloud. The group will critique the paper and give the author feedback about possible revision. Go to work." Group assignments are often solely limited to this stage (Gebhardt, 1979). There is nothing inherently wrong with such an assignment. Certainly, the task represents one of the end goals of using peer instruction to teach writing. However, such an assignment presupposes a variety of skills that are as yet unlearned by both the group and its individual members (Newkirk, 1984). These skills are developed as part of a trifold structure of peer editing and evaluation that consists of (1) goal-setting, (2) peer evaluation, and (3) self-evaluation (Beaven, 1977).

While there is no doubt that the efficient use of peer groups can simultaneously allow for more student writing while reducing the grading burden on teachers, there is no guarantee that the feedback such groups offer is of sufficient quality to enable a given member to learn what she needs to learn from the group. The weakness of live feedback from peer groups is that it can be blatantly useless, uninformed, and often thoroughly unconstructive: "That's a dumb thing to say." It may be irrelevant: "Gee, I like your colored pencils." And it can be erroneous: "You don't put the title of a song in quotes, you underline it." For peer instruction to be effective the teacher must be prepared to teach students how to give meaningful and informed feedback and must also develop methods for monitoring, facilitating, and evaluating the effectiveness of the feedback emerging from each group (George, 1984; Newkirk, 1984; Wiener, 1986).

To edit each other's papers profitably, students must have acquired such skills as giving and taking critical feedback, articulating their perceptions of the specific strengths and weaknesses in a manuscript, and distinguishing among the stages of the revision process. The class as a whole must first be taught the concepts behind such feedback skills (Bruffee, 1978). If editing groups have not learned how to give meaningful critical

feedback to an author, they are condemned to offer comments that are, at best, superficial and, at worst, incorrect and misleading.

Stages of the Evaluating Process

Too often a student author arrives at an "edit-group" with a manuscript that at best represents a sketch of an idea. Moreover, the untrained editing group tends to ignore the fundamentals of the revision process, which include, at the very least:

1. *The Rewriting Stage.* (The manuscript is assumed to be in a state of flux.) In extreme cases, this may mean writing a whole new draft. It may mean a whole new approach to the idea. It assumes a conceptual flexibility that allows for the logical reordering of ideas by cutting and pasting, rearranging parts of a paper into a new linear sequence, and adding, substituting, or deleting major sections when necessary.
2. *The Editing Stage.* (The manuscript is assumed to be in a comparatively stable form as far as overall organization is concerned.) This stage focuses on the logical coherence and linguistic flow of organizational structure. It concerns itself precisely with such matters as introductions and conclusions, transitions, development and demonstration of ideas, and appropriateness of diction and syntax.
3. *The Proofing Stage.* (The manuscript is assumed to be a comparatively finished conceptual and syntactic statement.) This stage focuses on producing a clean copy for an audience in terms of the conventions of standard usage.

Obviously, these three stages of the revision process overlap one another in varying degrees depending on the competency of the author and the nature of the manuscript. But with beginning writers, it is crucial to distinguish all three of these stages.

A particularly difficult distinction for students is that between the rewriting and editing stages. Ofen, rewriting becomes a superficial cleaning of the manuscript. An exercise that can aid students in breaking down their conceptual rigidity and reordering their linear representation of thought is the "scissors and tape" exercise, which frees students from the idea that a manuscript, once written, is inviolate.

When students arrive in class with multiple copies of their manuscripts for their response group, they are asked to distribute them, and the response group is asked to divide into groups of three. The authors are then requested to cut apart a copy of their texts, separating them into individual

paragraphs. Initially, there may be considerable resistance to this idea. ("What are we doing this for? I worked all night on this paper!") But once the separation has been accomplished, the group can examine the order in which the paragraphs were written. The author is responsible for rethinking the order and for justifying it to the group. Almost without exception, students will discover that additional information is needed and that transitional paragraphs or sentences are necessary. Whether or not the original order is revised, students come to understand that there is nothing sacred about the overall organization and linear progression of a draft.

Response Groups vs. Edit Groups

The problem with the edit-group concept is that by collapsing the writing process into one stage, the edit-group tends to focus on the very last steps of preparing a manuscript for an audience (Flanigan & Menendez, 1980). As a result, the edit-group tends to limit itself to performing only comparatively superficial cosmetic surgery on introductions and conclusions, transitions between paragraphs, awkward syntax, and grammatical lapses.

Part of the difficulty that many teachers have experienced with the use of so-called edit-groups is inherent in the term "edit." Webster's *New World Dictionary* defines *edit* as "to make ready for publication." The edit-group concept ignores the necessity of giving the individual writer feedback about the predrafting activities and drafting procedures that a writer must have successfully completed in order to produce a manuscript worthy of revision (Gebhardt, 1979). Without training in responding to these preliminary activities, groups know too little about writing to be able to offer constructive aid in the final stages of the composing process: rewriting, editing, and proofreading.

Perhaps the term "response group" better suggests the wide variety of feedback skills that small groups must master before they can profitably and successfully assist the student author in the last step of revising the manuscript. This term sidesteps the assumption that the function of small groups is limited to superficially "fixing" individual members' manuscripts. Before a response group can assist in the final step of revising a manuscript and preparing it for an audience, the group must have mastered a wide variety of skills. Members must have learned to give and receive critical feedback; to evaluate a writer's predrafting and drafting strategies and make suggestions for their improvement; to articulate their perceptions of specific strengths and weaknesses within a manuscript; to critique the underlying conceptual framework and organization of a man-

uscript; and, finally, to differentiate between the rewriting, editing, and proofing stages of revision (Flower et al., 1986).

The teacher facilitates the learning of these critical skills by carefully sequencing group tasks. Ideally, each assigned group task represents a specific skill that must be mastered if group members are to learn to give critical feedback about one another's writing. Depending on the type of writing being taught and on the age, ability, and experience of the students, each teacher must necessarily devise her own sequence of tasks for response groups.

OPERATIONAL GROUP RULES
AND CRITICAL RESPONSE SHEETS

When small groups enter the working stage, they are ready to engage in group tasks designed to provide peer feedback that will help each individual master a variety of writing skills. At this time it is valuable to specify operating rules (Wiener, 1986) that limit and direct the nature of the feedback given in response to the written work submitted by each group member. The following set of rules may be helpful:

1. Each group member is responsible for bringing three legible copies of her writing for the other members of the group to read. (Two members share one copy.)
2. Each member is responsible for bringing to class three specific questions about her draft that she would like the group to discuss/answer. "Students *always* know where they had difficulty as they were writing their own essays." (George, 1984, p. 324)
3. Each member is responsible for reading her writing aloud to the group.
4. Each member is responsible for listening carefully and following along as a piece is read.
5. Each member should consult the critical response sheet in order to keep in mind the purpose of the session.
6. Responses to the writing should come from every member of the group. Everyone's opinion is valuable. Group members should agree to disagree.
7. Responses to another's writing should be positive as well as negative. Look first for what is good in the writing, and then go back to see how that writing could be better. Couch criticism in positive terms.

8. Criticism should be specific and illustrated by a discussion of particular passages in the author's manuscript.
9. Each member should make written comments in response to the student's manuscript. Comments given orally may be forgotten.
10. The author of a piece of writing is required to listen to the opinions of the group members without responding to them. There should be no rebuttal of the "But I did that because . . . " type. This rule has to be emphasized *again and again*. An incredible amount of group time is wasted in defensive self-justification of an author's text. Professional writers are just as guilty of this as student authors.
11. The author is responsible for accepting or rejecting the opinions of the group members. She is not required to follow the advice of the group.

In addition to the operational rules, which remain constant for each assigned group feedback task, the teacher needs to provide a written list of questions defining types of critical responses appropriate to the particular writing assignment. All members of the group need to be working on a composition of the same type, and the distinctions among these types and their characteristics must be taught. Having a "common vocabulary" helps ensure criticism that is both concrete and on target (Flanigan & Menendez, 1980). For example, critical questions about the establishment of scene and character are more likely to be appropriate to narrative writing, whereas questions about the statement and definition of logical premises are more likely to be appropriate to argumentative writing.

The following critical response questions were devised to help group members give one another feedback on a childhood experience paper:

1. Are scenes *sufficiently* established in terms of time and space?
2. If you change scenes, are *transitions* from one place to another accomplished economically?
3. Once the scene is established, are the details *elaborated*?
4. Are your *characters* well visualized? Could the reader pick them out of a line-up?
5. Are your characters sufficiently *realized*? That is, could the readers discuss their personalities?
6. Is your voice *authentic*? Are there any "words about words"? If you are enraged or disgusted, show us.
7. What is the *point* of the experience? In short, what "angle" or principle of selection have you used to establish the significance of the experience? Which details reveal this? Which details are irrelevant?
8. Is your narrative point of view an *appropriate vehicle* for establishing the significance of the experience?

9. Is the conclusion *satisfying* to your audience?
10. Is there an *appropriate title?*

The operational group rules and the critical response questions provide a procedural framework for both the teacher and the small group. The basic parameters and procedures remain the same no matter what type of writing assignment or which members of the small group are expected to provide feedback. Once this procedural framework has been established, the teacher can attend to the development, sequencing, and monitoring of group tasks and processes.

THE TEACHER'S ROLE

None of the discussion in this chapter pertaining to the use of peer groups to teach writing should be interpreted as dismissing the critical role of the teacher in the writing classroom. If the teacher cannot successfully teach the concepts that define the writing skills that students are trying to master, any attempt to teach writing is an irrelevant enterprise. The teacher must be able to structure, demonstrate, and validate the feedback process that is involved in each response group assignment.

1. The teacher needs to demonstrate the feedback task by critiquing an example of each student writing assignment in front of the whole class.
2. The teacher needs to provide a precise written definition of each feedback assignment and a list of critical response questions in order to assist the response group in defining the parameters of its task.
3. The teacher needs to validate the significance of the completed task in a lecture format or she can use the response groups to parent larger group structures for a class discussion of the significance of the completed feedback task.

Where peer group instruction is used to teach writing, response groups become the primary vehicles by means of which each student actually confronts and masters the skills of writing. The teacher continues to be responsible for designing what is learned.

APPENDIX 6–A:
A TAXONOMY OF GROUP STRUCTURES

SMALL GROUP DISCUSSION

Students use purposeful conversation to explore, teach, and learn about a subject of mutual interest. The use of an observer who reports back to the group about its behavior encourages the maximum participation and growth of all students.

```
      X
  X    X
   X X  X
      ← Observer
```

PANEL DISCUSSION

Three to six students from the class who have special access to information on a subject of interest are asked to express their individual views in front of the class. A variety of issues and special concerns are presented and explored from the differing perspectives of the panel members. Subsequently, the class as a whole is invited to question the panel.

```
                         Teacher
                          ↳ X
Student
Panel
      ↳ X X X X X

  X  X              X  X
  X  X              X  X
   XX     X  X       XX
          X  X
           XX
  X  X              X  X
  X  X              X  X
   XX               XX
```

EXPLORATORY DISCUSSION
(INSIDE–OUTSIDE GROUP)

Half of the class is seated in a circle with the other half standing behind them. Those class members inside the circle bring information to the group and discuss it. The members standing *listen* to the interchange. If they have something to contribute, they must "tap into" the group, exchanging places with a seated classmate. In a large class, the teacher may need to construct two of these inside–outside groups.

```
   X XXX X
  X X XXX X X
 X X       X X
 X X       X X
  X XXX X
   X XXX X
```

This taxonomy of group structures evolved from a noncited, anonymously authored handout that "floated around" the School of Education at Washington State University, Pullman, Washington, in the late seventies. Through the years, we have modified and adapted it significantly for our own purposes.

ROLE PLAYING

Students may understand a problem intellectually without understanding it operationally. Role-playing a situation — for example, whether unemployed migrant workers should receive welfare — helps students gain operational insight into their own behavior and that of others. Specific roles are assigned to students, action is outlined without scripting actual dialogue, and then the action is played out before the group. Role-playing dramatically illustrates how social problems affect individuals, allows students insight into others' feelings and reactions, and aids students in applying their own personal problem-solving skills to others' situations.

INTERVIEW

The teacher systematically questions and explores various aspects of a topic with two or more resource persons. Information is presented in an informal manner, problems are explored and analyzed, and students interact with respected professional resource people. This procedure models good interview techniques so that eventually class interviews can be conducted collectively and individually by the students themselves.

BRAINSTORMING

Students are asked to share spontaneously all their ideas on a specific subject. Ideas are recorded but not discussed. Quantity is preferred over quality. Any idea on the topic is recorded. No idea is considered inappropriate. Brainstorming encourages maximum student participation in a nonevaluative exercise that values all ideas about a subject.

7

Integrating Evaluation
into the
Composing Process

Evaluation specialists make a distinction between final or summative evaluation and formative evaluation. Formative evaluation is that response given to the author while the work is still being formed. It may, for example, be oral feedback given during the predrafting stage of the composing process as a result of discussing a proposed topic with peers. Richard Gebhardt (1979) stresses the importance of using peer response groups early in the writing process to locate interesting subjects, to generate details, to clarify focus, and to develop a sense of audience. It may be written or oral feedback given to the writer during the drafting or revision process (see Chapters 4 and 5). Richard Beach (1979) noted the particular effectiveness of between-draft evaluations by the teacher. Students' papers that had received between-draft feedback from teachers were ranked by a panel of judges as having a greater degree of change as well as being of higher quality than papers that received between-draft student self-evaluations or no between-draft evaluations. But whatever the approach, *formative* evaluation is feedback given *during* the composing process so that the author may revise her conception during the generation of the text.

Formative evaluation is one of the major components of the writing curriculum envisioned in this book; it is given to the writer while subjects are rehearsed and while texts are predrafted, drafted, and revised. The preceding chapter on group processes discussed specific structures and strategies for teaching young writers how to give significant formative feedback to one another. But a major issue remains unresolved. How does the teacher integrate final or summative evaluation into a process-based composing curriculum?

In contrast to formative evaluation, *summative* evaluation is the act of making judgments about a *finished* text and/or the writer's overall performance during a course. Unfortunately, summative evaluation is most often associated in students' minds and in many teachers' minds with awarding numerical or A-through-F grades. With rare exceptions, most teachers function within classroom environments that require assigning numerical

or letter grades at the end of each term. Frankly, we have no interest in tilting with the philosophic windmills of the graded versus the nongraded classroom controversy. However, to assume that awarding a numerical or letter grade is equivalent to or constitutes an adequate definition of summative evaluation is inefficient.

In *Webster's New World Dictionary*, the first definition of *evaluate* is "to find the value or amount of; determine the worth of; appraise." Only in the second definition, which is limited to mathematics, is *evaluate* defined as "to find the numerical value of; express in numbers [or letters]." To confuse the mathematical definition of evaluation with the more general definition is to obscure the primary purpose of summative evaluation.

First and foremost, summative evaluation is designed to provide students with *feedback* about the comparative worth of their work, its strengths and weaknesses, and the level of performance achieved in completed classroom tasks. In terms of the student's needs, the primary purpose of summative evaluation in the writing curriculum is to provide specific information about what the writer needs to learn, to be aware of, to focus on, or to practice the next time she engages in a writing task. From this perspective, the summative evaluation of one task or course serves as formative evaluation for the next task or course.

Certainly, when educational systems deal with large numbers of students, numerical or letter grades are convenient descriptors of how students' performance and abilities are related to educational norms. Such descriptions are necessary for placement, advancement, and certification of the level of the individual's achievement to society at large. But if a mathematical definition of summative evaluation dominates the evaluation techniques employed in the classroom, the evaluation system is pedagogically primitive. There are numerous other types of summative evaluation techniques that, depending on the nature of the task, can provide much more helpful feedback to the writer.

ALTERNATIVE STRATEGIES
FOR SUMMATIVE EVALUATION

In the writing curriculum described in this book, we apply various methods of summative evaluation — including contract learning, test-re-test, mastery learning, and revision.

Contract Learning

In contract learning, the teacher and the student specify and define a series of tasks that the student must complete to get credit for that portion

of the course. The key aspect of contract learning is that the student's grade is based solely on the *completion* of the agreed-upon tasks; the comparative level of the student's performance is not graded. Classroom tasks that emphasize practice, risk-taking, and the value of mistakes often profit from contract evaluation.

The journal, with its emphasis on significant rehearsal, clearly lends itself to contract evaluation. The students' daily journal exercises are ungraded (Chapter 2), yet the assignments must be completed to receive credit. The "journal checkoff sheet" (Figure 2–E, p. 46) serves as a contract by which the teacher and student confirm that the work has been done. When the student has satisfied the contract by completing her journal assignments, the teacher also complies with the contract by reading selected journal entries and giving ungraded formative feedback. It is important to note that contract learning assumes and demands significant engagement and investment on the part of the student. In the case of the journal, written "non-responses" are unacceptable.

Contract learning is unique in that it divorces evaluation from the *quality* of students' work and rewards them for the *quantity* of their work. If the student receives an incisive evaluation of her journal writing without the anxiety of being graded, the contract powerfully reinforces the writer's rehearsal and practice of basic writing skills. Moreover, it encourages the writer to take risks and make significant mistakes. Most importantly, contract evaluation of the journal promotes and rewards *fluency* — the regular production of significant quantities of prose.

Test–Retest

Retesting is a simple evaluation procedure that allows the student to take more than one test on the same material. The teacher prepares several tests about the same subject and gives one test to the entire class. If the teacher or the student is dissatisfied with the grade received, the student may take a second or even a third version of the test. She receives the highest grade scored on any of the tests taken.

Test-retest evaluation is particularly helpful in assisting students to learn the basics of formal systems of information that demand memorizing key definitions and facts. Due to the number of tests that have to be scored, test-retest evaluation is often associated with "objective" tests that rely on fill-in-the-blank, multiple choice, matching, or true-false answers. (Often these tests can be computer-scored.)

In a writing curriculum, the test-retest evaluation is particularly effective in assessing students' formal knowledge of the basics of standard English usage and in requiring those who are deficient to learn the formal

principles. In our introductory writing course, we review five critical areas of usage in the first five weeks of the term: (1) subject-verb agreement, (2) sentence fragments, (3) comma splices, (4) punctuation errors, and (5) pronoun referents. At the end of each review of a specific usage area, the students are immediately given a short multiple choice test that checks their *formal* understanding. (The students' ability to *produce* error-free prose is fostered and monitored in their peer response groups.) If students do not receive at least a 70 percent correct score on the test, they are required to attend a two-hour review session in the Writing Center. After the review session, students immediately take a second test on the particular usage area. If they do not pass this test, they are mandatorily referred to the Writing Center for individualized tutoring before taking yet a third version of the test.

In schools where a writing center or a learning skills center is not available as a backup system for the teacher, the test-retest procedure can be implemented inside the individual classroom. In this case, while students who have already passed the test are engaged in a substantive in-class writing assignment, those who need further work in a specific usage area are tutored by the teacher in a subgroup, perhaps with the assistance of programmed usage textbooks such as Blumenthal's (1973) *English 2200, English 2600, English 3200* texts. (These programmed texts are keyed to different levels of usage problems.) Those who are tutored in class have the additional responsibility of completing the in-class writing assignment outside of class on their own time; the completion of this work is *carefully* checked at the beginning of the next class period.

The unique aspect of retesting is that it allows the student some latitude to fail tests without penalty; failure can be one step in the learning process. The test-retest procedure is extremely powerful when the teacher is attempting to guarantee that every student has learned the basics that are necessary to the progression of the course as a whole. It is an extraordinarily efficient procedure in that it automatically "tracks" those students who need additional work in specified areas. Rather than having a minority of students monopolize critical class time, with this evaluation procedure the responsibility for learning key information is placed on the individual student.

Mastery Learning

Mastery learning evaluation in its most basic form consists of establishing competency criteria for any specified subject area or skill. Its power resides in denying the "normal curve of distribution" which assumes that on a typical assignment a few students will make F's and A's, a larger

number of students will make D's and B's, and the majority of students will cluster in the C range. In contrast, mastery learning assumes that on a given assignment the teaching objective is for an overwhelming percentage of the class to reach basic competency. Mastery learning assignments are graded pass/fail.

Mastery learning does not attempt to test for minor discriminations of failure or excellence. When the competency criteria are clearly defined in terms of specified performance objectives, it allows both teacher and students to go for the jugular vein — that information and those skills that *must* be mastered if students are to function successfully in the classroom. For example, in our regular freshman composition courses, we have a specified set of competency criteria for acceptable prose in terms of mechanics: On major, out-of-class writing assignments, no paper will be accepted that has more than one spelling error per typed page, or more than two usage errors per typed page, or more than two punctuation errors per typed page. The reader may remember that when an individual student's prose falls below these competency levels, the paper is returned to the student's response group for further editing and revision — and no one in the response group is eligible to receive a grade until the student's writing in question is brought to the level of competency in terms of mechanics (see Chapter 5).

Mastery learning is a particularly effective evaluation strategy because of the ease with which it can be combined with other evaluation procedures. In the case of the test-retest evaluation of five basic principles of usage, for example, the student *must* score at least 70 percent correct in each of the five test areas. No student can receive a passing grade in the course until she has *mastered* the key definitions of correct usage.

The combination of mastery learning evaluation and revision lies at the heart of our writing curriculum. In the progression of a regular freshman composition course, we typically assign four major out-of-class papers and four in-class essays. Three of the out-of-class papers and three of the in-class essays must demonstrate mastery competency in terms of (a) central idea, (b) development, (c) organization, (d) audience, (e) conceptualization, and (f) mechanics. Students who fall below the mastery standards on more than one out-of-class paper or one in-class essay must rewrite and revise the work until it meets the competency criteria. Not every piece of writing profits from being graded on a numerical or A-through-F basis. Evaluating in-class and out-of-class papers on a mastery basis allows students, particularly the better students, to engage difficult subjects and experiment with differing rhetorical stances and organizational structures.

Even a Nobel-prize-winning author like Hemingway wrote a lot of bad novels, and sometimes we learn more from our mistakes than from our

successes. If you want to limit the growth of the potentially excellent writers in your classes, grade every paper they write on an A-through-F basis. Our best students learn all too quickly to produce technically correct, bland versions of the five-paragraph essay that reflect little or no investment in or engagement with the topic. Mastery evaluation of student writing not only demands competency but also allows and encourages students to take a chance on stumbling into a substantive and often significant statement about their relationship to the world.

In our experience, mastery learning in no way reduces the performance drive of the "A" and "B" students (they have a high ego investment in their role as "good students"), but it places real pressure on "C" and marginal students to focus on learning the basics. The pressure is on — either the student passes or fails.

Revision

In our regular freshman composition courses, all major out-of-class papers are revised by the author on the basis of substantive feedback received from the student's peer response group. Moreover, the writer's final text is edited by the peer group for correctness at the level of usage. In contrast, the in-class essays written over a three-day period that focus on teaching the drafting process (day one, zero drafting; day two, problem-solving drafting; day three, final drafting) are not revised but are submitted directly for evaluation. Regardless of whether the students have revised their texts with the assistance of their peer groups, the text that the teacher evaluates is presumed to be a final text. Only those papers or essays that do not meet the competency criteria are mandatorily required to be revised. (Three of four out-of-class papers and three of four in-class essays must meet the basic competency standards.)

In the foregoing context, revision as an evaluative procedure is subordinated to mastery learning and directed toward guaranteeing that the weaker students in the class are pulled up, often "screaming and yelling," to basic standards of competency. But revision can also be used as a summative evaluation procedure in and of itself, designed to promote, encourage, and demand excellence. Students in our freshman composition courses who have met the basic competency criteria on three out-of-class papers and three in-class essays have guaranteed themselves a C in the course — assuming that they have fulfilled their journal contract and passed their five usage tests. How to determine final numerical or letter grades will be discussed in the next section, but to receive an A or a B in the course, students must produce two or more pieces of writing in the progression of

the term that are *worthy of being revised* by standards of *absolute* excellence.

A piece of writing meets the standards of absolute excellence if, when it is successfully revised with the teacher's editorial assistance, the writing is worthy of being read and appreciated by a knowledgeable audience. We often encourage students to submit exceptional pieces of revised writing to both student and professional publications. In addition, when a student successfully completes a final revision of this order, we commonly make copies for the class and ask the author to read the final text aloud. The "ah-*ha!*" response of the class to a truly fine piece of writing not only serves as appreciation of the author's accomplishment, but it also validates absolute standards of excellence for the writer and the class as a whole.

When revision is used as a summative evaluative procedure to assess for absolute excellence, it is extraordinarily powerful. It is also tricky to implement. The teacher has to develop a "nose" for spotting the potentially revisable piece of writing. We require that at least one of the pieces of writing that students revise be selected from their out-of-class papers or in-class essays, but the students' journal entries are also eligible for revision. The key to implementing revision as a summative evaluation procedure in this context is that the initial or baseline piece of writing selected as "worthy of revision" must capture a pivotal moment in the individual's life, or represent an unusual perspective on a commonplace idea or occurrence, or embody an original idea or unusual experience. The defining words are *capture, represent, embody*; what the teacher is looking for is a text that already engages a significant idea or experience *in writing*.

After reading a student journal entry, the teacher may have an intuition that there is a big fish lurking somewhere in the vicinity — but beware. The piece of writing worthy of revision is a fish that has already been hooked. The teacher's task is to help the student land the fish successfully. All students have had meaningful experiences and participated in memorable events. Moreover, the journal, the out-of-class writing assignments frequently derived from significant journal entries, and the in-class essays derived from the source-sheet subjects are designed to *encourage* students to write about the defining ideas and experiences of their lives. But not all students will produce writing "worthy of revision" in the progression of a course. When the teacher works with a piece of writing worthy of revision, by definition she works with writing that has already been produced — not a prototext of writing that might be produced. Sometimes students are not ready to write about the obviously significant events and ideas to which they indirectly refer. Teachers can only encourage; their role in the classroom is not that of therapists, spiritual guides, or personal friends.

If teachers will limit themselves to working with students to revise

pieces of writing that *already* capture, represent, or embody a significant idea or experience, they will avoid the embarrassment of encouraging students to invest time and energy in trying to revise "ideas" that they cannot realize in quality writing—in short, revisions that fail. Also, by limiting revisions to writing that already demonstrates quality, the teacher avoids the problem of students who wish to revise anything and everything, including the phone book, in hopes of raising their grades. The teacher is a trained professional and her editorial energy and time are valuable. *Both* the teacher and the student must agree that a piece of writing is worthy of revision.

A practical aside: If a teacher chooses to integrate the "worthy of revision" procedure into the writing curriculum, she needs to be a real "hardcase" about establishing time deadlines for submitting revisions. We have a firm and almost immutable policy about revision deadlines. For the first two-thirds of the term, after a piece of writing has been identified as worthy of revision, the writer has two weeks in which to set up an editing conference with the teacher and submit a first substantive revision. In the last third of the term, the student has one week to set up an editing conference and submit a first substantive revision. Moreover, no first revision can be submitted in the final week of classes. The reasons for carving such a policy in stone are twofold. First, revising a piece of writing into finality is an organic process that may require two or more editorial sessions with the teacher. The student must have time for ideas to incubate for reflection, and for the unconscious generation of solutions to problems of form and content. Revising for finality marches to the beat of an internal drummer and tends to be neutered by immediate, desperation-fraught deadlines. Second, if the teacher does not establish absolute time deadlines for submitting revisions, too many students put off revising their potentially excellent texts until the latter part of the term—an obvious overload situation for the teacher.

Such firm deadlines for submitting revisions of "potentially excellent texts" often have a dramatic effect on the development of individual writers. The reader may remember that one of the journal assignments is to revise and turn in a copy of an observation/description each week. Among these already-revised observation/descriptions and other journal entries, the teacher will find pieces of writing "worthy of revision" within the first several weeks of the term. In our own experience these potentially excellent texts are produced not only by "A" and "B" students but by "C" students as well. Working early in the term on revising short, comparatively simple but potentially excellent texts, with the teacher's assistance, can completely transform students' attitudes toward and participation in the composing process. Suddenly they find themselves functioning as real writers, writing

and rewriting in an attempt to say something significant in the best possible way. Such an experience early in the course can become a seed crystal that precipitates entirely new standards of competence that restructure students' engagement in the act of writing. Many a prototypic "C" student begins to internalize standards of excellence that transform her into a "B" or even an "A" student. And many a prototypic "A" or "B" student who has been coasting on mere writing *skills* begins to engage writing as a vehicle in which cognitive development and excellence become inextricably intertwined. In short, enforcing a schedule of revision early in the term not only protects the teacher from end-of-term burnout but promotes the metamorphosis of students who are merely taking a required composition course into self-directed writers pursuing excellence.

Using revision as a summative evaluation technique to assess a limited number of quality texts has three unique strengths. First, it fosters absolute excellence in writing of an order that is seldom seen in a classroom. Many of the pieces of writing identified as "worthy of revision" are already "A" papers in the context of traditional classroom norms. During the revision process, they evolve into texts of an entirely different order of quality — benchmarks by which all subsequent writing by the author will be assessed. Second, because the teacher chooses to work only with those pieces of writing that are worthy of revision, she establishes a true editorial relationship with the students. The teacher is on the students' side, radically invested in their success, attempting to help them transform a potentially excellent text into a fine piece of writing by anyone's standards. This is a rare form of intimacy in the classroom. And third, evaluation by revision teaches students that the final payoff in a written work revised to completion is a sense of finality that is both conceptual and aesthetic. Once a writer has experienced finality, a topic fully accounted for and rendered, she tends to internalize that sense of completion as the ultimate standard of excellence for her own and others' writing.

TRANSLATING SUMMATIVE EVALUATION PROCEDURES INTO FINAL GRADES

The applications of contract learning, test-retest, mastery learning, and revision in the previous discussion were designed to be illustrative. Each teacher must devise and weight her evaluation procedures to implement specific course objectives and must adjust them to fit the actual skill levels of particular student populations. But whatever the course objectives or the nature of the students, the teacher needs to integrate a variety of summative evaluation techniques into the writing curriculum. Mere A-

through-F grading of a specified number of essays only reinforces the one-shot-draft "neurosis" that reduces student writing to a parody of mature prose. In contrast, a full-spectrum evaluation system develops and tests a wide range of specific skills and levels of achievement. Above all, in a process-based composing curriculum a sophisticated evaluation system encourages, demands, and rewards a mature composing process.

Once a teacher has designed the summative evaluation procedures that are necessary to assess and reinforce the specific skills required by a mature composing process, it is fairly easy to translate a combination of evaluation procedures into a final numerical or letter grade. For instance, consider the course requirements and sample grade record for a regular freshman composition course, as shown in Figure 7-A.

With such a detailed course requirements/grade record, it becomes a simple arithmetical procedure to translate a variety of summative evaluative techniques into a final numerical or letter grade. We suggest that the teacher maintain a folder on each student, with the grade record stapled to the inside of the folder. The teacher files in the folder all completed usage tests, final versions of essays, papers, and successful revisions and keeps a running account of the student's work on the grade record. At any point in the term, both the student and the teacher can assess the student's progress at a glance.

Once the teacher has constructed a variety of summative evaluation procedures to meet specific course objectives and the needs of specific student populations, it is fairly easy to weight these evaluation procedures to emphasize particular skills. For instance, consider how the course requirements and sample grade record for a remedial freshman composition course (see Figure 7-B) differ from those of the regular freshman composition course (shown in Figure 7-A).

The two evaluation systems stress different teaching objectives. In the regular freshman composition course, the formal knowledge of basic usage is an exit requirement for which students receive no credit. In the remedial course, the same usage tests are worth 25 percent of the course grade; moreover, considerably more instructional time is spent teaching usage in class. To allow the time for this additional instruction in usage, the out-of-class papers are reduced in number from four to three, and the emphasis on revising texts "worthy of revision" is reduced from 25 percent of the final grade to only 10 percent. The different weighting of the summative evaluation procedures in the remedial course shifts the emphasis to learning basic usage principles and mastering the competency criteria for writing. In contrast, the regular freshman composition course requirements and grade record assume mastery of basic usage principles and emphasize mastering basic competency criteria for writing and revising for absolute excellence.

Figure 7–A: Course Requirements and Sample Grade Record
for a Regular Freshman Composition Course

Name _____   Freshman Composition, Sec. _____

Term _____   Year_____

I. You must pass all 5 of the usage tests
    at the 70% level or better to be
    eligible to receive a passing grade in
    the course.

Test No.

1	2	3	4	5

complete ☐
incomplete ☐

Test No.: 1 = subject/verb agreement
           2 = sentence fragments
           3 = comma splices
           4 = punctuation errors
           5 = pronoun referents

II. Your journal will be checked on
     the average of every 2 weeks.
     When checked, each up-to-date
     journal is worth 4 points.

Week

2	4	6	8	11

20 possible points

Score _____

III. Of the 4 in-class essays derived
      from the source sheet subjects,
      3 of the 4 essays must meet
      the basic competency standards.
      Each of the 3 acceptable essays
      is worth 8.3 points. If your
      initial version of your essay does
      not meet the competency
      standards, it must be revised
      until it does.

In-class Essays

1	2	3	4

25 possible points

Score _____

Note: The maximum possible score is 25 points
(8.3 x 3 essays.) Writing 4 acceptable essays
will not give you a score of 33 -- take chances,
have fun.

IV. Of the 4 out-of-class papers,
     3 of the 4 must meet the basic
     competency standards. Each
     of the 3 acceptable papers is
     worth 10 points. If the
     initial version of your paper
     does not meet the competency
     standards, it must be revised
     until it does.

Out-of-Class Papers

1	2	3	4

30 possible points

Score _____

Note: The maximum possible score is 30 points
(10 x 3 papers). Writing 4 acceptable papers
will not give you a score of 40 -- take chances.
Engage complex & challenging subjects.

Paper No.: 1 = Childhood Experience Paper
           2 = Interview Paper
           3 = Library Paper
           4 = Final Paper
               (cannot be revised)

REQUIRED CLASSWORK -- TOTAL SCORE _____

V. To receive a grade higher than a C in
   the course, you must successfully
   revise 2 or more pieces of writing
   produced during the course that are
   worthy of revision. These revised
   texts must meet standards of absolute
   excellence. Variable points are
   awarded for these revised texts
   depending upon substance, quality,
   conceptual complexity, and so forth.

Revision 1

Revision 2

Revision 3

Revision 4

Revision 5

REVISIONS
25 possible points
Score _____

Final Grades

100 – 90 = A
89 – 80 = B
79 – 70 = C
69 – 60 = D
59 – 50 = F

Required classwork: _____
Revisions: _____

Final Score   _____
Final Grade   _____

Figure 7–B: Course Requirements and Sample Grade Record
for a Remedial Freshman Composition Course

Name _____   Freshman Composition, Sec. _____

Term _____   Year_____

I. You must pass all 5 of the usage tests at the 70% level or better to be eligible to receive a passing grade in the course. Each successfully completed test is worth 5 points.

Test No.

1	2	3	4	5

25 possible points

Score _____

complete ☐
incomplete ☐

Test No.: 1 = subject/verb agreement
2 = sentence fragment
3 = comma splices
4 = punctuation errors
5 = pronoun referents

II. Your journal will be checked on the average of every 2 weeks. When checked, each up-to-date journal is worth 4 points.

Week

2	4	6	8	11

20 possible points

Score _____

III. Of the 4 in-class essays derived from the source sheet subjects, 3 of the 4 essays must meet the basic competency standards. Each of the 3 acceptable essays is worth 6.7 points. If your initial version of your essay does not meet the competency standards, it must be revised until it does.

In-class Essays

1	2	3	4

20 possible points

Score _____

Note: The maximum possible score is 20 points (6.7 x 3 essays). Writing 4 acceptable essays will not give you a score of 27 -- take chances, have fun.

IV. Of the 3 out-of-class papers, 2 of the 3 must meet basic competency standards. Each of the 2 acceptable papers is worth 12.5 points. If the initial version of your paper does not meet the competency standards, it must be revised until it does.

Out-of-Class Papers

1	2	3

25 possible points

Score _____

Note: The maximum possible score is 25 points (12.5 x 2 papers). Writing 3 acceptable papers will not give you a score of 33 -- take chances. Engage complex & challenging subjects.

Paper No.: 1 = Childhood Experience Paper
2 = Interview Paper
3 = Final Paper
     (cannot be revised)

REQUIRED CLASSWORK -- TOTAL SCORE _____

V. To receive a grade higher than a B in the course, you must successfully revise 1 or more pieces of writing produced during the course that are worthy of revision. These revised texts must meet standards of absolute excellence. Variable points are awarded for these revised texts depending upon substance, quality, conceptual complexity, and so forth.

Revision 1
Revision 2
Revision 3

REVISIONS
10 possible points

Score _____

Final Grades

100 – 90 = A
89 – 80 = B
79 – 70 = C
69 – 60 = D
59 – 50 = F

Required classwork:_____
Revisions: _____

Final Score   _____
Final Grade   _____

These sample course requirements and grade records are only two examples of ways to manipulate weighting particular summative evaluation procedures within a writing curriculum. For each different course, the teacher needs to tailor the summative evaluation procedures to implement specific teaching objectives and match the skill levels of particular students. But translating these evaluation procedures into a final numerical or letter grade that reflects the overall level of the individual student's performance then becomes a simple mathematical procedure.

ESTABLISHING COMPETENCY CRITERIA
FOR ASSESSING STUDENT WRITING

The foregoing discussion of summative evaluation procedures has repeatedly referred to "competency criteria" for the assessment of individual pieces of writing. Now that the reader has an overall picture of a sophisticated evaluation system, it is time to discuss competency criteria in depth.

One of the students', particularly weaker ones', perennial gripes is that they do not understand why they receive the grades that they do on their writing. Admittedly, it is difficult for teachers to be consistent in grading when they have to confront multiple sets of writing assignments on a Sunday afternoon. But the student complaint, "I don't know what the teacher is looking for," reflects a deeper problem.

Essentially what students are saying is that they do not understand the basic criteria by which all writing is evaluated. One of the fundamental characteristics of mature writers is the ability to evaluate the quality of their own writing, both texts in process and completed texts. The ability to assess the strengths and weaknesses of one's writing is a critical component in the development of a writer. Mature writers do not always produce successful texts, but typically they can identify their major problems. Unless writers can isolate and understand the problems in their writing, they have little or no chance of resolving them (Flower et al., 1986). For many students, writing their way through a sequence of composition assignments is like playing a game of chess without fully understanding the rules. Not only do they commit some of the same basic strategic errors over and over, but they make different types of mistakes on different assignments. For example, on the first in-class essay, the student may have a clearly identified central idea and thesis but does not define any of the concepts subordinated to her thesis and instead merely lists them like items on a grocery list. After considerable feedback from the teacher, the student may proceed in the next essay to define in detail individual concepts but does not subordinate them to a central idea. This type of nonaccumulative progression

through a sequence of writing assignments drives both the students and their teacher to distraction.

Clearly what is required is a set of basic competency criteria that can be applied to all types of writing. If students are to become successful writers, they must learn that there are basic criteria by which all writing is evaluated, whether it takes place in an English course, in a biology course, in the "real world" of job-related writing, or in the context of personal correspondence. These criteria need to be operationally defined and redefined for students throughout the progression of the course. Additional stylistic, bibliographical, and research requirements may come into play in specialized subject areas, but the *basic competency criteria* by which all writing is assessed remain the same for all writers in all situations.

In our classes, we use a modified version of Paul Diedrich's (1974) analytic scale and use six key criteria to assess all writing: (1) central idea, (2) development, (3) organization, (4) audience, (5) conceptualization, and (6) mechanics. Each criterion is defined in terms of high, middle, and low competency. These basic competency criteria are shown in Figure 7–C.

After students have been presented with an operational definition of competency criteria that can be applied to all the writing that they produce, the real problem is to teach these criteria in the context of the students' own work. Initially, we adopted two strategies. First, we developed a master set of heuristic questions that were keyed to each individual criterion, and we handed them out with the competency criteria at the beginning of the term. (See "Two Sides of the Same Coin," in Appendix 7–A at the end of this chapter.) Then, throughout the semester we reproduced sample student essays from other classes and asked students to critique them using the competency criteria.

We would like to be able to report that these measures were successful in assisting students to internalize the competency criteria as formative criteria for producing prose and as summative criteria for evaluating prose. Unfortunately, posttests at the end of the term, in which students were asked to apply the criteria to a piece of their own writing and to two other student papers, demonstrated that a majority of the students could not apply the criteria with any consistency. We concluded that two additional measures were necessary. First, students need to *practice* applying the criteria to real pieces of writing again and again under *controlled conditions* in which they are given feedback about and held accountable for their summative evaluations of substantive texts. Second, if students are to make the necessary self-investment to internalize the competency criteria, they need to be *personally involved* in the summative evaluation procedures by which a significant portion of their grade is determined.

Figure 7–C: Basic Competency Criteria

CRITERION 1: CENTRAL IDEA

HIGH   The text has one clear central idea.

The central idea controls the development of the text and is sufficiently limited to be manageable within the limits of the assignment.

MIDDLE   The text does not have one clear central idea.

Multiple ideas may receive equal attention in the text and its topic may be too broad to be covered within the limits of the assignment.

LOW   The text has no central idea.

The reader is unable to determine the text's central idea. There is little or no apparent control over the content of the text.

CRITERION 2: DEVELOPMENT

HIGH   The text's central idea is sufficiently and logically developed.

The text offers sufficient detail to support the central idea to the reader's satisfaction. Subordinated ideas clearly relate to the central idea and are also sufficiently supported. The main points are given greatest emphasis; others are emphasized in proportion to their importance.

MIDDLE   The text's central idea is not sufficiently and logically developed.

The reader senses gaps in the factual and logical development of the central idea. Generalities and abstractions may be used when more concrete and specifc detail is needed.

LOW   The text's central idea is given no support.

The text may merely repeat the central idea without developing it, or the supporting evidence may be confusing and difficult to relate to the central idea.

CRITERION 3: ORGANIZATION

HIGH   The order and method of presentation are clear.

Sentences and paragraphs are sequential and readable. Appropriate transitions signal the relationships of various divisions of the text.

MIDDLE   The order and method of presentation are sometimes forced or even unclear.

Occasionally the text is difficult to read.

LOW   There is no apparent order or method to the text.

Whether the text is one long paragraph or many short ones, the reader cannot see a relationship of ideas; nothing appears sequential.

Figure 7–C: (*Continued*)

CRITERION 4:   AUDIENCE

HIGH   The text clearly takes its audience into account.

The text's purpose, diction, and style are consistent and appropriate for its intended audience.

MIDDLE   The text is not consistent in its awareness of audience.

The text's purpose, diction, and style are not consistent, and at times they are not appropriate for the intended audience.

LOW   The text exhibits no awareness of audience.

CRITERION 5:   CONCEPTUALIZATION

HIGH   Concepts are synthesized into a coherent plan.

Individual concepts are precisely defined. Concepts are precisely interrelated in a complex plan, scheme, pattern—for example, by means of causes and effects or comparisons and contrasts of size, duration, and number.

MIDDLE   Concepts are minimally interrelated.

Individual concepts are for the most part adequately defined, but they are only loosely interrelated to an organized plan.

LOW   Concepts are merely labeled.

Individual concepts are not adequately defined in terms of their essential characteristics, nor are concepts logically related one to another.

CRITERION 6:   MECHANICS

HIGH   The text adheres to accepted standards of grammar, spelling, punctuation, capitalization, and usage: for research writing, bibliographical format is correct.

MIDDLE   Occasional errors in mechanics mar the text.

The text has some annoying errors in spelling or other mechanics. Errors in grammar and usage may interfere with the reader's ease of comprehension.

LOW   The text contains errors on almost every line.

Errors are so numerous that the text is difficult to read and often impossible to understand.

These criteria were developed by Professors Roland Huff, Ronald Reed, and King Buchanan with the assistance of the heads of all academic departments at Lubbock Christian College, Lubbock, Texas, 1986. They were adopted as college-wide criteria for the assessment of writing in all subject areas.

If students are unable to judge for themselves the strengths and weaknesses of their finished work, it is unlikely that they will learn from their mistakes and use that knowledge to guide themselves to produce increasingly sophisticated texts in the future. Even if a returned paper is accompanied by extensive written comments, the teacher's summative evaluation — the grade — seems to have only minimal effect on the next paper written by the student unless the teacher confers with each writer about her finished paper (Beach, 1980; Bereiter & Scardamalia, 1982; Bracewell, Scardamalia, & Bereiter, 1978; Hansen, 1978).

Students also need to learn how to evaluate their finished texts so that they can engage in the act of appreciating their achievement. Without informed judgment, there can be little significant appreciation. We know that immature writers spend little or no time reading back through their completed work and valuing it (Flower & Hayes, 1980; Pianko, 1979); mature writers do. Without the reinforcement of appreciating what they have achieved, few writers would continue to write. The act of judgment is a critical component of a mature composing process.

INTEGRATING SUMMATIVE EVALUATION
INTO STUDENTS' COMPOSING PROCESSES

There are at least three ways in which integrating summative evaluation into the students' composing process is profitable. First, continuing development as a writer requires evaluating that which is already written. Second, justifying a summative evaluation of one's own or a peer's text in front of a group requires a perspective-taking that sharpens social skills and a sense of audience. Third, a student who evaluates texts summatively internalizes much more realistic standards by which to produce and appreciate writing than does a student who writes solely for a teacher's grade-book.

Peer Groups and Holistic Scoring

The College Entrance Examination Board uses "holistic" scoring to assess student writing (for an extended discussion of CEEB procedures, see Godshalk, Swineford, & Coffman, 1966). The first step in holistic scoring is to establish a set of competency criteria that all evaluators understand and can accept. After evaluators have adopted the criteria, they practice reading and scoring sample student essays. The readings are done quickly (two minutes for sophisticated readers), and the essays are scored holistically on a numerical scale. For example, if the rating scale ranges from 1 to

6, the reader assigns the essay a single whole number on that continuum — taking into account all of the competency criteria.

After scoring each sample student essay or set of essays, the readers compare the holistic scores they assigned each student essay and discuss any divergence in their scoring. The training process continues until the readers reach reliability; that is, most of the readers, most of the time, will assign a given student essay a similar score. When the timed readings have reached inter-reader reliability, ideally no more than a three-point spread on a six-point scale, the actual scoring of student essays is fairly simple. Each essay is read quickly on a timed basis and scored by multiple readers, and the scores are averaged to generate a reliable score.

The first step in integrating holistic scoring into the writing curriculum is to establish a common set of competency criteria. The logic of the criteria is essential. In our classes, we use the previously described analytic scale based on central idea, development, organization, audience, conceptualization, and mechanics. After students have discussed, understood, and agreed upon the criteria, the most difficult part of introducing holistic scoring as a summative evaluation procedure in the classroom is training students to be reliable readers.

In classes already divided into peer response groups of six, each student essay can be read and independently scored by half a dozen students. A six-member group is large enough to allow for and yet balance out divergent opinions. However, unless peer readings can be made reliable (ideally involving no more than a three-point spread on the six-point scale), the average-scoring of the student essay is not significant.

Selecting Sample Student Essays

The quickest way to train students to be reliable readers is to have them practice reading selected sample student essays. Choosing these sample essays carefully is critical; the teacher should select them from large numbers of student essays written the term *before* the one in which she introduces holistic scoring into the writing curriculum. The essays need to be chosen with the following five criteria in mind:

1. All sample student essays should be selected from the same types of writing assignments that the students will be evaluating. General subjects, mode, and time constraints also need to be the same.
2. The teacher should not try to select the sample student essays without help. Even a trained reader is not likely to be a reliable reader all the time. Ideally, five or six teachers would score significant numbers of

student papers, and the sample student essays would be selected from those group scores.

3. A number of sample student essays need to be selected to serve as "boundary" essays. If a six-point scale is used, a boundary essay is one that falls between a 1 and a 2, or between a 3 and a 4, or between a 5 and a 6. The trained readers should all agree on the borderline status of the boundary essays. We suggest that three essays be found for each of the three boundary lines and that a brief justification be attached to each essay explaining why the trained readers considered it a boundary essay. The boundary essays are used throughout the course to assist students in defining common standards for scoring. When scoring a paper, students first determine whether it is a high, middle, or low paper. The students' repeated readings and discussions of the boundary essays then serve as touchstones to help establish whether the given paper is a 1 or 2, a 3 or 4, or a 5 or 6.

4. After the boundary essays have been chosen, complete sets of sample student essays need to be constructed. Given that the teacher is using a six-point scoring scale, it is useful for training purposes to have sets of student essays consisting of six papers that force a spread of high, middle, and low scores. If possible, the teacher should construct ten sets of these essays, six for initial training and four for periodic retraining and reinforcement.

5. Although it is not absolutely essential, typing the boundary essays and the sets of training essays aids speed and ease of reading. In actual practice, when students are scoring their peers' in-class essays, they will be reading handwritten essays.

Admittedly, it is initially time-consuming to select and duplicate the boundary essays and the sets of training essays. But once the sets of essays have been reproduced, they can be reused to train class after class. The actual training of students to be reliable readers is much less time-consuming and takes place during class.

Training Procedures for Holistic Scoring

Early in the course, students are introduced to the modified Diedrich analytic evaluation scale — the basic competency criteria. After considerable discussion of the terms and definitions of the criteria, the concept of holistic scoring on a six-point scale is explained. When reading and scoring sample student essays, readers are encouraged first to assign a high (6-5), middle (4-3), or low (2-1) score, and then to determine whether the essay

should be assigned the higher or lower score within that category. The boundary essays that fall between 6 to 5, 4 to 3, and 2 to 1 scores are discussed at length in order to establish common standards.

After the holistic scoring procedures have been explained, the class scores two sets of six sample student essays. For training purposes, all members of the class are provided with duplicated copies of all of the essays. These sets of sample essays are carefully chosen to force a spread of scores across the six-point scale, and students are particularly encouraged to award scores at both the high and low ends.

For the first set of essays, students are given four minutes to read and score each essay. (We alert the students when three of the four minutes have passed.) After each paper has been scored, the class compares scores. Those members of the class whose scores represent extreme deviations from the norm are asked to explain their reasoning. After a class discussion of the essay's scoring, with an emphasis on "reliability" rather than "correctness," students spend four minutes scoring another essay and repeat the procedure of comparing the scores and discussing the reasons for extreme deviations of readers' responses. When the first set of six papers has been scored in this manner, students reread the boundary essays, and the teacher leads a discussion that clarifies in greater depth the function of the boundary essays and the nature of holistic scoring in general. The class then proceeds to score and discuss each essay of the second set of sample essays.

After this general introduction to holistic scoring, the class is divided into their six-member peer response groups. Each member of each group is given a third set of six sample essays. After scoring each sample essay, group members compare their scores and discuss extreme deviations. When the first six essays have been scored and discussed in this manner, the groups repeat the procedure with a fourth set of six essays.

This training procedure, which may stretch over a period of a week, establishes a high degree of reliability between the scores in each group. At this point, each response group proceeds to score three sets of six sample student essays, but this time each group is provided with only one copy of each of the six essays. Each member spends four minutes reading an essay and scoring it; she then passes it to a member sitting next to her. After *all six* essays have been scored, the members of the group compare scores and discuss any essays that have produced extremely disparate scores. Each student reads independently; the group provides checks on criteria and a structure for organizing the activity.

For a more detailed description of holistic scoring, the reader may wish to consult Miles Myers' (1980) *A Procedure for Writing Assessment and Holistic Scoring.*

Holistic Scoring of In-class Essays

After having been trained to be reliable readers, students apply holistic scoring to the in-class essays of their peers. First, students spend three class days drafting an in-class essay (Huff, 1983). Three days are allotted to draft the essay since research suggests that more than one class period is desirable if in-class essays are to serve as useful vehicles of writing development (Hartvigsen, 1981; Sanders & Littlefield, 1975). Moreover, the three days spent drafting the essay give the teacher time to conference with students who are having problems or are working on revisions. (Students who spend extensive time in conference with the teacher are expected to make up that drafting time at home, and the completion of their drafts is checked at the beginning of the next class.)

At the end of the third day of the in-class writing assignment, students are expected to turn in their completed essays. On the next day of class, they are organized into their six-member response groups for the purpose of holistically scoring the essays. To reinforce and update reader reliability, the class rereads the boundary essays and scores three or more sample essays that trained readers have identified as high (5 or 6), middle (4 or 3), and low (2 or 1) essays. After students have scored the "training essays," scores are correlated and disparate scores are discussed.

Subsequently, each group scores the essays written by one of the other groups. The essays are identified by Roman numerals I through VI and by part of the student identification number rather than by the author's name. In order to get a full spread of scores, it is particularly important to reemphasize that any paper higher than the 6 to 5 boundary essay is a 6, and any paper lower than the 2 to 1 boundary essay is a 1. It is also helpful to inform students that anyone receiving a low overall score (below an average of 3.0) on her paper will be allowed to revise and resubmit the essay.

The actual procedure of scoring essays is quite simple. Each member of the group is provided with a scoring chart (see Figure 7–D) and a student essay. After students record the student identification number of the essay beside the corresponding Roman numeral on the scoring chart, they are given four minutes to read the essay. At the end of that time, they record their score for the essay on the score sheet and give the essay to the student next to them. This method of passing the essays around in daisy-chain fashion eliminates the need to have more than one copy of each essay. The procedure is repeated until all of the essays have been scored by each member of the group. The groups then exchange papers and retrieve their own essays, at which time they are asked to write their own names on their papers next to their student identification numbers.

Figure 7–D: Peer Scoring Chart

Group # ___3___   Name ___Martha Rice___
                    Student I. D. ___463 - 00 - 9971___

Your code letter, "a" through "f": __b__   (Each group member selects a different code letter.)

Paper #	Score Given to Sample Essay					
	1	2	3	4	5	6
I			✓			
II				✓		
III			✓			
(IV)				✓		
(V)	✓					
(VI)				✓		

Paper #	Student I. D.	Score Given to Peer Essay					
		1	2	3	4	5	6
I	5-4972				✓		
II	8-1131						✓
III	6-3536		✓				
IV	5-8998			✓			
V	3-1902			✓			
VI	6-2322						✓

Score assigned by writer to his or her own essay: | 4 |

The final scoring task is for each writer, after having read and evaluated six other essays, to score her own essay. It is critical that students learn to make accurate and credible summative judgments about their own finished texts.

When students have finished scoring their own essays, all score sheets and essays are passed to the teacher. The entire peer evaluation procedure can be accomplished in one fifty-minute period if the teacher uses a timer for the reading of the essays and *stringently* enforces the four-minute time

limit for reading the essays. Slow readers will be pushed to complete reading longer essays within the time limit, but they *must* assign a score when time is up, even if they have not completely finished reading the essay. (Remember, Educational Testing Services allows readers only two minutes to read essays of comparable length.)

The Teacher's Role in Peer Evaluation

Although it involves a fair amount of paper shuffling, the teacher's role in peer evaluation is not difficult and after practice can be completed in an hour to an hour and a half — a far cry from the time it would take to grade and comment on a full set of student essays. The teacher constructs a master scoring chart for each group's work (e.g., five charts for a class of thirty students) and lists the six peer-assigned scores given to each essay (see Figure 7–E). Then the teacher uses a calculator to average the scores for each essay and records them to the nearest first decimal place on the master scoring chart.

Ideally, the spread of scores is no more than three points, but a spread of four points can be common — balanced by a score of a 2 and a 5, for example, which cancel each other out. However, if the group's scoring of an individual essay has a radical disparity — for instance, a cluster of 1's and 2's set off against a cluster of 3's and 4's — the teacher needs to intervene on behalf of the writer, read the essay, and assign it a score herself. If in the teacher's opinion the essay warrants a higher score than the average peer score, she may adjust the score upward. We encourage teachers not to adjust the score downward because it tends to destroy the credibility of peer scoring in the eyes of the students.

Figure 7–E: Master Scoring Chart

Group # ___3___   Date _____

Paper #	Student I. D.	Reader–Assigned Scores							Author's Self–Score
		a	b	c	d	e	f	Average	
I	5-4972	3	4	3	4	4	3	3.5	4
II	8-1131	6	6	5	6	6	5	5.7	5
III	6-3536	3	2	3	2	4	2	2.7	3
IV	5-8998	5	3	3	4	3	3	3.5	3
V	3-1902	3	3	3	4	4	3	3.3	4
VI	6-2322	6	6	6	6	5	5	5.7	6

After recording the average score of each essay for all the groups on the master scoring charts, the teacher records in another column the score that the writer assigned her own essay. Essays are returned with the average (P)eer score and the (W)riter's score juxtaposed on the first page — for example, P2.7/W3. If there is an extreme divergence between the two scores, the need for a conference with the writer is indicated. For the teacher's purposes, she records the peer score and the writer's score on the essay and on each student's grade record. Ideally, this averaging and adjusting of the group scores takes place within 24 hours, and the essays are returned the following class day.

At the beginning of the next class session, the teacher returns the essays to the individual authors. She also hands out duplicated copies of two master scoring charts to each group: (1) the chart that shows the six scores assigned by another group to each of this group's essays, so that the students can see how their peers rated their papers, and (2) the chart that shows the scores this group assigned to the essays of another group. This second chart allows each group member to compare her scorings with those of the group and identify any patterns of divergence. Did she consistently score essays too high or too low? A consistent but unpatterned divergence from the group norm indicates that the group member needs to set up a conference with the teacher; the student has not internalized the evaluation criteria. If more than two members of a group are unreliable evaluators, the teacher may wish to conference with the entire group and provide them with special training in reliable reading.

After students have had a chance to compare the group scoring of their own essays with their individual scoring and to analyze their reliability as readers, the teacher passes out duplicated copies of three or four problem essays, that is, essays that produced widely divergent scores. The class as a whole is asked to read and rescore these essays. After each essay has been scored, individual scores are correlated and the essay is discussed in some depth. If the teacher chooses the problem essays carefully, the discussion of the reasons for the divergence in scores can illuminate for the students a variety of conceptual, organizational, and stylistic issues.

When students have been trained to be reliable readers and have gone through this process of peer evaluation once, it is fairly effortless to repeat the sequence of (a) writing a three-day in-class essay, (b) spending one class day in peer evaluation, and (c) analyzing the scores and selected problem essays in a follow-up class session. This cycle, which is aimed at the student's internalizing evaluative strategies and criteria, needs to be repeated at scheduled intervals throughout the course. It is important to note that this process of peer evaluation is designed only for evaluating in-class essays, which limit time constraints, types of subjects, and modes; out-of-

class papers are harder to score due to extreme variations in student investment and length of text (the timed four-minute reading is no longer
feasible).

Translating Peer Scorings into Grades

In our classrooms, we do not actually award letter grades for in-class
essays, but rather assess them on a mastery basis for competency. Any
average score below 3.0 requires that the essay be rewritten until it meets
competency standards. Three out of four in-class essays must meet competency standards for the student to receive full credit for this portion of the
course. If, however, a teacher wishes to assign a grade for the essays, the
six-point scoring scale can be translated into letter grades. In this case, the
averaging of the scores to the nearest first decimal point is crucial. In our
experience, 6 to 4.9 equals an A; 4.8 to 3.7 equals a B; 3.6 to 2.5 equals a
C; 2.4 to 1.3 equals a D; and 1.2 and below equals an F. This adjusted
grading scale tends to compensate for the lack of unanimous scores of 6 at
the high end of the scale and students' tendency to avoid giving scores of 1
at the low end of the scale except in extreme cases. (Individual teachers
need to establish their own adjusted grading scales in accordance with the
realities of their classrooms.)

BUT: DOES IT WORK?
IS IT WORTH IT?

Yet the question remains, "Does peer evaluation work?" Fortunately,
in addition to the testimony of teacher experience, there is empirical evidence of its effectiveness. Hadley and Huff (1984), Lynch (1982), Millet
(1969), Sager (1973), and Thompson (1981) have all reported success in
teaching students to use analytic rating scales to evaluate their own and/or
each other's writing. In a current review and analysis of the research,
Hillocks (1986) states:

> Apparently, the active application of criteria and subsequent suggestions
> for improvement in their own and others' writing enabled the students to
> internalize criteria which then served as guides for their own indepen-
> dent writing. (p. 158)

Hillocks concludes:

These studies indicate rather clearly that engaging young writers actively in the use of criteria, applied to their own or to others' writing, results
not only in more effective revisions but in superior first drafts. . . . Most
of them show significant gains for experimental groups, suggesting that
the criteria learned act not only as guides for revision but as guides for
generating new material. (p. 160)

The second question likely to be raised by practicing teachers is, "Can
the instructional time consumed by peer evaluation be justified?" Our
subjective response is that anything that cuts a teacher's grading responsibilities in half is worth it. But from a more objective perspective, peer
evaluation plays an essential role in teaching students how to write for a
number of reasons. First, if the holistic scoring of the writer's essay has
been determined by peer readers, the writer begins to realize that real
writing is judged by the effect that it has on a real audience — not by a
grade awarded by a teacher. Second, if the peer scores of the writer's essay
are reliable — the majority of the readers agree on the essay's score — the
students begin to understand that the comparative quality of a piece of
writing is not just a matter of opinion, and that there are real criteria by
which all writing is judged: focus on central idea, development and support, organization, match to needs of audience, conceptualized plan of the
text, and mechanics.

Peer evaluation is at least as important for the student evaluators as it
is for the writer. Only by weighing and considering a variety of texts of
assorted quality can young writers begin to internalize operationally the
criteria by which to judge what a substantive and successful text looks like
and reads like. Without criteria by which to define good writing, the
young writer is hopelessly adrift in the struggle to produce a quality text.
Learning how to evaluate a text is just as important as learning how to
produce one; the two orders of knowledge are interpenetrating aspects of
the composing process.

APPENDIX 7–A
TWO SIDES OF THE SAME COIN:
TRANSLATING COMPETENCY CRITERIA INTO
THE PRODUCTION OF QUALITY PROSE

[This student handout is given to members of the class at the same time they receive the description of the competency criteria used to *evaluate* the final products of writing.]

The criteria by which writing is evaluated and the principles by which competent writing is produced are two sides of the same coin. The competency criteria for evaluating finished pieces of writing need to be internalized as principles that guide and assist you in composing particular texts.

The competency standards for evaluating writing in this class are based on six criteria: (1) central idea, (2) development, (3) organization, (4) audience, (5) conceptualization, and (6) mechanics. To help you internalize these criteria, the following questions attempt to transform the criteria into principles designed to guide you in writing competent prose.

The type of questions we suggest you ask yourself during the writing process are derived from research on the composing processes of mature writers. These are, in fact, the type of questions that successful writers ask themselves during the production of competent prose. These questions are not designed to be answered on a "yes" or "no" basis. Nor will all of the questions be relevant to the writing of any particular piece of prose. Rather, the purpose of the questions is to create a "field of awareness" during the composing process that alerts you to both the problems and the possibilities in the conceptual and organizational structure of your text as it evolves.

If you make a habit of asking the following questions during the writing process, you will find that after awhile they ask themselves. You will have internalized the criteria for evaluating writing as a way of conceptualizing and structuring your thinking. If you do not learn to ask these types of questions during the composing of a text, they will come back to haunt you as the criteria by which your writing will be evaluated. The trick is to ask the questions before you are judged by the answers. They are two sides of the same coin. Following are types of questions that need to be asked during the writing of a text:

THE WRITER'S QUESTIONS

1. *Central Idea*
    A. What is the central idea or thesis of your text?
    B. Are all of your major ideas clearly subordinated to the central idea?

C. Could one of your subordinated ideas better serve as the central idea?

D. Does your first paragraph clearly establish the central idea of the text? Could you just as well start with your second paragraph?

2. *Development*

A. Are all of your major ideas demonstrated with concrete examples or specific evidence? Could you use more interesting or humorous examples and evidence?

B. Are there transitions that lead the reader logically and naturally from one idea to another, from one paragraph to another?

C. Where do you need to add a paragraph? Where do you need to delete a paragraph? Is each paragraph adequately developed?

3. *Organization*

A. Are all of your ideas relevant? If the text has three major ideas, could you get by with two? Or do you need a fourth?

B. Would the progression of the text profit from a reordering of the sequence of the major ideas? Where could you reorder the sequence of your paragraphs?

C. Are there places in the text where what follows doesn't connect with what comes before — where the flow of the text breaks?

D. Does the conclusion clearly tell the audience what you expect them to think or do? Could you end the text with the next-to-the-last paragraph?

4. *Audience*

A. How old are the members of this audience? How are they dressed? How well-informed are they about this topic? Do they all hold the same basic opinions about the topic?

B. How well-informed are you about the topic? How are you dressed? How formal or informal is the word choice and syntax of the paper? Are the diction and style appropriate to the relationship between you and the audience?

C. Is the intended audience likely to believe or accept what you say? How might you change your stance to communicate better with the audience? How might a member of the audience be changed by reading this text?

D. Is your point of view consistent and appropriate?

5. *Conceptualization*

A. Are you interested in this topic? Does it represent at some level a problem you are invested in exploring? Is this topic worth writing about?

B. Do you know enough to write about this topic? Are all of your assertions and arguments supported with convincing evidence? Do you need to go to the library? (Don't kid yourself.)

C. Are your major ideas related in ways that you have not shown — by means of causes and effects or comparisons and contrasts of size, duration, and number? Would making such relationships explicit strengthen and enrich the text?

D. Have you adequately replied to and accounted for arguments or theories that differ from your presentation of the topic?

6. *Mechanics* (When writing out-of-class papers, *do not* concern yourself with mechanics until after you have produced a working draft of your paper as a whole.)

A. Assuming you have already produced a working draft, have you proofread your text for the following items?

1. Subject–verb agreement
2. Sentence fragments
3. Comma splices
4. Punctuation errors
5. Pronoun referents
6. Spelling and typographical errors

B. With an appropriate style guide *in hand*, have you checked your citations and bibliography for correct form?

References

Adams, D., & Kline, C. (1975). The use of film in teaching composition. *College Composition and Communication, 26*, 258–262.

Beach, R. (1976). Self-evaluation strategies of extensive revisers and nonrevisers. *College Composition and Communication, 27*, 160–164.

Beach, R. (1979). The effects of between-draft teacher evaluation versus student self-evaluation on high school students' revising of rough drafts. *Research in the Teaching of English, 13*, 111–119.

Beach, R. (1980). *The self-assessing strategies of remedial college students.* Paper presented at the annual meeting of the American Educational Research Association, Boston, MA.

Beach, R. (1982). Pragmatics of self-assessing. In R. Sudol (Ed.), *Revising: New essays for teachers of writing* (pp. 71–83). Urbana, IL: National Council of Teachers of English.

Beaven, M. (1977). Individualized goal setting, self-evaluation, and peer evaluation. In C. Cooper & L. Odell (Eds.), *Evaluating writing: Describing, measuring, judging* (pp. 135–156). Urbana, IL: National Council of Teachers of English.

Bereiter, C., & Scardamalia, M. (1982). From conversation to composition: The role of instruction in a developmental process. In R. Glaser (Ed.), *Advances in instructional psychology: Vol. 2* (pp. 1–64). Hillsdale, NJ: Lawrence Erlbaum Associates.

Berlyne, D. (1966). Notes on intrinsic motivation and intrinsic reward in relation to instruction. In J. Bruner (Ed.), *Learning about learning* (pp. 104–105). Washington: U. S. Department of Health, Education, and Welfare, Office of Education.

Blake, R., & Mouton, J. (1961). Comprehension of own and outgroup positions under intergroup competition. *Journal of Conflict Resolution, 5*, 304–310.

Blatt, M., & Kohlberg, L. (1973). The effects of classroom moral discussion upon children's level of moral judgement. In L. Kohlberg (Ed.), *Collected papers on moral development and moral education.* Cambridge, MA: Moral Education and Research Foundation, Harvard University.

Blumenthal, J. C. (1973). *English 2200: A programmed course in grammar and usage* (4th ed.). New York: Harcourt Brace Jovanovich.

Blumenthal, J. C. (1973). *English 2600: A programmed course in grammar and usage* (4th ed.). New York: Harcourt Brace Jovanovich.

Blumenthal, J. C. (1973). *English 3200: A programmed course in grammar and usage* (4th ed.). New York: Harcourt Brace Jovanovich.

Boiarsky, C. (1982). Prewriting is the essence of writing. *English Journal, 71*, 44–47.

Bracewell, R., Scardamalia, M., & Bereiter, C. (1978). *The development of audience awareness in writing*. (ERIC Document Reproduction Service No. ED 154 433.)

Braddock, R., Lloyd-Jones, R., & Schoer, L. (1963). *Research in written composition*. Urbana, IL: National Council of Teachers of English.

Bridwell, L. S. (1980). Revising strategies in twelfth grade students' transactional writing. *Research in the Teaching of English, 14*, 197–222.

Britton, J., Burgess, T., Martin, N., McLeod, A., & Rosen, H. (1975). *The development of writing abilities (11–18)*. London: Macmillan Education Ltd.

Bruffee, K. (1978). The Brooklyn Plan: Attaining intellectual growth through peer-group tutoring. *Liberal Education, 64*, 447–469.

Burke, K. (1969). *A rhetoric of motives*. Berkeley: University of California Press.

Clifford, J. (1981). Composing in stages: The effect of a collaborative pedagogy. *Research in the Teaching of English, 15*, 37–53.

Cooper, C., & Odell, L. (Eds.). (1978). *Research on composing: Points of departure*. Urbana, IL: National Council of Teachers of English.

Corbett, E. P. J. (1971). *Classical rhetoric for the modern student* (2nd ed.). New York: Oxford University Press.

Corey, G., Corey, S. C., Callanan, P. J., Russell, J. M. (1982). *Group techniques*. Monterey, CA: Brooks/Cole.

Crawford, J., & Haaland, G. (1972). Predecisional information seeking and subsequent conformity in the social influence process. *Journal of Personality and Social Psychology, 23*, 112–119.

Dabrowski, K. (1964). *Positive disintegration*. Boston: Little, Brown.

Denn, R. J. (1982). The Delphi technique: Revising as problem solving. In R. Sudol (Ed.), *Revising: New essays for teachers of writing* (pp. 140–143). Urbana, IL: National Council of Teachers of English.

Diedrich, P. (Ed.). (1974). *Measuring growth in English*. Urbana, IL: National Council of Teachers of English.

Dixon, J. (1967). *Growth through English: A report based on the Dartmouth Seminar*. Reading, England: National Association for the Teaching of English.

Egan, G. (1973). *Face to face*. Monterey, CA: Brooks/Cole.

Elbow, P. (1973). *Writing without teachers*. New York: Oxford University Press.

Emig, J. (1971). *The composing process of twelfth graders*. Urbana, IL: National Council of Teachers of English.

Faigley, L., Miller, T., Meyer, P., & Witte, S. (1981). *Writing after college: A stratified survey of the writing of college trained people* (Tech. Rep. No. 1). Austin: University of Texas.

Festinger, L. (1957). *A theory of cognitive dissonance*. Stanford, CA: Stanford University Press.

Field, J. P., & Weiss, R. H. (1984). *Cases for composition*. Boston: Little, Brown, & Company.

Figg, K. M. (1980). Introducing invention techniques: A middle school writing assignment. *English Journal, 69*, 60–61.

Flanigan, M., & Menendez, D. S. (1980). Perception and change: Teaching revision. *College English, 42*, 256–266.

Flower, L. (1979). Writer-based prose: A cognitive basis for problems in writing. *College English, 41*, 19–37.

Flower, L. (1981). *Problem-solving strategies for writing.* New York: Harcourt Brace Jovanovich.

Flower, L., & Hayes, J. R. (1980). The cognition of discovery: Defining a rhetorical problem. *College Composition and Communication, 31*, 21–32.

Flower, L., & Hayes, J. R. (1981). Plans that guide the composing process. In C. Fredericksen & J. Dominic (Eds.), *Writing: The nature, development, and teaching of written communication: Vol. 2.*, 39–58. Hillsdale, NJ: Lawrence Erlbaum Associates.

Flower, L., Hayes, J. R., Carey, L., Shriver, K., & Stratman, J. (1986). Detection, diagnosis, and the strategies of revision. *College Composition and Communication, 37*, 16–55.

Frondizi, R. (1963). *What is value?* LaSalle, IL: Open Court.

Frost, R. (1964). *Complete poems of Robert Frost.* New York: Holt, Rinehart & Winston.

Fulwiler, T. (1982). Teaching teachers to teach revision. In R. Sudol (Ed.), *Revising: New essays for teachers of writing* (pp. 100–108). Urbana, IL: National Council of Teachers of English.

Garibaldi, A. (1979). The effective contributions of cooperative and group goal structures. *Journal of Educational Psychology, 71*, 788–795.

Gebhardt, R. (1979). *Teamwork and feedback: Broadening the base of collaborative writing.* Paper presented at the annual meeting of the Conference on College Composition and Communication. (ED 174 994.)

George, D. (1984). Working with peer groups in the composition classroom. *College Composition and Communication, 35*, 320–326.

Godshalk, F., Swineford, F., & Coffman, W. (1966). *The measurement of writing ability.* New York: College Entrance Examination Board.

Gunderson, B., & Johnson, D. (1980). Promoting positive attitudes toward learning a foreign language by using cooperative learning groups. *Foreign Language Annals, 13*, 39–46.

Hadley, D., & Huff, R. (1984). *Peer evaluation and holistic scoring.* Unpublished manuscript.

Hairston, M. (1982). The winds of change: Thomas Kuhn and the revolution in the teaching of writing. *College Composition and Communication, 33*, 76–88.

Hansen, B. (1978). Rewriting is a waste of time. *College English, 39*, 956–960.

Hartvigsen, M. K. (1981). *A comparative study of quality and syntactic maturity between in-class and out-of-class writing samples of freshmen at Washington State University.* Unpublished doctoral dissertation, Washington State University, Pullman, WA.

Haswell, R. H. (1983). Minimal marking. *College English, 45*, 600–604.

Hawkins, T. (1976). Group inquiry techniques for teaching writing. *College English, 37*, 637–640.

Hawkins, T. (1980). The relationship between revision and the social dimension of peer tutoring. *College English, 40,* 64–68.

Hayes, J. R., & Flower, L. (1980). Identifying the organization of writing processes. In L. Gregg & E. Steinberg (Eds.), *Cognitive processes in writing* (pp. 3–30). Hillsdale, NJ: Lawrence Erlbaum Associates.

Healy, M. K. (1982). Using student writing response groups in the classroom. In G. Camp (Ed.), *Teaching writing: Essays from the Bay Area Writing Project.* Montclair, NJ: Boynton Cook.

Heilman, R. (1970). Except he come to composition. *College Composition and Communication, 10,* 230–238.

Hilgers, T. L. (1980). Training college composition students in the use of freewriting and problem-solving heuristics for rhetorical invention. *Research in the Teaching of English, 14,* 293–307.

Hillocks, G. (1975). *Observing and writing.* Urbana, IL: National Council of Teachers of English and ERIC Clearinghouse on Reading and Communication Skills.

Hillocks, G. (1982). The interaction of instruction, teacher comment, and revision in teaching the composing process. *Research in the Teaching of English, 16,* 261–278.

Hillocks, G. (1986). *Research on written composition: New directions for teaching.* Urbana, IL: National Conference on Research in English and ERIC Clearinghouse on Reading and Communication Skills.

Hodges, K. (1982). A history of revision: Theory versus practice. In R. Sudol (Ed.), *Revising: New essays for teachers of writing* (pp. 24–42). Urbana, IL: National Council of Teachers of English.

Huff, R. (1983). Teaching revision: A model of the drafting process. *College English, 45,* 800–819.

Hull, G. (1981). Effects of self-management strategies on journal writing by college freshmen. *Research in the Teaching of English, 15,* 135–148.

Inhelder, B., & Sinclair, H. (1969). Learning cognitive structures. In P. H. Mussen, J. Langer, & M. Covington (Eds.), *Trends and issues in developmental psychology* (pp. 2–21). New York: Holt, Rinehart & Winston.

Johnson, D. (1980). Group processes: Influences of student-vs-student interaction on school outcomes. In J. McMillan (Ed.), *The social psychology of school learning* (pp. 123–168). New York: Academic Press.

Johnson, D. (1986). *Reaching out: Interpersonal effectiveness and self-actualization* (3rd ed.). Englewood Cliffs, NJ: Prentice-Hall.

Johnson, D., & Ahlgren, A. (1976). Relationship between students' attitudes about cooperation and competition and attitudes toward schooling. *Journal of Educational Psychology, 68,* 92–102.

Johnson, D., & Johnson, F. (1975). *Joining together: Group theory and group skills.* Englewood Cliffs, NJ: Prentice-Hall.

Johnson, D., & Johnson R. (1980). Integrating handicapped students into the mainstream. *Exceptional Children, 46,* 89–98.

Johnson, D., Johnson, R., Holubec, E., & Roy, P. (1984). *Circles of learning:*

Cooperation in the classroom. Alexandria, VA: Association for Supervision and Curriculum Development.

Johnson, D., Johnson, R., Johnson, J., & Anderson, D. (1976). The effects of cooperative vs. individualized instruction on student prosocial behavior, attitudes toward learning and achievement. *Journal of Educational Psychology, 68*, 446–452.

Johnson, D., Johnson, R., & Maruyama, G. (1983). Interdependence and interpersonal attraction among heterogeneous and homogeneous individuals: A theoretical formulation and a meta-analysis of the research. *Review of Educational Research, 53*(1), 5–54.

Johnson, D., Maruyama, G., Johnson, R., Nelson, D., & Skon, L. (1981). The effects of cooperative, competitive, and individualistic goal structures on achievement: A meta-analysis. *Psychological Bulletin, 89*(1), 47–62.

Kant, I. (1949). *Fundamental principles of the metaphysic of morals* (T. K. Abbott, Trans.). New York: Bobbs-Merrill. (Original work published 1785.)

Kinneavy, J. (1971). *A theory of discourse*. New York: Norton.

Kinney, J. (1979). Classifying heuristics. *College Composition and Communication, 30*, 351–356.

Kirby, D., & Liner, T. (1980). Revision: Yes, they do it; yes, you can teach it. *English Journal, 69*, 41–45.

Kline, C. (1975). Students rate profs in accord with grade expectations. *Phi Delta Kappan, 57*(1), 54.

Knoblauch, C. H., Brannon, L. (1981). Teacher commentary on student writing: The state of the art. *Freshman English News, 10*, 1–3.

Kroll, B. (1978). Cognitive egocentrism and the problem of audience awareness in written discourse. *Research in the Teaching of English, 12*, 269–281.

Lamberg, W. (1980). Self-provided and peer-provided feedback. *College Composition and Communication, 31*, 63–69.

Larson, R. L. (1968). Discovery through questioning: A plan for teaching rhetorical invention. *College English, 30*, 126–134.

Lauer, J. M. (1979). Toward a meta-theory of heuristic procedures. *College Composition and Communication, 30*, 268–269.

Lauer, J., Montague, G., Lunsford, A., & Emig, J. (1985). *Four worlds of writing* (2nd ed.). New York: Harper & Row.

Laughlin, P., & McGlynn, R. (1967). Cooperative versus competitive concept attainment as a function of sex and stimulus display. *Journal of Personality and Social Psychology, 7*, 398–402.

Lynch, D. (1982). Easing the process: A strategy for evaluating compositions. *College Composition and Communication, 33*, 309–314.

Macrorie, K. (1968). *Writing to be read*. Rochelle Park, NJ: Hayden.

Macrorie, K. (1976). *Telling writing* (2nd ed.). Rochelle Park, NJ: Hayden.

Maimon, E. (1979). Talking to strangers. *College Composition and Communication, 30*, 364–369.

Marder, D. (1982). Revision as discovery and the reduction of entropy. In R. Sudol (Ed.), *Revising: New essays for teachers of writing* (pp. 3–12). Urbana, IL:

National Council of Teachers of English.

McCrimmon, J. (1970). Writing as a way of knowing. *The Promise of English: NCTE 1970 Distinguished Lecturers*. Urbana, IL: National Council of Teachers of English.

McLuhan, M. (1962). *The Gutenberg galaxy, the making of typographic man*. Ontario: University of Toronto Press.

Millerton, N. N. (Ed.). (1973). *The daybooks of Edward Weston*. New York: Aperture.

Millet, N. C. (1969). On snarles and straghteners. *Illinois English Bulletin, 57*, 13–18.

Moffett, J. (1968a). *A student-centered language arts program, K–12*. New York: Houghton Mifflin.

Moffett, J. (1968b). *Teaching the universe of discourse*. New York: Houghton Mifflin.

Moffett, J., & Wagner, B. J. (1983). *Student-centered language arts and reading, K–13: A handbook for teachers* (3rd ed.). Boston: Houghton Mifflin.

Muller, H. (1967). *The uses of English*. New York: Holt, Rinehart & Winston.

Murray, D. (1968). *A writer teaches writing*. Boston: Houghton Mifflin.

Murray, D. (1978a). Internal revision: A process of discovery. In C. Cooper & L. Odell (Eds.), *Research on composing: Points of departure* (pp. 85–103). Urbana, IL: National Council of Teachers of English.

Murray, D. (1978b). Teach the motivating force of revision. *English Journal, 67*, 56–60.

Murray, D. (1978c). Write before writing. *College Composition and Communication, 29*, 375–381.

Myers, M. (1980). *A procedure for writing assessment and holistic scoring*. Urbana, IL: ERIC Clearinghouse on Reading and Communication Skills and the National Council of Teachers of English.

National Assessment of Educational Progress. (1977). *Write/rewrite: An assessment of revision skills; select results from the second national assessment of writing*. Denver, CO: Education Commission of the States. (ERIC Document Reproduction Service No. ED 075 822.)

National Council of Teachers of English. (March 1976). Guidelines for nonsexist use of language in NCTE publications. *English Journal, 65*(3), 23–26.

Newkirk, T. (1977). James Britton and the teaching of writing in selected British middle and secondary schools. *Dissertation Abstracts International, 38*, 2622–A.

Newkirk, T. (1984). Direction and misdirection in peer response. *College Composition and Communication, 35*, 301–311.

Nold, E. (1982). Revising: Intentions and conventions. In R. Sudol (Ed.), *Revising: New essays for teachers of writing* (pp. 13–23). Urbana, IL: National Council of Teachers of English.

Paull, M., & Kligerman, J. (1973). *Invention: A course in pre-writing and composition*. Cambridge, MA: Winthrop.

Peckham, L. (1978). Peer evaluation. *English Journal, 67*, 61–63.

Piaget, J., & Inhelder, B. (1969). *The psychology of the child* (H. Weaver, Trans.). New York: Routledge & Kegan Paul.

Pianko, S. (1979). Reflection: A critical component of the composing process. *College Composition and Communication, 30,* 275–284.

Pirsig, R. (1974). *Zen and the art of motorcycle maintenance: An inquiry into values.* New York: Morrow.

Price, G. (1980). A case for the modern commonplace book. *College Composition and Communication, 31,* 175–182.

Progoff, I. (1975). *At a journal workshop.* New York: Dialogue House.

Rest, J., Turiel, E., & Kohlberg, L. (1969). Relations between level of moral judgment and preference and comprehension of the moral judgment of others. *Journal of Personality, 37,* 225–252.

Rohman, D. G., & Wlecke, A. (1964). *Prewriting: The construction and application of models to concept formation in writing.* East Lansing, MI: Michigan State University.

Rubin, D., & Piché, G. (1979). Development in syntactic and strategic aspects of audience adaptation skills in written persuasive communication. *Research in the Teaching of English, 13,* 293–316.

Sager, C. (1973). *Improving the quality of written composition through pupil use of rating scales.* Unpublished doctoral dissertation, Boston University, Boston, MA.

Sanders, S. E., & Littlefield, J. H. (1975). Perhaps test essays can reflect significant improvement in freshman composition: Report on a successful attempt. *Research in the Teaching of English, 9,* 145–153.

Scardamalia, M., & Baird, W. (1980). *Children's strategies for composing sentences.* Paper presented at the annual meeting of the American Educational Research Association, Boston, MA.

Scardamalia, M., & Bereiter, C. (1979). *The effects of writing rate on children's composition.* Paper presented at the annual meeting of the American Educational Research Association.

Scardamalia, M., & Bereiter, C. (1983). The development of evaluative, diagnostic, and remedial capabilities in children's composing. In M. Martlew (Ed.), *The psychology of written language: A developmental approach* (pp. 67–95). London: John Wiley & Sons.

Shuman, R. (1982). H. G. Wells' *The outline of history*: A study in revision. In R. Sudol (Ed.), *Revising: New essays for teachers of writing* (pp. 43–51). Urbana, IL: National Council of Teachers of English.

Sommers, N. (1979). The need for theory in composition research. *College Composition and Communication, 30,* 46–49.

Stallard, C. (1974). An analysis of the writing behavior of good student writers. *Research in the Teaching of English, 8,* 206–218.

Stewart, D. (1972). *The authentic voice: A pre-writing approach to student writing.* Dubuque, IA: William C. Brown.

Strunk, W., & White, E. (1972). *The elements of style.* New York: Macmillan.

Thompson, R. F. (1981). Peer grading: Some promising advantages for composi-

tion research and the classroom. *Research in the Teaching of English, 15,* 172–174.

Turiel, E. (1973). Stage transition in moral development. In R. Travers (Ed.), *Second handbook of research on teaching.* Chicago: Rand McNally.

Veit, R. C. (1982). *The little writing book: Cases for rhetorical expression.* Englewood Cliffs, NJ: Prentice-Hall.

Vygotsky, L. S. (1962). *Thought and language* (E. Hanfmann & G. Vaker, Trans. and Eds.). Cambridge: Massachusetts Institute of Technology Press. (Original work published 1934.)

Wagoner, D. (Ed.). (1974). *Straw for the fire: From the notebooks of Theodore Roethke, 1943–63.* Garden City: Anchor Press.

Webster's new world dictionary of the American language. (1968). New York: World Publishing.

Wheeler, R., & Ryan, F. (1973). Effects of cooperative and competitive classroom environments on the attitudes and achievement of elementary students engaged in social studies inquiry activities. *Journal of Educational Psychology, 65,* 402–407.

Wiener, H. S. (1986). Collaborative learning in the classroom: A guide to evaluation. *College English, 48,* 52–61.

Windhover, R. (1982). A holistic pedagogy for freshman composition. In R. Sudol (Ed.), *Revising: New essays for teachers of writing* (pp. 87–99). Urbana, IL: National Council of Teachers of English.

Winterowd, W. R. (1975). *The contemporary writer: A practical rhetoric.* New York: Harcourt Brace Jovanovich.

Woodson, L. (1982). *From cases to composition.* Glenview, IL: Scott, Foresman, & Company.

Young, R. E., Becker, A. L., & Pike, K. L. (1970). *Rhetoric: Discovery and change.* New York: Harcourt Brace Jovanovich.

Zinsser, W. (1980). *On writing well: An informal guide to writing nonfiction* (2nd ed.). New York: Harper & Row.

Index

Page numbers followed by *n.* indicate footnotes or reference notes.

About the Authors

Senior author **Roland K. Huff** received his bachelor's degree from Hiram College and his M.A. and Ph.D. from Indiana University. His research interests include the nature of the composing process, post-modern rhetoric, and the Dickensian imagination. He has directed graduate programs in rhetoric and composition at Washington State University and Eastern Washington University. Currently, he is director of writing programs at the University of Winnipeg in Canada.

Charles R. Kline, Jr., now a writing consultant, was formerly Associate Professor of English education and rhetoric at The University of Texas in Austin, and visiting researcher, Institut de Recherches Herméneutiques, Université de Neuchâtel, Switzerland. He received his Ph.D. in English and education from the University of North Carolina.